Beyond
Right
and
Wrong

Beyond Right and Wrong

A STUDY IN MORAL THEORY

HARRY K. GIRVETZ

University of California,
Santa Barbara

 THE FREE PRESS
A Division of Macmillan Publishing Co., Inc.
New York

COLLIER MACMILLAN PUBLISHERS
London

THE FREE PRESS
A Division of Macmillan Publishing Co., Inc.
866 Third Avenue, New York, N.Y. 10022

Collier–Macmillan Canada Ltd., Toronto, Ontario

Library of Congress Catalog Card Number: 73–1858

Printed in the United States of America

printing number

1 2 3 4 5 6 7 8 9 10

Library of Congress Cataloging in Publication Data

Girvetz, Harry K   1910–
    Beyond right and wrong.

    Includes bibliographies.
    1. Ethics. I. Title.
BJ1012.G55   170   73–1858
ISBN   0–02–911770–4

What advantage can there be in possessing everything except what is good, or in understanding everything else while of the good and desirable we know nothing?

Plato, *Republic*, VI, 504

Contents

vii

Preface

My debts are many. Among historical philosophers I have been helped most by the insights of Kant, as the reader who perseveres to the final chapters of this book will discover. The colossus of Königsberg would doubtless be critical of the use to which I put him, as of my reluctance to accept him totally. But the immortals among philosophers must surely be reconciled to having their names used in vain, especially since, not being gods, they are unable to issue a commandment forbidding the practice —and would have as little luck as the gods if they did. In this century, in my judgment, no one has contributed as much to our understanding of the ethical experience as John Dewey. Even though I have been forced to conclude that he fails us in the end, Dewey has, I believe, taken us farther along the way than any other philosopher of our time. I owe most to Henry Waldgrave Stuart, who taught me philosophy at Stanford when I was a student there many years ago. Not wishing, as he said, to add another book to the heap that few read and fewer understand, he unfortunately deferred to those of us who are more rash, leaving only a few essays in which, as the title of one of them suggests, he proposed "a reversal of perspective in ethical theory." Much of what is said in the following pages is indebted to these essays. Finally, I am deeply grateful to my colleagues, Professors George Geiger, Richard Taylor, and Ralph Ross, who were kind enough to read and comment on my manuscript.

The issues dealt with in this book are of such urgent concern to students and thoughtful people in general that they ought to

be presented in a manner that addresses itself to the perplexities
of a larger circle than professional philosophers. I hope the latter
will therefore overlook the inclusion of familiar background
material and the omission of those more detailed analyses that
belong properly in a treatise intended exclusively for specialists.
I attempt a notoriously difficult task—to write for serious students of philosophy in a way that will not discourage inquiring
lay readers troubled, as they think about moral issues, by the
Hobson's choice between skepticism and dogmatism that faces
them, yet unwilling or unable to cope with the often formidable
and tedious philosophical discussions which deal with such problems. Such readers can skim Chapters six to eight, or even skip
them, without serious loss of continuity. However, these and the
preceding chapters on emotivism and the interest theory of value
are not rigorous, and the reader who omits them will lose a sense
of the difficulty encountered in finding a basis on which we
might claim for moral judgments an objectivity that avoids
dogmatism and survives the criticism of philosophically sophisticated skeptics. The material referred to deals with recent chapters
in the history of moral theory. But they are not closed chapters
and, in any case, it is important in philosophy to reckon with its
past, if only, as we are often reminded, because the errors of able
thinkers can be more instructive than the truths of lesser ones.

I may raise more problems than I solve. And I shall no doubt
be charged with neglecting problems that are crucial. But these
are the risks that one takes in an area beset by notoriously intractable difficulties.

Introduction

The fears and tensions, the doubts and perplexities that once prompted W. H. Auden to call ours the Age of Anxiety have many sources. To find ourselves reaching for an abundance of which people hardly even dared dream—as we are in America— only to have success jeopardized by the polarization of the world into armed camps, is surely reason enough for frustration. When, its guns hardly cooled from a catastrophic war, the world wastes its substance on weapons and lives uneasily in the shadow of the atomic bomb, one hardly need look deeper for the cause of unrest.

And yet our perplexities would not be removed even if, by a miracle of understanding, the differences that threaten and sometimes involve us in international conflict could be reconciled. These perplexities have been longer in preparation than the present crisis, and victory for what we call, and sometimes miscall, the free world would not banish them; indeed it might even exacerbate them.

The deeper sources of our perplexities and anxieties can be variously described. They spring from the phenomenon of consciousness itself, torn between the role that Santayana assigned spirit as Nature's comment on herself, and soaring pretensions that spurn nature and nature's ways. They issue from man's yearning for immortality and his suspicion that he is like "the lightning which doth cease to be ere one can say, it lightens." They stem from the endless quarrel of science and folklore, of

1

fact and fancy, bred by the impact of what is on what we would
have things be. Indeed here there is a double impact, for "what
is" embraces more than the corporeality of heavenly bodies and
the elliptical orbits in which they travel, the vast age of the
earth, the variability of species and all the countless facts which,
when they were first announced, disturbed our prejudices and
preconceptions; "what is" embraces in the Great Society a
dynamic technology compelling us endlessly to reorient ourselves
to the always strange new world we are ourselves creating.

All these are related ways of explaining the predicament of
modern man, but in the end we understand this predicament
best—at any rate we grapple with it in its most fundamental
form—when we state it in terms of the problem of value. If the
problem was first posed by the Greeks (as nearly all problems
were), it is nevertheless more acute for us, in our time, for our
culture.

We are in need of a new ethic. The absolutisms of the past
will no longer do for us: it becomes increasingly difficult to
breathe life into the old authorities. We cherish their wisdom,
we profit from their insights; but we no longer accept them as
infallible guides. Wherever men have a free choice the very
principle of infallibility is in eclipse. The great integration of
values achieved in the Middle Ages is irrevocably gone,
however nostalgically some may yearn for its revival. The later
gospel of progress in which the Enlightenment sought a substitute for Providence has been shaken in our century by wars and
depression and the slow recognition that accumulation, mechani-
cal improvement and middle-class prosperity are not ends in
themselves. The Marxist certitudes of the 1930's are shattered,
although there are some who still play with the pieces. For us
there is no easy reliance on codes of conduct immune to the
influence of time and place, no simple recourse to fixed standards
and rules, no comfortable appeal to the "true" good, no com-
placent resort to the law of progress—in short, no ready-made
formula for moral rectitude which contains in advance the
answers to all our questions concerning the guidance of conduct.
Far more than earlier generations, we are skeptical of such prescriptions: in part because in an increasingly secular world the

claim of revealed religion has lost its hold on most of us; in part because standards of conduct have changed dramatically in our lifetime and, possessed of historical perspectives not available to our ancestors, we know how rules and standards have changed in the remoter past; in part because legions of ethnologists have overwhelmed us with the sheer multiplicity of moral codes.

Once Voltaire could speak of "the principles of morality common to the human race." In our time, in the concluding paragraphs of her now classic *Coming of Age in Samoa,* Margaret Mead writes:

[Our] children . . . must be taught that many ways are open to them, no one sanctioned above its alternative, and that upon them and upon them alone lies the burden of choice. . . . it is unthinkable that a final recognition of the great number of ways in which man, during the course of history and at the present time, is solving the problems of life, should not bring with it in turn the downfall of our belief in a single standard.[1]

Does this mean that we are to be left without a basis for distinguishing morally between one way of life and another? In rejecting moral dogmatism are we to be driven to moral skepticism? This is no remote academic question. Everywhere incompatible ends beckon us—which shall we choose? Plausible ideologies, each propounding a different way of life, invite our adherence—with which shall we ally ourselves? We are torn by conflicting loyalties—to which shall we give ourselves? Must the choice be arbitrary? Must the decision be left to subjective preference? Must we conclude that anything goes? Is there no *objective,* i.e., demonstrable sense in which one alternative is better than another? These are fundamental questions; failure to answer them is surely a basic source of our disquiet. This is the harassing problem of value as modern man faces it in the Western world.

Unhappily, in attempting to extricate ourselves from this predicament, we have received little help from those whose province is the science of man and less help from contemporary philosophers. For decades the weight of much of their testimony has been on the side of an extreme form of relativism which treats all moral judgments as a reflection of personal or cultural bias and therefore as subjective and arbitrary. Although there has been a retreat from the more extreme positions, it is important to review this testimony, part of which limits itself to an examination of moral judgments and part of which, in questioning the objectivity of *all* cognitive claims, applies *a fortiori* to the claims implicit in *moral* judgments. Anthropologists espousing what has come to be known as "cultural relativity," logical positivists and language analysts affirming the essential meaninglessness of moral statements, ideologists such as Marx and Mannheim questioning the objectivity of the social sciences, Freud probing the subconscious—all in their diverse ways have argued against an "objective" basis for moral judgment or evaluation. The case must be examined. But before it is examined some broader issues require attention.

A discussion of conduct and of the criteria by which we distinguish between good and bad conduct must not become lost in labyrinthine metaphysical speculation, yet it must begin with certain assumptions about the nature of man and man's place in the world. For, if that place is a special one in some large design, then all questions of conduct will be resolved by reference to the outlines of that design. If, as a recent work on metaphysics declares, the universe has "a definite objective to realize" and the history of man is "nothing if not an attempt to work out that objective," ethics will be an adjunct of theology or metaphysics: its deliberations will consist of descrying those broader purposes by which the universe is governed and drawing the proper inferences.

Such is our capacity for self-esteem that it has taken two revolutions, the Copernican and the Darwinian, to shake, if not to shatter man's conviction that he is the focus of the universe. The heliocentric theory of Copernicus banished the notion that the planet man inhabits is the center about which all the heavenly bodies revolve. By the time his successors completed the revolution that Copernicus started, earth had been relegated to the status of an insignificant planet, a mere speck of dust (it is now usual to say), virtually lost in the vast recesses of space. But, removed from the physical center of the universe, consigned though he might be to humble and inconspicuous quarters, man was not yet prepared to relinquish the lofty place to which he had become accustomed. The great nature-philosophers of the seventeenth century, and Descartes, who was their missionary, enthusiastically proclaimed the reign of natural law and the ubiquity of the system of nature—by which they meant the physical world—but they excepted man. Man was something special and apart. Whatever the place of his body—and Cartesians were prepared to assign man's body, along with all animal organisms, to the realm of physical nature (*res extensa*)—the mind or soul of man, the seat of his awareness and source of his knowledge, was not part of the system of nature. Consciousness, all the activities of reasoning, thinking, judging, doubting, feeling, were so little a part of nature that they had nothing in common with it. Mind is ultimate and irreducible; mind and matter are completely different in kind: one cannot be understood in terms of or derived from the other. The autonomy of man, at least so far as his distinctive attributes are concerned, was thus preserved.

It remained for Darwin to provide a scientific basis for including man within the system of nature by showing that man is part of the evolutionary process and is related by descent to simpler organisms. To be sure, the thesis that all species have a common ancestry and hence are genetically related did not, as Darwin first formulated it, expressly include man. For reasons of expediency Darwin limited himself in *The Origin of Species* to only a perfunctory reference to the origin of man. He simply promised that "Much light will be thrown on the origin of man and his history."[2] It was not until 1871, twelve years after the appearance of his magnum opus, that Darwin's *Descent of Man* was published. In it he set out to establish not only that man is descended from simpler organisms, but that, like other species, man is a product of *natural selection.* The latter point is crucial and requires brief comment.

Quite apart from his explanation of the origin of man, the view that living species are genetically related and have a common ancestry is by no means original with Darwin. Darwinism and evolutionism are commonly treated as synonymous, but this is an error. Although Darwin was the first to amass overwhelming evidence in favor of the evolutionary hypothesis, others had already taken evolution seriously. Indeed, had Darwin confined himself merely to confirming the notions of common origin and the variability of species, his critics would have been limited for the most part to those who subscribed to a literal interpretation of the account of creation in the Book of Genesis and believed that Darwin had challenged the authority of the Bible. But Darwin accomplished much more. Darwin's originality and greatness rest primarily on his discovery of *how* evolution occurs. It is his explanation in terms of *natural selection* with which Darwinism, so-called, is properly identified. It was this account that provoked the bitterest hostility, since it appeared to dispense entirely with a Creator in explaining the origin of species. No purpose is at work. Given the great fecundity of all living species, there is normally a pressure of numbers on available resources and a consequent struggle for survival; organisms undergo heritable variations which may or may not help them in the struggle for survival (or competition for a mate); those which undergo beneficent variations are likelier to survive and transmit them to their offspring; such changes are thereby preserved and as they accumulate new species emerge—this in its essentials is what is meant by natural selection.

The details of Darwin's account of natural selection, along with the gaps in his explanation which were later filled, need not detain us here. The important point is that Darwin has no need to refer in this kind of explanation to a purposeful or guiding agency. The heritable variations (later called mutations) which give organisms an advantage in the struggle for survival and enable them to reproduce and transmit such variations to their offspring are *random;* they are blind and purposeless and do not happen *in order to* further the survival of the organism. Although

Darwin sometimes lapsed into a teleological idiom his final verdict was that such variations occur by "chance," by which he meant not that they occur without a cause, but that they are "accidental as far as purpose is concerned."[3] In point of fact, the overwhelming majority of mutations are harmful rather than helpful to the survival of the organism, as emphasized by the distinguished geneticist, R. A. Fisher, when he spoke of "a storm of adverse mutations."

In other words, natural selection provides an explanation of evolutionary change without postulating a teleological principle; there is no need for a "vital force" (*élan vital*) or "inherent tendency" or "inner perfecting principle" or "entelechy," or any other of the agencies which have been invented to "prove" that evolution is somehow goal-oriented. It is always tempting, of course, to pass from the adaptive nature of many of the characteristics of an organism, the complex structure of the eye, for example, to the conclusion that such adaptations are evidence of purposeful guidance. The lizard appears to be provided with a coloration that blends it with its background *in order* to protect it from its enemies; the ears of predatory animals are cupped forward so that they may more readily detect their prey; the neck of the giraffe is elongated so that it may reach the higher foliage. And, of course, the temptation to invoke a guiding agency or principle to account for a creature as complex (and "Godlike") as man is overwhelming. Even A. R. Wallace, who independently formulated the principles and conclusions for which Darwin has become celebrated, including natural selection and the descent of man, recoiled from explaining the origin of man without purposeful intervention. However, if the origin of man with all his distinctive endowments can be explained solely in terms of the operation of such natural processes as natural selection, the old Cartesian dichotomy is broken down: Man is now one with nature, subject to the operation of the same blind, impersonal laws that govern the rest of nature. Not only does he inhabit a nondescript planet, as the Copernican revolution forced him to conclude; his origins, it turns out, are as humble as the humblest beast in the field. We must acknowledge, wrote Darwin in the memorable final passage of *The Descent of Man,*

. . . that man with all his noble qualities, with sympathy that feels for the most debased, with benevolence which extends not only to other men but to the humblest living creature, with his godlike intellect which has penetrated into the movements and constitution of the solar system—with all these exalted powers—Man still bears in his bodily frame the indelible stamp of his lowly origin.[4]

Some have interpreted Darwinism as degrading man, as reducing him to the level of the merely animal and the crudely physical. Those who do ignore one of the fundamental insights which Darwin's work makes possible. Darwinism does indeed lead to the conclusion that the system of nature is all-inclusive, but it also requires us to see that nature is not limited to manifesting itself in the movements of physical particles or changing configurations of energy in space. Nature is not, like a machine, a closed system, the parts of which move to their predetermined and predictable places according to inexorable law. Nature cannot be viewed as finished and complete but is always, as William James suggested, "in the making." Besides those samenesses, repetitions and recurrences which make prediction possible, there is also novelty in nature. This is indeed the essence of evolutionary doctrine, broadly interpreted: namely, that nature is not limited to repeating itself, that not even the movements of heavenly bodies, not to mention the histories of organisms and societies, are characterized by complete periodicity. In the fullness of time nature can and does manifest itself in *new* ways. Such novel configurations[5] are continuous with and derivative from simpler configurations and yet qualitatively distinct, that is to say, so different *in kind* that generalizations which suffice for a description of their antecedents will not do for the consequents: generalizations of a different order are required and with them sciences other than physics—for example, biology, psychology, sociology.

Once in possession of this insight it has become possible for philosophy to treat man (and all his works) as part of the system of nature without doing violence to his peculiarly human attributes. To say that man derives from simpler organisms is not to say that he is identical with them in kind, any more than organisms in general can be identified with the inorganic world. A nineteenth-century philosopher, Feuerbach, made a bad pun: "Man ist was er isst"—man is what he eats. Those who would derive materialism from such evidence, are also guilty of bad philosophy—although no worse than the philosophy of those who conclude that if man descended from simians he must, as Disraeli once expostulated, be an ape or a monkey.

To note man's antecedents, both causal (as Feuerbach did in the case of the chemical ingredients man absorbs from his food) and historical (as in the case of his subhuman ancestry), is to affirm his oneness with nature and thereby to rescue him from the obscurities of dualism. But this does not denigrate man; rather it testifies to the fecundity of nature: in man nature manifests itself in ways unknown to chemists and biologists, and even psychologists (as psychology is conventionally understood) and sociologists. In him nature reveals itself in ways requiring the still groping procedures of the moralist, of the aesthetician, and —in at least one sense of this calling—of the theologian. For, in man, nature presents itself not only as a configuration of physical particles, nor merely as an organism, but as a self-conscious agent capable of differentiating between good and evil, of appreciating beauty and of finding meaning in God.

However, for the naturalist, *it is only to man* that such distinctions are relevant and meaningful. And this will be the assumption of the discussion which follows. Such a discussion will therefore be found incomplete by those who believe with the editor of a survey of theologically and metaphysically oriented ethical standpoints—a kind of orientation in near eclipse among contemporary philosophers—that "Good and Evil are not hypotheses or attributes of the mind alone but relations within reality."[6] Once we agree that more complex and qualitatively distinct phenomena may derive from simpler antecedents, it no longer becomes necessary to make the category of value coextensive with the category of being in order to render man and his values intelligible.

If one accepts the evolutionary in contrast to the creationist view of man's origin it becomes easy to see that moral consciousness need no longer be regarded as an original or native endowment. Man did not begin as a moral agent; moral awareness is a level of experience man—some men—have *achieved*. Twenty-five thousand years ago man was hardly distinguishable from other mammals in his ability to cope with his environment; indeed in many respects he was inferior. Since then man has not changed biologically; his present command over nature can be understood only in terms of social evolution. Conduct on the moral level, in which man may be said to achieve command over himself, is a product of social evolution in quite the same sense. The latter no less than the former derives from a specific kind of social organization, is thwarted by some social institutions and fostered by others. In short, moral awareness is a *cultural* phenomenon, expressing itself in different ways at different levels of social development, just as in the life history of the individual it takes on different forms in the passage from childhood to maturity.

Much speculation about ethics, especially that part which has been theologically influenced, is vitiated by failure to appreciate this elementary point. Nowhere is this failure more obvious than in the efforts of missionaries to Christianize the aborigines—as though the moral insights which inform Christianity emerged in a cultural vacuum. The assumption that man, simply and solely as being man, engages in moral deliberation or has a moral "sense" has indeed blocked the appearance of what may well be called a *science of ethics,* for such a science—having accepted moral deliberation as a natural phenomenon—would begin by asking: (a) under what social conditions does man become capable of acting as a moral agent, (b) given these conditions, what kind of juncture or "situation" evokes that manner of deliberation we call moral? To answer these questions will require us to identify moral deliberation somewhat more precisely than is ordinarily the case and to discover that there are significantly different levels of morality which have generally been confused in the traditional approaches to ethics. Traditional ethics has been so preoccupied with defining *what* is good or *what* is right

—on the assumption that "good" and "right" are constants discernable to all who care to look—that it has generally neglected inquiry into *how* men come to distinguish between good and evil, right and wrong. It is this gap which contemporary analysis must fill. Once this is done we shall be in a much better position to understand the nature of moral judgments and, perhaps, to escape a skeptical relativism without embracing the opposite extreme of dogmatism. Implied, as will be seen, is the possibility of affirming a position that can without contradiction be called *objective relativism*. First, however, the case for relativism must be examined in several of its extreme forms. To examine them is to deal with much that has been stimulating, original, and valuable in modern thought. It is also to discover how we have been led into a *cul de sac*, so far as understanding the data of ethics is concerned.

Part One

Sources
of Moral
Skepticism

Chapter One

Cultural Relativity

During the twentieth century anthropological field studies have documented in impressive detail a bewildering variation in custom and belief, often to the neglect of uniformities. Amid the rich profusion of cultural differences there has seemed to be no value accepted by one group which has not been ignored or rejected by another, no practice followed in one part of the world which has not been shunned or ignored elsewhere. Inventories of such differences are too commonplace to recite. They led eminent anthropologists such as Margaret Mead, Melville Herskovits, and Ruth Benedict to espouse what is generally known as *cultural relativity*. Even though a later generation of anthropologists has come to regard cultural relativity as greatly oversimplified and misused in its first formulations, as so often happens among unwary readers, the classical version tends to overshadow amendments and corrections. It is therefore still a standpoint to be reckoned with—all the more so in that some of the attempts to refute it share its vulnerability.

Cultural relativity may be construed in a number of different senses. No anthropologist would quarrel with cultural relativity understood as the *methodological* postulate that ethnologists, to comprehend a culture, must view it, so far as possible, from the standpoint of those who partake of it, and try to understand the specific practices of a society from the point of view of the function they serve. More controversial is the *epistemological* version of cultural relativity which affirms that the content of all knowledge—even of perception, which is to say, the way we experience time, distance, weight, etc.—is culturally conditioned.[1] A new science, the sociology of knowledge, is founded on this quasi-Kantian assumption. From this it is easy to derive the corollary that all *value judgments* are culturally conditioned, although one may subscribe to cultural relativism as a moral or value theory without defending cultural relativism as an epistemological standpoint.

Cultural relativism as a generalization about values and value judgments is epitomized in William Graham Sumner's famous dictum that "The mores can make anything right." In *Folkways* he wrote that "for the people of a time and place their own mores are always good . . . for them there can be no question of the goodness of their mores. The reason is because the standards of good and right are in the mores."[2] Melville Herskovits, who was one of its most distinguished later exponents, is more explicit:

Evaluations are *relative* to the cultural background out of which they arise. . . . The principle [of cultural relativism] briefly stated, is as follows: *Judgments are based on experience, and experience is interpreted by each individual in terms of his own enculturation.* (p. 63) . . . Cultural relativism is a philosophy which, in recognizing the values set up by every society to guide its own life, lays stress on the dignity inherent in every body of custom, and on the need for tolerance of conventions though they may differ from one's own. Instead of underscoring differences from absolute norms that, however objectively arrived at, are nonetheless a product of a given time or place, the relativistic point of view brings into relief the validity of every set of norms for the people whose lives are guided by them, and the values these represent. (p. 76)[3]

The essence of this position is, as Richard Brandt has noted in his *Hopi Ethics*, that two people may assert "contradictory ethical views without either being mistaken."[4] More explicitly, the cultural relativist tells us that time and place vary and we are inescapably creatures of our time and place. We cannot transcend these conditions. We are culture-bound and therefore incorrigibly biased. We cannot be other than we are and we are what our experience under determinate social conditions has made us. Therefore, when we claim that we judge those who partake of other cultures *objectively,* we are guilty of conscious or unconscious pretense: we are making claims for our values which they may just as rightfully make for theirs.

Imbedded in this position are two distinguishable and not necessarily related assertions. First of all, the cultural relativist is stressing the diversity of moral conduct and moral codes. Awareness of diversity in moral *practice* obviously antedated William Graham Sumner, much as modern ethnology may have heightened such awareness. Athenians hardly needed professional ethnologists to remind them of how their moral values and practice differed from the Spartans! Presumably, the cultural relativist's stress on diversity refers to differences in the moral assumptions underlying diverse practices, to differences in what Richard Brandt refers to as "basic ethical axioms." That is to say, there may be agreement on principles or values, even though practices differ because there is a difference in awareness of or access to the relevant conditions or facts. If, in spite of having the same factual information, two groups still diverge in their moral practice, it may be inferred that they start from different moral assumptions. Presumably an advocate of slavery like Calhoun and an abolitionist like Garrison had much the same knowledge of or access to the facts pertaining to slavery; they diverged in their basic moral axioms. Obviously the presence or absence or degree of such divergence is more difficult to establish than the mere prevalence of differences in moral practice. And clearly the issue is a critical one since, if all differences among men of goodwill—not to mention evil men—could be reconciled by appeal to facts, the task of securing agreement would be immensely simplified. In any event, cultural relativists stress such differences in basic moral principles. Secondly, cultural relativists like Herskovits subscribe to *ethical* relativism, the view that there are no trans-cultural standards by reference to which the standards of a group may be judged. Such a conclusion is implicit in cultural relativity as formulated by its best known advocates.

Cultural relativism as thus understood is the product of a laudable protest against ethnocentrism. It is a repudiation of the kind of narrow provincialism that consists of elevating the value judgments of one's group and uncritically judging others by them. It reminds cultural chauvinists that there are ways of life at least as good as their own. It undermines absolutism. Whatever the follies of our era, it is surely only in our time that individuals in any number have overcome cultural bias sufficiently to view the values of other cultures with even this much impartiality and detachment. The upshot is tolerance of others, which we badly need, although, as has often been remarked, when the relativists preach tolerance the bias of their own subculture is showing, since few social groups value tolerance. Even so, the cultural relativist properly corrects our tendency to confuse difference with inferiority and to disparage those who are guilty of the sin of not being like us. And he properly reminds us that we have been much too patronizing about pre-industrial and pre-literate cultures which may be neither as "simple" and childlike nor as "backward" as was once assumed. There is real nobility in the plea of Ruth Benedict in her widely read *Patterns of Culture* that "social thinking [take] . . . adequate account of cultural relativity" with the promise that "we shall then arrive at a more realistic social faith, accepting as grounds of hope and as new bases for tolerance, the coexisting and equally valid patterns of life which mankind has carved for itself from the raw materials of existence."[5]

But the question always haunts us: shall we accept as an "equally valid pattern of life" carved out by mankind "from the raw materials of existence" the pattern evolved in Nazi Germany? Or Stalin's Russia? Or Brezhnev's Prague? Or Wallace's Deep South? Or, to get closer to home, our own decaying cities? Must we abandon all trans-cultural value judgments? And, if so, what are the consequences for *intra*-cultural judgments? After all, in our pluralistic society there are many subcultures: the austere routine of a priestly order, the way of life found in our ghettoes and barrios, the life style of prosperous suburbia, the ways of the Amish; there are also the subcultures of the Mafia, the skid rows, the "gay" colonies and art colonies and (increasingly) the student communities of our large cities. Should not tolerance, like charity, begin at home? And, if it is to be extended to subcultures, why not to individuals? Why should differences among individuals ever be treated as invidious differences? Although this is no doubt contrary to his intention the relativist's position appears to culminate in moral skepticism.

In fairness to that position it must be noted that cultural relativists are careful to repudiate suggestions that theirs is a counsel of nihilism: if cultures differ in *what* is found valuable or judged to be good, there is this *formal* resemblance, namely, that they all distinguish between good and bad, right and wrong. The multiplicity of norms and rules must not obscure the fact, the relativist reminds us, that standards *do* prevail; moral distinctions *are* made. "To say that there is no absolute criterion of value or morals . . . does not mean that such criteria, in differing *forms,* do not comprise universals in human nature. . . . Morality is a universal, and so is enjoyment of beauty, and some standard for truth."[6]

But we are hardly reassured. Many will affirm, with Herskovits, the dignity of *other* sets of customs and deny that dignity is, as he says, "inherent in *every* body of custom." (My emphasis.) Waiving such ambiguities as may lurk in the term, we might still wish to question the "dignity" of torture rites practiced by the Penitentes of New Mexico, a last surviving sect of the Flagellants of medieval Spain. Ruth Benedict describes the Good Friday ritual in which they identify themselves with the crucified Savior:

The climax of the rite is the crucifixion of the Christ, impersonated by one of the members of the cult. The procession emerges from the house of the Penitentes at dawn of Good Friday, the Christ staggering under the weight of the tremendous cross. Behind him are his brethren with bared backs who lash themselves at every slow step with their great whips of bayonet cactus to which are fastened barbs of cholla. From a distance their backs look as if covered with a rich red cloth. The 'way' is about a mile and a half, and when they reach the end the Christ is bound upon the cross and raised. If he, or one of the whippers, dies, his shoes are placed upon his doorstep, and no mourning is allowed for him.[7]

The Penitentes are a small and remote sect, but morally repugnant, if not quite so bizarre, practices have been found among larger groups closer to home—the Klu Klux Klan, for example, or the jackbooted storm troopers of Nazi Germany.[8]

Response to the cultural relativists has usually taken the form of charging them with ignoring significant trans-cultural values in their preoccupation with variety and difference. Thus, a distinguished ethnologist, Clyde Kluckhohn, notes that no group tolerates cruelty. In-group cruelty is never accepted as an end in itself, and even out-group cruelty is justified only if it serves some purpose. Again, all groups celebrate marriage in one form or other; and death is memorialized in every culture.

Kluckhohn wrote:

Every culture has a concept of murder, distinguishing this from execution, killing in war, and other "justifiable homicides." The notions of incest and other regulations upon sexual behavior, of prohibitions upon untruth under defined circumstances, of restitution and reciprocity, of mutual obligations between parents and children—these and many other concepts are altogether universal.[9]

It can also be argued against those who stress the diversity of moral belief that the differences cited by ethnologists are often apparent rather than real. Brandt's reference to differing attitudes towards parricide is an excellent example. We regard parricide as a heinous crime. In contrast are certain primitive societies in which sons may kill their fathers without reproof. Clearly the practices are diametrically opposed. However, if we get behind the act to the meaning it has for those who practice parricide, we may learn that it is committed from a sense of filial duty (possibly in a spirit of self-sacrifice) based on the belief that if one's father is done away with while still vigorous and healthy, he will inhabit this kind of body in the next life instead of a frail and enfeebled one. Clearly the values involved are not as diverse as they first appeared!

Kluckhohn concluded: "It seems increasingly clear and increasingly important that some values, perhaps entirely of a broad and general nature, transcend cultural differences,"[10] and he placed himself squarely in agreement with the judgment of a fellow anthropologist, Ralph Linton, that "Behind the seemingly endless diversity of culture patterns there is a fundamental uniformity."[11] And, of course, there *are* certain universal needs— for food, sex, shelter, etc.—and certain universal requirements (e.g. care of infants) for survival. However, such "cultural imperatives," as Malinowski called them, are hardly ignored by relativists. "We can agree," wrote Herskovits, "that certain cultural uniformities do arise out of the similarities in the situations with which all human beings must cope, such as some kind of family to care for the young, or even some system of belief with which to achieve a sense of security in an otherwise over-powering universe."[12]

Those who would answer the relativists with inventories of trans-cultural values betray the weakness of their case in seemingly innocent qualifications such as Kluckhohn's reference above to these values as "perhaps entirely of a broad and general nature." It turns out that within these broad limits bewilderingly diverse preferences and practices call for evaluation. The fact that all men have hunger drives and try to satisfy them hardly provides us with an objective standard for evaluating the cannibalism of the Miranhas, whose chief explained "When I have killed an enemy it is better to eat him than to let him go to waste." It is notorious that all kinds of taboos obstruct the satisfying of the hunger drive. Here, where the strongest of survival imperatives is presumably operative, some foods will be rejected even by the undernourished and hungry. Milk is not acceptable to the peoples of Southeast Asia, beef is rejected by the Hindus in a land where starvation is rampant, insects loaded with vitamins, although relished in other countries, would not be eaten by vitamin-starved Euro-Americans. In Africa, the Kikuyu limit their diet to vegetables and, since they lack the knowledge of nutritive values available to a Euro-American vegetarian, they are smaller, weaker, and more prone to disease than their neighbors, the Masai of Kenya, whose diet includes milk, blood, and flesh. Worse, the average Masai woman is as strong as the average Kikuyu man.[13] Yet vegetarianism has prevailed among the Kikuyu over the centuries. Given such a multiplicity of dietary laws, reference to man's need for food hardly provides us with a trans-cultural standard of value. Sex practices, despite the universality of the sex drive, are even more diverse. Clearly, even if cultural relativists erred in stressing differences to the neglect of uniformities, attempts to find universal values founder on the sheer variety of the ways in which men have gratified the needs they have in common.

Moreover, differences have often been obscured by verbal designations which suggest a similarity where none exists. There is little resemblance between the English Utilitarians' conception of the "greatest good to the greatest number," for whom it generally meant the prosperity of the English middle class, and the view of those for whom the "greatest number" included the working classes and the "greatest good" meant their welfare. There is still less resemblance between the English utilitarian ideal and the Nazi slogan: "Gemeinnutz vor Eigennutz" (the common good before the individual good). There is nothing in common between love of country expressed by salutes to the flag, oaths of loyalty and bumper strips which read: "America—love it or leave it," and love of country expressing itself in concern over polluted air and streams, blighted cities, and cheap commercial exploitation of the countryside. Yet both may be called "patriotism." S. E. Asch has written: "We do not know of societies in which bravery is despised and cowardice held up to honor, in which generosity is considered a vice and ingratitude a virtue."[14] But as Dr. Lazari—Pawlowska properly points out in response:

The author [Asch] does not take into consideration the obvious fact that the idea of bravery, although it may be known everywhere, refers to different acts in different cultures. An act that is not approved of is called not brave but rash, inconsiderate, etc. What some people condemn and call cowardice, others approve of and call prudent, careful behavior . . .[15]

Still, attempts to disprove cultural relativity by stressing trans-cultural uniformities persist. In the case of L. S. Feuer psychoanalysis is invoked to argue that differences are not what they seem to be and that behind the apparent diversity the same values prevail. Verbal reports, he reminds us, are notoriously untruthful. Philosophers (and presumably, ethnologists) tend to exaggerate the truth value of verbal reports as to ultimate values.

When the ascetic tells us, "I value my deprivation, I value my starvation," we might ask him to tell us his dreams and fantasies. We'll then find that his dreams depict with vivid symbolism a tremendous desire for food, and that they are filled with resentment against authorities who have pledged him to a life of deprivation. The deeper unconscious experiences of the ascetic are a rejection of the so-called values of the ascetic way of life. Simeon Stylites dreams of a soft, cool bed as he bakes on the pillar under the desert sun, Paphnutius longs for the voluptuous Thais, St. Jerome is tormented by the flesh.

People may overtly have accepted passivity as a norm of life, but their fantasies are then of self-assertion and a restored human pride. The Navajo dreams of a redeemer who will thrust out the white interloper, the Jews through centuries of passive acquiescence dreamed of an all-powerful Messiah. No group in its deepest psyche makes "weakness" and "submission" into values; their fantasies are of strength and revolt.[16]

Much of this is true. But surely not all differences can be disposed of in this way. And the judgments which Feuer believes the psychoanalysts would regard as examples of self-deceit are, not surprisingly those to which Professor Feuer himself is clearly hostile.

What, finally, may we conclude from such statements and counter-statements? Primarily, that we cannot settle the question of objectivity in moral judgment by a counting of noses, and that most parties to the controversy have begged the question of "validity" and what it means. This is as true of Ruth Benedict in her reference to "equally valid patterns of life" as of Ralph Linton's stress on a "fundamental uniformity." The issue is one that concerns theoretical or meta-ethics and not ethnology. *Ethical* relativism is not a necessary inference from *cultural* relativism any more than *objectivity* or absolutism is a necessary inference from the *universality* of ethical principles or practices. Slavery or the use of torture to purge individuals found guilty of "witchcraft" would not, if universal, establish the validity of the moral judgments on which such practices are based. Neither does the fact that North and South (including their churches) differed over slavery or that we differ with the inquisitors of the sixteenth century over the use of torture to secure religious conformity exclude the possibility of their validation or objective moral appraisal. Professor Paul Taylor has argued cogently: "Whether a given moral opinion is true or false depends not on who believes it or how many believe it, but on whether reasons can be given to justify it. And such reasons will not include counting the number of people who believe it."[17] This will have to be determined by a wholly different kind of enquiry which would begin not by taking the meaning of validity and objectivity in moral judgment for granted, but by asking how, if at all, we go about validating moral judgments.

It will be argued later that there *is* a trans-cultural basis by reference to which the prevalent precepts and practices in a given culture can be judged, and that such a basis can be formulated without *arbitrarily* elevating the standards prevalent in one culture (or subculture) above another. This will require us to challenge Herskovits's assumption that every set of norms has validity even *"for those people whose lives are guided by them."* (My emphasis.) Such a challenge will be undertaken in the sequel.

Chapter Two

Ideologism:
Marx and Mannheim

Reference was made earlier to cultural relativism understood in the broad epistemological sense as affirming that judgments of fact as well as judgments of value reflect a cultural bias. The content of all knowledge, the very way in which we experience the world, the actual information supplied us by our senses, is, on this view, in part a product of the cultural milieu. Two versions of this view, neither of them using the kind of evidence assembled by ethnologists, have had a powerful influence in undermining belief in the objectivity of moral standards. They are both based on what Karl Marx and Friedrich Engels called the "ideological" component of consciousness.

To understand the concept of ideology as interpreted by Marxists one must first reckon with Marx's theory of economic determinism. In the Marxist view, the bias built into our value judgments derives not so much from the culture as a whole as from the economic conditions that prevail in a culture at any given moment in its history and determine the sequence of events more or less uniformly in all cultures, however much cultures may otherwise differ. These economic conditions, distinguished by Marx as the *forces of production* and the *relations of production,* determine the manner of life of every social group—its institutions, its values, its artifacts. By the "forces of production" Marx meant the human and physical resources available to a society and the level of technology that prevails at any given time. By the "relations of production" he referred to the prevailing system of class relationships in which class is defined by reference to the way the individuals composing it are related to the means of production. This varies: one time the relationship may be that of master and slave; at another, lord and serf; in our day, employer and employee. But always it is a relationship of oppressors and oppressed. The moving force in history is the attempt of such classes to reconstruct society to suit their needs, and so long as the means of production are privately owned these needs will always be in conflict. History is thus a struggle of economic classes, a contest which now breaks out into open warfare, now subsides, depending on whether the hegemony of the property-owning class releases or frustrates the forces of production. There can be no abatement of the struggle until a victorious proletariat abolishes private ownership of the means of production and ushers in the classless society.

The theory of economic determinism—also confusingly known as the materialist interpretation of history—was given its classic formulation in two celebrated statements. In *Anti-Dühring* (1877–1878) Engels, Marx's devoted friend, disciple and collaborator, wrote:

The materialist conception of history starts from the principle that production, and with production the exchange of its products, is the basis of every social order; that in every society which has appeared in history the distribution of the products, and with it the division of society into classes . . . is determined by what is produced and how it is produced, and how the product is exchanged. According to this conception, *the ultimate causes of all social changes and political revolutions are to be sought not in the minds of men, in their increasing insight into eternal truth and justice, but in changes in the mode of production and exchange;* they are to be sought not in the *philosophy* but in the *economics* of the epoch concerned.[1] (Mostly my emphasis.)

And, in the *Critique of Political Economy* (1859) Marx wrote:

In the social production which men carry on they enter into definite relations that are indispensable and independent of their will; these relations of production correspond to a definite stage of development of their material powers of production. The sum total of these relations of production constitutes the economic structure of society— the real foundation, on which rise legal and political superstructures and to which correspond definite forms of social consciousness. *The mode of production in material life determines the general character of the social, political, and spiritual processes of life. It is not the consciousness of men that determines their existence, but, on the contrary, their social existence determines their consciousness.* At a certain stage of their development, the material forces of production in society come into conflict with the existing relations of production, or—what is but a legal expression for the same thing—with the property relations within which they had been at work before. From forms of development of the forces of production these relations turn into their fetters. Then comes the period of social revolution. With the change of the economic foundation the entire immense superstructure is more or less rapidly transformed. *In considering such transformations the distinction should always be made between the material transformation of the economic conditions of production which can be determined with the precision of natural science, and the legal, political, religious, aesthetic, or philosophic—in short ideological forms in which men become conscious of this conflict and fight it out.*[2] (My emphasis.)

Whether he is aware of it or not, the total outlook of an individual is shaped by his participation in the class struggle as thus described. His loyalty to his class, even if only subconsciously, transcends all other loyalties—to family, community, nation. His ideas and aspirations, the way he views his role as parent or spouse, defines justice, seeks rewards, fixes responsibilities, all are a function of his place in the economic structure of society. Accordingly, one cannot speak of man in general, only of specific men belonging to this or that class; one may not speak of justice in the abstract, only of bourgeois or proletarian justice; nor of universal principles of morality, only of the morality of a class; nor of good or bad art, only of good or bad "middle class" art or "people's" art. Objectivity, it turns out, is an illusion or deception; standards and norms masquerading as objective are really reflections of class interest. The following passage is perhaps their clearest formulation of ideological relativism:

We therefore reject every attempt to impose on us any moral dogma whatsoever as an eternal, ultimate, and forever immutable moral law on the pretext that the moral world, too, has its permanent principles which transcend history and the differences between nations. We maintain, on the contrary, that all former moral theories are the product, in the last analysis, of the economic stage which society reached at that particular epoch. And as a society has hitherto moved in class antagonisms, morality has always been a class morality; either it has justified the domination and the interests of the ruling class or, as soon as the oppressed class has become powerful enough, it has represented the revolt against this domination and the future interests of the oppressed.[3]

Historical examples abound, many of them persuasive. During the Middle Ages, the church condemned all lending of money for interest as usury. It later modified this position in what is known as the doctrine of *Damnum emergens* ("loss arising") which affirms that the lender deserves to be compensated for the risk he takes since the loan may not be repaid. Later this doctrine was superseded by the doctrine of *Lucrum cessens* ("profit ceasing") which permits the lender to charge interest, not only to cover his risk, but to compensate him for not having the use of the money. Even this proved to be too restrictive leading to the adoption of the doctrine of *Contractus trinus* ("threefold contract") which makes usurious practices even easier. Marxists urge, no doubt with considerable merit, that such changes were hardly the result of new moral insights, but rather responses to Europe's growing need, as it became urbanized and commercialized, for more capital and for more moneylenders to provide it. The moneylender himself was initially frowned upon by the medieval church; such a career was not for good Catholics, but for Protestants or, as the *Merchant of Venice* reminds us, for Jews. If we (including Catholics) no longer drive money changers out of the temple but honor our bankers ("moneylender" as a term is still tainted) as pillars of our society, how is our change of heart to be explained if not as a consequence of the triumph of the middle class and middle-class values?

What accounts for the spread of Protestantism if not the ascendancy of that same middle class? The Catholic Church was rooted in a feudal, agrarian society and failed to accommodate itself rapidly enough to the needs and aspirations of the newly emerging commercial middle class. "If it is proper to insist on the prevalence of avarice and greed in high places," writes R. H. Tawney in commenting on the Middle Ages, "it is not less important to observe that men called these vices by their right names, and had not learned to persuade themselves that greed was enterprise and avarice economy."[4] Merchants and manufacturers needed an ethic that stressed thrift, industry, austerity —virtues indispensable to success in business and industry. Protestantism, especially Calvinism with its discovery that success in the accumulation of wealth is a mark of one's favor in the eyes of God, provided the appropriate creed. It is no accident that Protestantism flourished in the very areas—North

Germany, the Lowlands, England—where the commercial and industrial revolutions were most advanced.

A final example will suffice. The institution of slavery was taken for granted by the Greeks. Among the Athenians, whose culture we praise above all others, it is estimated that as many as 50 percent of the population were slaves. Plato in his indictment of democracy complains that "The full measure of popular liberty is reached when the slaves of both sexes are quite as free as the owners who paid for them."[5] Aristotle held that slavery was both necessary and natural. The advent of Christianity, even after it became the official and nearly universal religion of both the eastern and western parts of the Roman Empire, did not fundamentally alter attitudes towards slavery. Over the centuries slavery gave way in Europe to serfdom and eventually to the wage system. In Euro-American society the United States was the last holdout. Awkwardly, for those who look to religious sources for moral guidance, the church in the North condemned slavery, the church in the South condoned it.

The following words, spoken by Senator James Hammond of South Carolina as the controversy over slavery in this country grew more intense, deserve to be recalled:

In all social systems there must be a class to do the menial duties. . . . Such a class you must have, or you would not have the other class which leads to progress, civilization and refinement. . . . We call them slaves. We are old-fashioned at the South yet; slave is a word now discarded by 'ears polite'; I will not characterize that class at the North by that term; but you have it; it is there; it is everywhere; it is eternal. . . . The difference between us is, that our slaves are hired for life and well compensated; there is no starvation, no begging, no want of employment among our people, and not too much employment either. Yours are hired by the day, not cared for, and scantily compensated, which may be proved in the most painful manner, at any hour in any street in any of your large towns. . . . Our slaves do not vote. We give them no political power. Yours do vote, and, being the majority, they are the depositaries of all your political power. If they knew the tremendous secret that the ballot-box is stronger than "an army with banners," and could combine, where would you be? Your society would be reconstructed, your government overthrown, your property divided. . . . You have been making war upon us to our very hearthstones. How would you like for us to send lecturers and agitators North, to teach these people this, to aid in combining, and to lead them?[6]

Senator Hammond's bitter tirade tells us, of course, that Marxists were not alone in stressing the class struggle.[7] But it also suggests, as Marxists have tirelessly urged, that the moral difference between slavery and the wage system, at any rate during the period when one replaced the other, was negligible. The transition occurred, Marxists aver, not because slavery affronted the conscience of high-minded men—their conscience seemed untroubled by the abuses of the wage system—but because slavery interfered with more profitable productive relationships and hence became economically untenable.

In all of the illustrations cited—the position of the church on usury, the rise of Protestantism, the abolition of slavery, one encounters appeals to high moral principles which turn out, according to the Marxist, to be reflections of class interest. Even that "kingdom of reason" proclaimed by the French revolutionists, in which "superstition, injustice, privilege, oppression were to be superseded by eternal truth, eternal right, equality based on nature and the inalienable rights of man," turned out, Engels wrote in *Anti-Dühring*, to have been "nothing more than the idealized kingdom of the bourgeoisie." "Eternal right" proved to be no more than "bourgeois justice"; "equality" no more than "bourgeois equality before the law" with property proclaimed as an essential right.[8] Engels concludes: ". . . the bourgeois vices hitherto practiced in secret, began to blossom all the more luxuriantly. Trade became to a greater and greater extent

cheating. The 'fraternity' of the revolutionary motto was realized in the chicanery and rivalries of . . . competition."[9]

The class bias which infuses the vocabulary of moral approval and disapproval confirms the Marxist position. Reinhold
Niebuhr in discussing what he calls the "confusion of manners
and morals" in an hereditary aristocracy notes that " 'Gentle-
man' and 'nobleman' in English and *adel* and *edel* in German
are significant examples of words to be found in all languages
which have the connotation of well-born and well-mannered, on
the one hand, and virtuous and considerate on the other."[10]
Others have called attention to the double meanings of such
terms as "villain," once a feudal tenant; "blackguard," one
who looked after the kettles; and "knave," a servant.[11] So, too,
the German *"schlecht"* for bad or poor as *"schlicht"* simply
designated a plebian as distinguished from an aristocrat. Clearly
the language of morals is often spoken with a class accent.

Despite what has just been said, it would be a mistake to
attribute to Marx the simplistic notion that individuals consciously and deliberately seek their own interest. Sophisticated
Marxists do not deal in conspiracy fantasies in which scheming
capitalists are depicted as tirelessly plotting their own advantage. Only a vulgarized Marxism (of which Marx and Engels
were innocent) views conduct in this way and in this respect
Marx was far more perceptive and subtle than such exponents
of the "selfish system" as Hobbes or Bentham. Marx wrote:

Only one must not form the narrow-minded notion that the petty
bourgeoisie on principle wishes to enforce an egoistic class interest.
Rather, it believes that the *special* conditions of its emancipation are
general conditions within the frame of which alone modern society
can be saved and the class struggle avoided.[12]

And, again, in the preface to *Capital* (first edition):

I paint the capitalist and the landlord in no sense *couleur de rose*. But here individuals are dealt with only in so far as they are the personifications of economic categories, embodiments of particular class relations and class interests. My standpoint, from which the evolution of the economic formation of society is viewed as a process of natural history, can less than any other make the individual responsible for relations whose creature he socially remains, however much he may subjectively raise himself above them.[13]

In the normal case the individual is not *consciously* seeking to serve an ulterior purpose or to mask his own narrow interests. He is not hypocritical or insincere; he really believes that he is judging by reference to objective principles. But this is, to use the well-known term that Marx borrowed from Hegel, a "false consciousness." As such it is what Marx and Engels called *ideological,* a distortion of reality:

Ideology is a process accomplished by the so-called thinker consciously, indeed, but with a false consciousness. The real motives impelling him remain unknown to him, otherwise it would not be an ideological process at all. Hence he imagines false or apparent motives.[14]

All morality is ideologically infected in this sense. For morality assumes that conduct is guided by the dictates of conscience. The appeal is to our sense of moral obligation, our respect for moral law, our ideals, to effect change, whether in individuals or in social conditions. But significant change, the doctrine of economic determinism teaches, is effected only by material (i.e., economic) forces and not by ideal principles. Therefore morality inverts the true relationship of cause and effect, treating ideas (or ideals) as causes when they are *really* effects. And since it is precisely this failing that defines the essential meaning of ideology, all morality is ideological. However, ideology is more than this methodological confusion of ideal effect with material cause. It is also subjective interest parading as objective judgment. It may do credit to human nature that we endlessly perpetrate this hoax, impelled as much to deceive ourselves as others, and, as will be noted later, we may well embarrass Marx and Engels by asking why. However, as far as Marxists are concerned, moral principles are relative —relative to class interest. For Marx that is the reality the obscuring of which is ideology.

In *The German Ideology* (1846), a work on which Marx and Engels collaborated, they wrote:

. . . in all ideology men and their circumstances appear upside down, as in a *camera obscura*. . . . In direct contrast to German philosophy [i.e. German Idealism] . . . we do not set out from what men say, imagine, conceive . . . in order to arrive at men in the flesh. We set out from real, active men, and on the basis of their real life-process we demonstrate the development of the ideological reflexes and echoes of this life process. . . . Morality, religion, metaphysics, all the rest of ideology . . . thus no longer retain the semblance of independence. They have no history, no development; but men, developing their material production and their material intercourse, alter, along with this, their real existence, their thinking, and the products of their thinking.[15]

Here the term "ideology" is used to refer to the philosophies with which Marx and Engels are in disagreement, in particular the idealism of Hegel, greatly influenced though they were by him. (Elsewhere the mechanistic materialism of Ludwig Feuerbach, by which they were also greatly influenced, is included.) Ideology thus refers to more than political economy and ethics; it embraces metaphysics and, of course, religion, jurisprudence, and art. These areas, at the very least, belong to the province of ideology because they ignore the "material," i.e., the economic forces governing our conduct and conditioning our judgments, and stress the role of ideas or ideals. And, as we have seen, for Marx the latter are merely reflections of material forces, mere epiphenomena—above Marx calls them "echoes" and "reflexes" —which as such exercise no decisive causal agency.

Although the generalizations of the natural sciences are exempted from the kind of class bias reflected in philosophy, art, and law, Marxists are ambivalent about the generalizations of the social sciences which often get relegated to the sphere of ideology. This poses a notorious problem for them. Marx thought of himself as a political economist dispassionately describing the dynamics of social change. Is dialectical materialism, the name given (though not by him) to his generalizations, an ideology? How could Marx and Engels, both middle-class intellectuals (Engels was a successful industrialist to boot), transcend their class bias? And, if they, why not others? The question is, of course, crucial. If Marxists answer negatively, affirming the incorrigibility of class bias, they are in the predicament of the Cretan who said that all Cretans are liars. If they answer affirmatively, who qualifies as the exception and by what criteria?

Marx and Engels confronted this issue. In the *Communist Manifesto* they wrote that, as the ruling class approaches dissolution,

A small section . . . joins the revolutionary class. . . . Just as, therefore, at an earlier period, a section of the nobility went over to the bourgeoisie, so now a portion of the bourgeoisie goes over to the proletariat, and in particular, a portion of the bourgeois ideologists who have *raised themselves* to the level of comprehending theoretically the historical movement as a whole."[16] (My emphasis)

Without pronouncing on the merits of Marx's view concerning the historical movement as a whole one may note that a basic problem is suggested in this concession, which Marx and Engels do not resolve. How do men raise themselves? What prompts them? And what kind of deliberation precedes such feats of moral insight? How could Robert Owen, described by Engels as "a man of almost sublime, childlike simplicity of character,"[17] have dedicated himself, almost uniquely among successful manufacturers, to building a society that might be worthy of human beings, even if this meant squandering his fortune on unsuccessful utopian experiments (e.g. New Lanarck) in America? Here, presumably, there has been an escape from the cave of class interests and private prejudices. In such cases one may perhaps find a clue that will further the quest for objectivity which the teachings of Marx otherwise discourage.

Marx and Engels were not ethical theorists and failed to pursue this clue, just as they failed to ask *why* men mask their class interest even from themselves. In the passage from the preface to *Capital* already quoted Marx, in the same sentence that declares the individual the creature of class relations and class interests, adds almost as an afterthought the significant qualification: "however much he may subjectively raise himself above them." Had he tried to account for this latter prompting he might have accomplished more in the area of moral theory than exposing our rationalizations and hypocrisies, significant though that disclosure may be.

It is important to note that Marx and Engels were not really consistent relativists. Not only did they lead lives completely dedicated to social improvement, their words are often glaringly at odds with a relativist position. Engels in the passage cited above (p. 29), in which moral ultimates are rejected, goes on to observe that there has been progress in morality—a judgment obviously presupposing an objective standard of value—and concludes by affirming the possibility of a "really human morality" which "transcends class antagonisms and their legacies in thought" once a stage of society is reached in which class contradictions are not only overcome, but even "forgotten . . . in practical life." It is quite impossible to reconcile such statements, and similar statements by Marx, not only with the words that precede them, but with Marx's dictum that "Communists preach no morality at all."[18] Marx rejected appeals to justice and equality, insisting that Marxism was a science and, as such, was descriptive and devoid of moral suasion and moral prescriptions, yet much of his writing, even if we ignore the young moralistic Marx of his *Economic-Philosophical Manuscripts* (1844), and other early writings is charged with moral fervor. Even though he repudiated his earlier work as too much under the spell of Hegel, we may agree with E. Kamenka that the theme of alienation expounded in the *Manuscripts* is implicit throughout his later work[19] and with it a fierce hatred of the way in which capitalism, as he believed, dehumanizes men by treating them— or their labor, which is a part of them—as a commodity or thing. He may have been limited by his experience of capitalism in its crudest phase and we may contest his judgment that capitalism is incapable of self-correction. Even so, his view of freedom as involving emancipation from economic as well as political bondage is not only more profound than the views of the political determinists of his day, but far more moving in its moral appeal. In truth, the scientist in Marx was often dwarfed by the prophet. The man who almost haughtily disdained moral advocacy was probably the most persuasive advocate of all time. "The philosophers have only *interpreted* the world, in various ways," he complained, "the point, however, is to *change* it."[20]

The legacy Marx left is accordingly mixed. For reformers and revolutionaries seeking radical social change he provided an inspirational ideology—for he was an ideologue as well as an ideologist (i.e. a student of ideologies). But for those who rejected his dream of a classless society as millenial or un-attainable, his positivism and his interpretation of the role of ideology provided another important basis for moral skepticism. What he gives us is a *sociology* of morals which is addressed not to how moral judgments are *validated*, but to their nonrational genesis. True, he believed that the proletariat, to the extent that the forward movement of history realizes itself in the satisfaction of their needs and aspirations, are capable of making what might be called "valid" moral judgments. But Marx's own concept of ideology led him to affirm that the proletariat have their own false consciousness, as when they fail to see the evils of capitalism and are taken in by the ideas and ideals of the ascendant middle class. It is, indeed, a mark of middle-class domination that it is able thus to propagate its views. Therefore, proletarian morality *as such* (if, indeed, there is a morality universally applicable to all proletarians) supplies no standard. The appeal must be to the "laws" of history, that is to the wave of the future. But the laws of history—if there are any—are written in notoriously illegible script. And the future is not yet. We have no way of distinguishing between the wave of the future and the wake of the past. And *ex hypothesi* the victims of a false consciousness are unable to know. As Sartre, himself a Communist, warns, the masses fight blindfolded: "They are in constant danger of going astray, of forgetting who they are, of being seduced by the voice of the myth-maker . . ."[21] Similarly, Lukacs: "Just as there were workers who were misled by Fascism, so there are workers today who fall for Cold War ideology."[22] One need not wonder that a vanguard is needed, especially since suffering no longer endows most Euro-American workers with special moral insight. Corrupt as capitalism is, the condition of workers, in defiance of the laws of history descried by Marx, has not progressively deteriorated. Accordingly, large masses of toilers no longer view themselves as outcasts; instead they join trade unions more concerned with the next round of wage negotiations than with their revolutionary vocation and unique mission to usher in the future. In *What Is to Be Done?* (1902) Lenin himself, arguing that socialism must be imposed from above, had warned—it would seem presciently—that the working class, if left to itself, would only develop a trade union consciousness.

Marx demolished the pretensions of ethical dogmatists. He taught us that we must reckon with the *sociology* and not merely the *psychology* of morals, that is to say, with behavior as *culturally* or *institutionally* conditioned and not merely with primal drives. In this respect he excels Freud, to whose views I shall shortly turn. But he leaves us, if we discount his apocalyptic visions, with a relativistic ethic which provides no place for the validation of moral judgments and, ironically, no basis for understanding his own powerful sense of moral commitment. It would be difficult to find a better example of what Polanyi has called "the chisel of skepticism driven by the hammer of social passion."

Even more ironically Marx provides no basis for understanding how self-interest becomes subordinated to class interest. He is aware of the problem. In *The German Ideology* he and Engels ask: "How does it come about that personal interests grow, despite the persons, into class interests, into common interests which win an independent existence over against individual persons, in this independence take on the shape of general interests, enter as such into opposition with the real individuals, and in this opposition, according to which they are defined as general interests, can be conceived by the consciousness as ideal, even as religious, sacred interests?"[23] A good question. But they fail to answer it. In the end it is this failure that precludes Marxism from providing the theoretical basis of an adequate ethic.[24]

A second version of ideologism is associated with the work of Karl Mannheim which, although not remotely comparable to Marxism in its impact on the course of events, did much to interest social scientists, and through them intellectuals in general, in the role of ideology. His understanding of ideology bears a striking resemblance to views expressed by American pragmatists—notably James, Mead, and Dewey—although it derives from German sources such as Hegel and Marx and has its own distinctive features.

"What we have hitherto hidden from ourselves," Mannheim writes in *Ideology and Utopia* (1929–1931), ". . . is that knowledge in the political and social sciences is, from a certain point on, different from formal mechanistic knowledge; it is different from that point where it transcends the mere enumeration of facts and correlations, and approximates the model of *situationally determined knowledge*."[25] (My emphasis.) By "situationally determined" Mannheim referred to the influence on the content of knowledge of the social "perspective" or life situation of the knower. Mannheim understood such social factors much more broadly than Marx. He would require us to reckon not merely with economic classes, but with such other group formations as occupations, sects, generations, races, nations, etc. In any case, once we attain the insight that knowledge *is* situationally determined, we (1) become capable of criticizing our "collective-unconscious motivations insofar as they determine modern social thinking"; (2) are able to evolve a "new type of intellectual history which is able to interpret changes in ideas in relation to social-historical changes"; (3) are able to evolve a new epistemology in which single, isolated selves do not stand in relationship to an independent object somehow disclosed to them in their singleness and solitude, but in which the social nature of thought is taken into account.[26] Mannheim varied in the kind of knowledge he regarded as situationally determined. The natural and formal (logic, mathematics) sciences are usually excepted, but even the rules of logic are called into question and treated along with all our intellectual tools as products of our social life. Claims made for the objectivity of the social sciences are therefore specious, a conclusion that applies *a fortiori* to the cognitive claims of moral judgments.

Mannheim formulated his notions about situationally determined knowledge in two concepts: *ideology* and *utopia*. "The

concept 'ideology',", he tells us, "reflects the one discovery
which emerged from political conflict, namely, the ruling groups
can in their thinking become so intensively interest-bound to a
situation that they are simply no longer able to see certain
facts which would undermine their sense of domination." That
is, "in certain situations the collective unconscious of certain
groups obscures the real condition of society both to itself and
to others and thereby stabilizes it."[27]

Mannheim distinguishes between two meanings of ideology
—the *particular* and the *total*. The former refers to the distor-
tions and deceptions we impute to an opponent when we regard
them not as deliberate lies or products of malicious cunning, but
as the unwitting outcome of his particular situation. The latter
refers to the ideology of an age or a social group and is distinguished by its inclusiveness, calling into question the "total
Weltanschauung." What is involved is not an occasional selfishly
motivated distortion, but "fundamentally divergent thought-sys-
tems and widely differing modes of experience and interpretation"[28] and hence not merely the content of thought but its
very structure. Thus, ". . . the dominant modes of thought are
supplanted by new categories when the social basis of the
group, of which these thought forms are characteristic, disinte-
grates or is transformed under the impact of social change."[29]
Groups differing in ideology presumably lack even common
criteria of validity. Accordingly, an understanding of "total"
ideological differences requires not a *psychology* of interests
dealing with the contingent motivations of this or that individual, but a *sociology* of *knowledge*, that is, a theory of cognition
concerned with explaining how *all* members of a group *must*
think as dictated by the place of the group in the social structure. Like all Germans, Mannheim was obviously nourished on
Kant; the foregoing is a kind of sociologized version of the
Critique of Pure Reason.

If ideological thinking is a way in which groups content with
the prevailing order strive to preserve it, utopian thinking re-

flects the opposite tendency of discontented groups to concentrate so exclusively on changing or destroying the social order that they see only what is to its discredit. Such thinking is incapable of correctly diagnosing a social problem because it is not concerned with what really exists, only with giving us a direction for action. "In the utopian mentality, the collective unconscious, guided by wishful representation and the will to action, hides certain aspects of reality. It turns its back on everything which would shake its belief or paralyse its desire to change things."[30]

Discovery of the ideological and utopian elements in thinking can occur only in a rapidly changing intellectual world where ideas and values heretofore taken for granted are in flux. It is a consequence, Mannheim notes, of the disappearance of a unitary intellectual world with fixed values and norms, coinciding with the discovery of the role of the unconscious in our thinking. Thus ours is an epoch in which all values and points of view appear in their genuine relativity. We are able to realize "once and for all that the meanings that make up our world are simply an historically determined and continuously developing structure . . . and are in no sense absolute."[31] For Mannheim, false consciousness is the consciousness that, in its preoccupation with changeless absolutes, "obstructs comprehension of a reality which is the outcome of constant reorganization of the mental processes which make up our worlds."[32]

Much of what Mannheim says is, of course, confirmed by common experience. Confronted as we often are with views irresolvably different from our own, there is often a disposition to conclude, after appeals to facts and rules of logic have failed, that our opponent simply doesn't *think* as we do. Appeals to logic seem pointless. Two intelligent, English-speaking adversaries, one a Bircher and the other a New Leftist are likely to conclude after extended debate that "We just don't speak the same language," and this is often true of adversaries less far apart. "The meaning of words had no longer the same relation to things," wrote Thucydides in describing the "commotion" on the eve of the Peloponnesian war. His comment is just as relevant to our time. In such circumstances, opponents abandon appeals to evidence and assail each other's motives, accuse each other of "rationalizing," exchange charges of paranoia, find each other blinded by group loyalties and past associations. The *ad hominem* argument takes over. Statements are tested in such contexts not by reference to evidence, but by citing the attributes of the author of the statement, his group affiliations and social background. Since *what* is said is too absurd to merit consideration, attention shifts from what is said to *why* it was said.

Considerations such as the foregoing have provided the basis for a relatively new discipline, the sociology of knowledge, the principal assumption of which is, in Mannheim's words, "that there are modes of thought which cannot be adequately understood so long as their social origins are obscured." The new discipline seeks to understand thought "in the concrete setting of an historical-social situation."[33] Mannheim, in a manner highly suggestive of John Dewey, cites a second feature of the sociology of knowledge. It understands that in their thinking the attitudes of men are not detached and merely theoretical or contemplative. They strive "in accordance with the character and position of the groups to which they belong to change the surrounding world of nature and society or attempt to maintain it in a given condition." It is this impulse to act or to oppose action which in certain areas "determines the selection of those elements of reality which enter into thought."[34] Thus there are two essential elements: (a) attachment to a group; (b) orientation towards action. Despite these observations Mannheim himself did not conclude that objectivity is unattainable. He believed that "a new type of objectivity in the social sciences is attainable not through the exclusion of evaluations but through the critical awareness and control of them."[35] Nevertheless, an approach which is concerned with the *origin* of beliefs rather than their *validity*, whatever its insights, is bound to encourage skepticism not only in the social sciences but in the whole domain of morality. As Mannheim said, "the sociological view regarding knowledge inevitably carries with it the gradual uncovering of the irrational foundation of rational knowledge."[36] A product of the multiplication of value systems, thought styles and world views, and of the "reciprocal unmasking" of the unconscious and irrational sources of the claims made for them, the sociology of knowledge has helped, as Mannheim conceded, to undermine "man's confidence in human thought in general."[37]

Both the insights of the sociology of knowledge and the sense of inadequacy with which it leaves us are suggested when we try to deal with statements like the following:

A Mysterious Providence has brought the black and the white people together from different parts of the globe, and no human power could now separate them. The whites are an European race, being masters; and the Africans are the inferior race, and slaves . . . they could exist among us peaceably enough, if undisturbed, for all time.[38]

These were the words of John C. Calhoun, addressing the U.S. Senate during the debate over slavery.

Another elitist, Edmund Burke, writing in behalf of the English aristocracy and its fitness to govern, declared in a passage too eloquent for abbreviation:

A true natural aristocracy is not a separate interest in the state, or separable from it. It is an essential integrant part of any large body rightly constituted. It is formed out of a class of legitimate presumptions, which, taken as generalities, must be admitted for actual truths. To be bred in a place of estimation; to see nothing low and sordid from one's infancy; to be taught to respect one's self; to be habituated to the censorial inspection of the public eye; to look early to public opinion; to stand upon such elevated ground as to be enabled to take a large view of the widespread and infinitely diversified combinations of men and affairs in a large society; to have leisure to read, to reflect, to converse; to be enabled to draw the court and attention of the wise and learned, wherever they are to be found; to be habituated in armies to command and to obey; to be taught to despise danger in the pursuit of honor and duty; to be formed to the greatest degree of vigilance, foresight, and circumspection, in a state of things in which no fault is committed with impunity and the slightest mistakes draw on the most ruinous consequences; to be led to a guarded and regulated conduct, from a sense that you are considered as an instructor of your fellow-citizens in their highest concerns, and that you act as a reconciler between God and man; to be employed as an administrator of law and justice, and to be thereby amongst the first benefactors to mankind; to be a professor of high science, or of liberal and ingenuous art; to be amongst rich traders, who from their success are presumed to have sharp and vigorous understandings, and to possess the virtues of diligence, order, constancy, and regularity, and to have cultivated an habitual regard to commutative justice: these are the circumstances of men that form what I shall call a *natural* aristocracy, without which there is no nation.[39]

Both Calhoun and Burke were intellectually gifted. Both were in their way public-minded men and both no doubt believed what they were saying. Burke was not even a member of the British aristocracy which he defended so eloquently. The sociology of knowledge requires us to disclose the ideological element in these statements and to unmask them as the unconscious deceptions they are. But, how can this be done except by reference to some standard that transcends the situation in which these men pleaded their cause? Thomas Jefferson would have rejected Calhoun's apology for slavery as he did Burke's advocacy of the rule of an hereditary aristocracy. Is there not a fundamental sense in which Jefferson was right and Calhoun and Burke wrong, not just about their facts but in their moral judgment? The sociology of knowledge leaves us with no basis for finding an answer.

Chapter Three

Freudian Psychology: Its Skeptical Implications

As if the testimony of distinguished social scientists were not enough, the formidable weight of Freudian psychology was likewise enlisted by its founder on the side of moral skepticism. To say this is not to detract from Freud's great contributions to our understanding of conduct. Thanks to the "Copernican revolution" he initiated, it is now possible to explore areas of experience and behavior which would otherwise have remained terra incognita. Freud's method of analyzing free associations, transference, dreams and errors provided those skilled in the use of his techniques with access to an inner life often suppressed or available to introspection only in distorted versions of the real thing. He repaired the neglect in his time of the role of the sex drive in the motivation of behavior, as he corrected sentimental idealizations of human nature which fail to reckon with man's aggressions. Much that parades as morality is sheer hypocrisy; Freud, like Marx, taught us to be on guard. It is difficult to exaggerate our indebtedness to him for his insights into the role of the unconscious and the extent to which irrational factors enter into conduct. In the foregoing accounts Marx, Engels, Mannheim, all refer to unconscious motivations; Freud probes the psychodynamics of such motivation and gives us a new understanding of its causes and consequences. Nevertheless, Freudian psychology suffers from serious limitations. And, in the absence of substantive revisions, its implications for moral theory are clearly skeptical. Concern here is not with the clinical aspects of psychoanalysis, but with Freud's larger speculations, sometimes called his "metapsychology."

At the outset Freud's account of motivation incorporated a thoroughly discredited hedonism. His defense of the pleasure principle reads like a rewrite of Bentham's *Principles of Morals and Legislation:*[1]

What do (men) demand of life and wish to achieve in it? The answer to this can hardly be in doubt. They strive after happiness. . . . This endeavor has two sides, a positive and a negative aim. It aims, on the one hand, at an absence of pain and unpleasure, and, on the other, at the experiencing of strong feelings of pleasure. . . . In conformity with this dichotomy in his aims, man's activity develops in two directions, according as it seeks to realize—in the main, or even exclusively—the one or the other of these aims.

As we see, what decides the purpose of life is simply the programme of the pleasure principle. The principle dominates the operation of the mental apparatus from the start.[2]

This was simply a restatement of what Freud had said earlier in his *Introductory Lectures on Psychoanalysis:*

We may ask whether in the operation of our mental apparatus a main purpose can be detected, and we may reply as a first approximation that that purpose is directed to obtaining pleasure. It seems as though our total mental activity is directed towards achieving pleasure and avoiding unpleasure—that it is automatically regulated by the *pleasure-principle*. (Freud's emphasis) [3]

It should be noted that Freud is not proposing a moral prescription, namely, that men *ought* to seek happiness or pleasure. Such *ethical* hedonism presupposes in the term "ought" some kind of moral obligation and prompts one to ask what "obligation" in this sense could mean. Freud is unconcerned with such questions. His *psychological* hedonism is intended as a description of how men do in fact behave. If we are so constituted that we must seek pleasure it is of course gratuitous to say that we *ought* to do so.

The notorious defects of hedonism as an account of motivation in conduct—quite apart from its inadequacy as an ethic—will be discussed in detail later. (See below, pp. 68–74.) Freud compounds these defects by exaggerating the role of the sex drive (libido), affirming that, consciously or unconsciously, the desire for erotic pleasure completely dominates man from the cradle to the grave (or womb to tomb). However broadly the sexual impulse may be understood by Freud (e.g., as infantile sexuality and "narcissistic" libido), his is the dubious thesis that it is not merely the "pleasure principle" but an *erotic* pleasure principle that always governs conduct.

Freud's use of what he called the "reality principle" is sometimes cited as exempting him from the foregoing criticism, as when Alasdair MacIntyre writes that "It is . . . in transcending the pleasure principle in the name of the claims of reality, of truthfulness, that the core of the Freudian ethic lies."[4] But Freud makes it quite clear that the reality principle (i.e., the claims of reality) which may replace the pleasure principle, "does not abandon the intention of ultimately obtaining pleasure." The reality principle simply "demands and carries into effect the postponement of satisfaction . . . and the temporary toleration of unpleasure as a step on the long indirect road to pleasure."[5] Freud is referring to the obvious fact that we sometimes have to tolerate pain or dis-pleasure (*Unlust,* poorly rendered by his translators as "unpleasure") or pass up pleasures in order to get greater pleasure in the end. His reality-principle simply places him in the tradition of the cautious Epicureans rather than the robust Cyrenaics; he is not thereby any less a hedonist.

In *Beyond the Pleasure Principle* Freud also acknowledges the presence of instinctive urges operating more or less independently of pleasure and pain. His experience after World War I with the war dreams of shell-shocked soldiers and a variety of related phenomena led him to postulate a "repetition compulsion" which "recalls from the past experiences which include no possibility of pleasure, and which can never, even long ago, have brought satisfaction even to instinctual impulses which have since been repressed."[6] Such repetition compulsions, found by him to be "more primitive, more elementary, more instinctive than the pleasure principle,"[7] and the instincts inherent in organic life, including the self-preservation drive with its manifestations in aggression, he now speculated might be related to a death instinct—Thanatos—which competes with the life instinct—Eros. In other words, with the large exception of the sex instinct, the instinctual life as a whole, including the self-preservative instincts, strives to return to an earlier state, which came to imply for Freud an original inorganic state. Therefore "the goal of all life is death."[8]

It is not useful to cite the farfetched arguments with which Freud embroidered this melancholy speculation. He begins by promising us that he is merely engaging in "an attempt to follow an idea consistently, out of curiosity to see where it will lead."[9] This is reassuring; he is trying the shoe on for size. But Freud has a disconcerting way of making off on long hikes while his readers are still wondering if the shoe fits. An extended argument follows which appears to be a serious defense of the plausibility of the death wish only to conclude with Freud confessing that he is not convinced of the truth of the hypotheses he has been advancing and has no intention of persuading others. In fact, he says disarmingly, "I do not know how far I believe in them."[10] However, twelve years later uncertainty has been dispelled. In his celebrated *New Introductory Lectures* (1932), a product of his most mature thought, he addresses himself to the same thesis, now "confirmed by sober and painstaking detailed research":

If it is true that . . . life once proceeded out of inorganic matter, then, according to our presumption, an instinct must have arisen which sought to do away with life once more and to re-establish the inorganic state. If we recognize in this instinct the self-destructiveness of our hypothesis, we may regard the self-destructiveness as an expression of a "death instinct" which cannot fail to be present in every vital process. And now the instincts that we believe in divide themselves into two groups—the erotic instincts, which seek to combine more and more living substance into ever greater unities, and the death instincts, which oppose this effort and lead what is living back into an inorganic state.[11]

One must concede, to be sure, that there is the germ of an idea in Freud's death instinct. Like so many of his observations this one provides us with a suggestive aperçu. The Europe that followed Freud's Vienna into a prolonged blood bath and re-enacted the tragedy a generation later could be said to have been possessed of a collective death instinct. The born loser is a familiar type—he has it made and self-destructively invites failure. We all know people who are their own worst enemies. It seems like an apt hyperbole to say that such people, along with those who seem accident prone, are afflicted with what Freud taught us to call a death wish. But it is difficult to take Freud's

excursion into metapsychology literally, and even admirers like
J. C. Flugel and Ernest Jones note[12] that few psychologists,
even among psychoanalysts, have found this somber amendment
to the pleasure principle acceptable. In any event, Thanatos is
hardly a star by which to guide the quest for an understanding
of moral obligation and, whatever the scope he finally gave to
the death instinct, the skepticism implicit in his pleasure principle remains. If such a principle governs our conduct, one kind
of pleasure or satisfaction is as good as another, as Bentham
recognized when he declared that "pushpin is a good as poetry."
Whatever yields the most gratification is best. There is no other
test.[13] True, Freud, not unlike Bentham before him, speaks of
"the improvement of the human lot," but clearly, if one can
maximize his pleasure at the expense of the human lot, Freud's
pleasure principle leaves one with no alternative.

The skeptical implications of Freudian psychology are not
an unintended consequence of his hedonism. They derive from
his theory of personality (the structural theory, so-called),
which he differentiates into what, in a now much used nomenclature, he calls the *id,* the *superego,* and the *ego.* The id, "a
cauldron full of seething excitations,"[14] is the locus of the individual's primitive passions and aggressions. These instinctual,
biological demands encounter the restraints imposed by society
first in the form of the authority of the father (or a father
substitute), then in the moral codes or ethical norms essential to
a viable social order. Although civilization could not survive
without rules and regulations to control our aggressive and
libidinal tendencies, such standards of conduct are felt, according to Freud, as inhibitive and repressive. They become internalized as the dictates of one's conscience, i.e., as imperatives
issued by what Freud calls the superego. The tension thereby
generated between our primal, instinctual drives and the external or internal "moral" restraints imposed by the superego
manifests itself in the ego's conscious or unconscious sense of

guilt and in a sense of moral obligation which is no more than a form of submission to authority, made easier when, by a putative identification of the self with the father, it is internalized as the voice of conscience likened, in a striking phrase, to a "garrison in a conquered city."[15]

If we waive the notorious difficulties inherent in Freud's variously defined concept of the ego, it turns out in the last reckoning to be a kind of tamed variant of the id, suppressing its primal passions in deference to the prohibitions of the superego and the external world and consoling itself by pretending that its now secret instinctual drives are morally bad. In Freud's words, the ego "is the better organized part of the id, with its face turned towards reality."[16] Concerning his concept of the ego Karen Horney concludes:

Freud denies—and on the basis of the libido theory must deny—that there are any judgments or feelings which are not dissolvable into more elemental "instinctual" units. In general his concept means that on theoretical grounds any judgments about people or causes must be regarded as rationalizations of "deeper" emotional motivations. . . . It means that theoretically there is no liking or disliking of people, no sympathy, no generosity, no feeling of justice, no devotion to a cause, which is not in the last analysis essentially determined by libidinal or destructive drives.[17]

Clearly a strong case can be made out for characterizing Freud as a *reductionist,* seeking to understand man exclusively in psychological—ultimately biological—terms and denying any unique or distinctive quality to man's moral experience. Criticizing Freud's "Homo psychologicus" for being as abstract as the "Homo economicus" of the classical economists, Erich Fromm aptly observes: "It is impossible to understand man and his emotional and mental disturbances without understanding the nature of value and moral conflicts."[18] But Freud was unconcerned with such conflicts in so far as they involve questions concerning the *validity* of moral judgments; for him the last word is said when their *motivation* is disclosed. Not some, but all value judgments are, he believed, mere rationalizations of our unconscious, irrational desires: ". . . man's judgments of value follow directly his wishes for happiness" and "are an attempt to support his illusions with arguments."[19] Not inconsistently, he characterized his own ardent commitment to the pursuit of truth as his "illusion" and his "mythology." Whatever his practice, his theory required him to regard the sense of obligation, whether to the cause of truth or any other cause, as the reflection of secret guilt feelings. Fromm justly concludes that "while psychoanalysis has tremendously increased our knowledge of man, it has not increased our knowledge of how man ought to live and what he ought to do."[20] The failure, if it is one, is underscored when we note the words Freud wrote to his devoted disciple, Princess Marie Bonaparte: "The moment a man questions the meaning and value of life he is sick, since objectively neither has any existence."[21] It may be concluded that there is no place in the Freudian scheme of things for an autonomous moral life even though, in a permissible use of the *ad hominem* argument, one may say that Freud's personal example was the best refutation of his theory.

Freud was a reductionist in another related sense, namely, in his view of institutional influences as external to the individual and hence in his essentially mechanistic view of society as an aggregate of individuals who possess their basic identity apart from the social relationships of which they partake. Such a mechanistic reductionism was perfectly consonant with the individualism of the Enlightenment to which he was heir. We may agree without reservation with Philip Rieff that "His [Freud's] work was an attempt to strengthen our inner resources against what he considered obsolete cultural systems of inhibitions."[22] However, in his laudable zeal to overcome the tyranny of certain unhealthy social restraints, Freud neglected the extent to which the institutional life of man enters into and is constitutive in a positive way of his very nature. Although it would be unfair to ignore Freud's occasional concessions to the influence of culture,[23] these are obscured by his overwhelming psychological bias and his assumption that the role of culture is invariably alien and restrictive rather than directive and creative. As is well known, Freud and orthodox Freudians find their explanation for conduct, both individual and collective, in the biography of the individual, his infantile experiences and instinctual drives, and in mechanisms of repression which assertedly are common to and function in the same way for all men.

The point is a crucial one. The foregoing parallels the criticism of Freudian revisionists such as Fromm, Horney, and Sullivan, whose views concerning the implications of orthodox Freudianism for moral theory I share. But the issue has occasioned vigorous and even bitter disagreement. Marcuse charges in a long polemic that the revisionist criticism of Freud "constitutes a blank [sic] discarding of his theoretical conception" and that it "consecrates a false picture of civilization and particularly of present-day society."[24] Dr. Franz Alexander, defending Freud against the charge of reductionism (or psychologism), contends that Freud was "fully aware of the fact that the development of human personality can be understood only if one considers the influence of the prevailing social standards and values to which it is subjected." He cites in support of Freud's interpretation of conscience: "Freud considered conscience (Ego Ideal, later called Superego) as the precipitate of parental influences which transmit to the child the standards and values of the society in which he matures."[25] Similarly, Ernest van den Haag urges that

To say that Freud "found there was just no room for including the [social] environmental factor in his frame of reference"[26] is in my

opinion a profound misunderstanding. In Freud's theory, the environmental factor transmitted through the primary group is internalized
quite early. It is *part* of the "frame of reference"—wherefore it need
not be added later.[27]

The same view was taken by Hans Meyerhoff who called
Freud's asserted neglect of the role of culture a "scientific
myth."[28]

However, this only shows that, to use Freud's own words,
"Men do not always take their great thinkers seriously even
when they profess most to admire them." Freud's text speaks
for itself. To be sure, there are qualifications which seem to
reject psychologism, but they are parenthetical or of the nature
of *obiter dicta* or are canceled out by what is said later. Thus,
in the Introduction to *Group Psychology and the Analysis of
the Ego* (1921), a work often cited as refuting those who charge
him with reductionism, Freud writes that "only rarely and under
certain exceptional conditions is individual psychology in a
position to disregard the relations of [the] individual to others."[29]
He adds that "Group psychology is therefore concerned with
the individual man as a member of a race, of a nation, of a
caste, of a profession, of an institution . . . of a crowd."[30] A
sociologist could hardly ask for more. However, in the end we
have this crucial retraction: "His [the primal father's] sexual
jealousy and intolerance became in the last resort the causes
of group psychology."[31]

The point requires brief elaboration. Freud is often defended against the charge that he neglects the role of social
relationships by citing, as van den Haag does above, the central
place in his treatment of the individual of the role of the family.
His analysis of the structure and dynamics of the family as a
primary group has been hailed not only as one of his greatest
scientific achievements but as his most significant contribution
to social psychology.[32] But in a basic sense that differentiates

it from other social groups, the family is a *biological* group. Moreover, it is significant that Freud treats the dynamics of the relationship between parents and children not as culturally variable—at any rate, in a basic sense (differentiating the Ashanti of Central Ghana, for example, from twentieth-century Euro-Americans, the Nayar caste of southern India, and the fifteenth-century villagers of Vinci where Leonardo was born)[33] —but as exhibiting a uniform bio-psychological pattern (of libidinal object choices, identification, hostility, ambivalence, the Oedipus and castration complexes, etc.). It is even more significant that, for Freud, as Hall and Lindzey point out, "The dynamics of family organization is reflected in the dynamics of all organized groups. For Freud, the family is the prototype for every association among people, whether the association be political, economic, social, recreational, or religious in character.[34] In sum, it is difficult indeed to derive from Freud's preoccupation with the family a true recognition of the role of social conditions in determining conduct.

I turn to Freud's text. His criticism of Communist views concerning aggression affords an instructive example of a failure to take cultural variations seriously. He does not limit himself to characterizing the assumption that aggressive tendencies will disappear with the abolition of private property as "psychologically untenable." Although aggression might thereby be deprived of one of its instruments, in abolishing private property,

We have in no way altered the differences in power and influence which are misused by aggressiveness, *nor have we altered anything in its nature.* Aggressiveness was not created by property. It reigned almost without limit in primitive times, when property was still very scanty, and it already shows itself in the nursery almost before property has given up its primal, anal form; it forms the basis of every relation of affection and love among people (with the single exception, perhaps, of the mother's relation to her male child). If we do away with personal rights over material wealth, there still remains prerogative in the field of sexual relations, which is bound to become the source of the strongest dislike and the most violent hostility among men who are in other respects on an equal footing. If we were to remove this factor, too, by allowing complete freedom of sexual life and thus abolishing the family, the germ-cell of civilization, we cannot, it is true, easily foresee what new paths the development of civilization could take; but one thing we can expect, and that is that this indestructible feature of human nature will follow it there.[35]

We may be grateful for a proper caution against the kind of innocence about human nature displayed by Communists. But the passage cited above goes far beyond such warnings. Clearly human nature in its basic aspects is viewed by Freud as a constant, quite insulated from even the most profound cultural or institutional changes.

Typically, when Freud found that women (presumably Viennese) are more jealous and envious than men, he assumed that the phenomenon was constant and universal—a dubious thesis—and promptly attributed it to the female's sense of deprivation in not possessing a penis (a calamity she discovers as an infant), her consequent wish for the next best, namely, sexual intercourse, and her envy of other women who have been gratified.[36] Freud might have but did not look for an explanation elsewhere—for example, in the subordinate status of women in Viennese society at the time his observations (assuming them to have been accurate) were made.

Whether it be his treatment of such a local phenomenon or his explanation of more widespread phenomena such as totemism and the taboo against incest, it is difficult to avoid the conclusion that, for Freud, man is basically no different today than when, as a member of a putative primal horde, he and his brothers, driven by an incestuous desire for their mother, slew their father in a fit of jealousy and (according to Freud) in their ensuing remorse, bequeathed to all generations that came after (by a hereditary mechanism no one has discovered) the legacy of guilt we now experience as the promptings of conscience.[37] Social institutions, culture, have made no real difference except to restrain the instinctual drives that rage in man as furiously as ever. Civilization is thus a mere gloss and the morality it imposes a specious appearance. This is not to deny that, as E. W. Burgess observed, Freud's work "has had a wholesome effect upon sociologists prone to ascribe all behavior to cultural conditioning."[38] But even a warm admirer like Rieff concedes that: "Freud never articulated a truly social psychology. Against the main drift of contemporary social science, his concern remains the individual and his instincts."[39]

There is, as much of the foregoing suggests, a simple test of the seriousness with which the influence of culture is taken, which is not to be found in the number of references to culture, as Meyerhoff failed to see when he protested that "in his later writings [Freud] addressed himself almost exclusively to cultural problems and insisted that all psychology was group psychology."[40] It is to be found in the *importance attached to cultural difference and institutional change*. What is the impact of such variation and change on conduct? If, despite great cultural diversity and change, conduct in its basic manifestations is treated as constant, it is clear that cultural influence is regarded as negligible and the explanation for conduct will be sought in the generalizations of psychology, no matter how numerous the references to society or "civilization." This was in fact the tendency of classical liberals from Locke to Mill, as evidenced by the extent to which their conclusions about society are deduced from psychological assumptions about individual human nature and their treatment (implicit in all strictly hedonistic accounts) of men as homogeneous whenever and wherever they live.[41] Although Freud's emphasis on the irrational in conduct removes him from that tradition, he otherwise shared this tendency. It is significant that for the most part he wrote about civilization in general and not about civilizations (in the plural) and their differing discontents. It is even more significant that when he does address himself in *Civilization and Its Discontents* to cultural change it is treated, often highly suggestively to be sure, as an evolution (undifferentiated by time and place) paralleling the development of the individual, including the emergence of a cultural superego, of a set of demands manifest in the ethics of a culture which ignores the needs of the cultural id, of a repudiation or martyrdom of great leaders (e.g., Jesus Christ) suggestive of primal parricide, etc. Although we are cautioned not to forget "that after all we are dealing only with analogies,"[42] there is no gainsaying that the behavior of the whole is thought of by Freud as closely resembling the behavior of the individuals that constitute it, which, whether or not it involves the fallacy of composition, would clearly leave us with a case of psychologizing the social instead of socializing the psychological.

If the criticism is, as I believe, a fair one, there is little basis in Freudian theory for understanding man *when he acts qua moral agent,* since this is, as will be seen in detail later, *essentially* a social process. In other words, a mechanistic reductionism, *regardless of the terms in which individual human nature is described,* since it regards the facts of psychology as sufficient and neglects man as a social being—we need not go so far as Émile Durkheim and A. L. Kroeber and reify social relationships with terms like "group mind" or "social substance"[43]—is precluded from understanding man when he makes authentic moral judgments.

However, in the final analysis, it is not necessary to take sides in the controversy over Freud's reductionism. Even those who exempt Freud of reductionism can hardly fail to concede that, to the extent that Freud reckons with social factors, they are cast in a negative role; they inhibit and restrain the individual, they cannot enhance or fulfill him. If the individual is altered by his social relationships, this appears to be in the unhappy direction of becoming guiltridden, not distinguishable in kind from the neurotic extreme typified by the parson in *Rain* or the Reverend Arthur Dimmesdale of Hawthorne's *Scarlet Letter*. The superego which represents the demands of morality and of society and speaks through the voice of conscience tyrannizes over the ego. It comes on as a forbidding (in the double sense) policeman. It addresses us always in the imperative mood: "Thou shalt not!" What it represents is in Freud's own term "ego-alien." It is not self-imposed *by* the ego but inflicted *on* it. It is no accident that, when Freud did turn his attention briefly to group psychology, he took two authoritarian institutions as his models, the Catholic Church and the Army; apparently these were for him paradigms of society as a whole.[44] The sadism which the individual would otherwise discharge against others becomes through the superego a kind of self-aggression: "the more a man checks his aggressiveness towards the exterior [others] the more severe—that is, aggressive—he becomes ["Nemesism"] in his ego ideal [superego].[45]

If all this had been limited in its application to prigs, prudes, moral snobs, phony evangelists, and other assorted imposters, and to rigid, authoritarian codes stressing punctilious conformity, we could be grateful without reservation for Freud's brilliant exposés. But, unfortunately, Freud's account of the superego and the morality that speaks through it is not limited to bogus moralizers and well-known neurotic types who, like Lord Angelo in *Measure for Measure*, while obsessive about moral rectitude, are secretly consumed with lust ("O, what may man within him hide/Though angel on the outward side!")[46]; nor to Freud's presumably guiltridden patients; nor to the restrictive codes parading as morality we call Pharisaism or Puritanism. We are told that *even ordinary normal morality has a harshly restraining, cruelly prohibiting quality.*[47]

We have good grounds, says Freud's loyal follower and chief biographer, Ernest Jones, "for supposing that to the activity of the superego we are mainly beholden for the imposing structure of morality, conscience, ethics, aesthetics, religion—in short to the whole spiritual aspiration of man that sunders him most strikingly from the beast."[48] But the spiritual aspirations to which Dr. Jones refers somehow in all of Freud's ruminations about them never escape the dark shadow cast over them by Freud's view of the superego as heir to the Oedipus complex. Dr. Jones's summary of that legacy as viewed by Freud is helpful:

The child, faced with the hopelessness of his oedipus wishes [carnal desires for the mother, jealousy and hatred of the father, fear of castration, etc.] both because of the inexorable privation and because of the fear of punishment, effects a renunciation of them on condition that he permanently incorporates something of the parents within himself. This image of love and dread, derived from both parents, though more especially from the one of the same sex, then constitutes the superego, which continues to exercise its function of watching, threatening and if necessary punishing the ego when there is any likelihood of its listening to the now forbidden and repressed oedipus wishes of the id. Freud thus termed the superego the heir of the oedipus complex: its derivative and substitute.[49]

A different view of social control, manifesting itself in the self-scrutiny that lies at the heart of moral deliberation, will be defended later in this volume. It will stress the importance of honesty and self-knowledge in such criticism and to that extent will rely heavily on Freud's great contributions to such self-criticism. However, it will find its inspiration not in Freud's negative view, but in the kind of positive view of social control expressed by another great teacher, George H. Mead, who, after the brilliant analysis of social interaction for which he became renowned, concluded:

And thus it is that social control, as operating in terms of self-criticism, exerts itself so intimately and extensively over individual behavior or conduct, serving to integrate the individual and his actions with reference to the organized social process . . . in which he is implicated. . . . That is to say, self-criticism is essentially social criticism, and behavior controlled by self-criticism is essentially behavior controlled socially. *Hence social control, so far from tending to crush out the human individual or to obliterate his self-conscious individuality, is, on the contrary, actually constitutive of and inextricably associated with that individuality;* for the individual is what he is, as a conscious and individual personality, just in as far as he is a member of society, involved in the social process of experience and activity, and thereby socially controlled in his conduct. (My emphasis.)[50]

To return to Freud. Freudians with an ethical bias will protest that Freud was morally motivated, pointing out that the goal of psychoanalysis it to bring the unconscious to the level of awareness and thereby to extend the area of rational control. Professor Herbert Fingarette argues persuasively that "there is a moral outlook with respect to guilt and responsibility which is compatible with the data and theories of psychoanalysis."[51] He points out, for example, that the aim of therapy is not to "loosen conscience" or eliminate feelings of guilt from human experience. To remove or reduce guilt feelings in the case of evil acts or wishes would be to encourage them, whereas the aim of the analyst is the opposite, i.e., where possible to eliminate or modify the wish. Hence, the psychoanalyst "far from relaxing our moral judgments in fundamental questions is, in fact, aiming at helping us to be moral (and rational)."[52] In *The Future of an Illusion* (1928) Freud himself refers to the "love of man and the decrease of suffering"[53] and similar references may be found elsewhere in his writings. In his *Introductory Lectures on Psychoanalysis* (1917) Freud rejected the charge that he ignored the positive aspects of moral life:

It is not our intention to dispute the noble endeavors of human nature, nor have we ever done anything to detract from their value. On
the contrary; I am exhibiting to you not only the evil dream-wishes
which are censored but also the censorship, which suppresses them
and makes them unrecognizable. We lay a stronger emphasis on what
is evil in men only because other people disavow it and thereby make
the human mind, not better, but incomprehensible. If now we give up
this one-sided ethical valuation, we shall undoubtedly find a more correct formula for the relation between good and evil in human nature.[54]

Perhaps so. Thanks in part to Freud (and to bitter experience)
we no longer question "civilized" man's capacity for savagery.
But what Freud gives us is a *psychology* of morals that precludes an ethic, which is to say, any meaningful distinction
between the good and evil referred to in the foregoing passage.
Denied, often if only by implication, is the possibility that the
biological and psychological raw material of instinctual drives,
and their repression, is at least in part transformed as man
becomes civilized and acquires a *moral* stature, so that new
concepts and categories are required for a full understanding
of the pertinent data. Freud exposed our hypocrisies and punc-
tured those self-serving pretensions that often masquerade as
duty and speak with a spurious voice of conscience. He taught
us to reckon with and respect the power of impulse and the
final futility and fearful cost of suppressing impulses that are
part of our nature. But it is not a vulgarization of his teaching
—as some apologists charge—to note that duty, conscience, the
sense of obligation, tend, in his treatment, to vanish as distinctive and authentic moral categories. Nor do we dismiss his
basic insight when we argue that their role, like the role of
social institutions, need not be merely negative and repressive,
as Freud suggests, but liberating and enhancing. "It is difficult
to see," writes Morris Ginsberg, "how such a conception of
human nature can ever provide the basis for a rational ethnic,"
and he concludes that "psychoanalysts suffer from what might

be called an 'ought phobia'."[55] I fail to see how one can ignore this verdict.

Doctrines change. Revision has its day. Freud's primitive drives, sexual and aggressive, are now supplemented even among faithful Freudians, by motivational "hierarchies" and "derivative motivations" which have undergone "delibidinization" and "de-aggressivation" (sic) and are regarded as possessing their own autonomy or semi-autonomy so that they "can be triggered independently into action."[56] There is a new willingness in Freudian circles to reckon with the social environment ("object relationships"), even if tinged with a reluctance to admit that it was ever neglected. But the course has not been an easy one. In many circles Freudian psychology has enjoyed a certain immunity from criticism just because it challenged a dissembling and unwholesome sex ethic and because it has promised therapeutic results for notoriously intractable illness. The sheer genius of the master tends to render criticism supererogatory, and it is often difficult to catch up with the soaring flights of his vivid imagination. One recalls the memorable remark of Kroeber when, twenty years after, referring to his devastating review of Freud's *Totem and Taboo*, he described it apologetically as "too suggestive of breaking a butterfly on the wheel."[57] All this may be why, in a statement where changes in recent theory such as those just referred to are recorded, the author concludes:

Psychoanalysis still adheres to a view of motivation as built on drives rooted in the biology of the organism. However much derived motivations are recognized, psychoanalytic theory still views behavior as essentially motivated by and occurring in the context of bodily drives. Drives for security, success, prestige, status, seem, relative to these basic drives, "superficial" to the psychoanalyst. He thinks rather of castration fear, oedipal wishes, cannibalistic impulses, homosexuality, or a drive to rend and destroy. It is often said that the analyst's preoccupation with these primitive impulses stems from his almost exclusive concern with disturbed personalities. But the analyst believes that the normal person, too, is occupied with dealing with such impulses.[58]

Amendments have not yet provided a bridge between the theory of psychoanalysis and moral theory, and efforts like Fromm's[59] to build such a bridge are often disparaged as sentimental moralizing. During his prolific lifetime, as has been seen, the master himself changed, but not, I believe, in a way calculated to direct us to an understanding of the authentic moral life.

Chapter Four

Subjectivism: The Interest Theory of Value

If ethnologists, pioneers in the sociology of knowledge, and orthodox Freudian psychologists have in their different ways left us without a basis on which to establish the validity of value judgments, they have not lacked help in our time from professional philosophers, especially in the English-speaking world. Moral skepticism is, of course, nothing new in the history of philosophy. The famous *Homo mensura* of Protagoras (c. 490–421 B.C.), his dictum that man is the measure of all things, reminds us of its antiquity. So, too, does Thrasymachus in the *Republic* when he argues that there is no justice except the interest of the stronger, and Callicles in Plato's *Gorgias* when, not unlike Nietzsche more than two thousand years later, he describes moral precepts as means by which the weak restrain the strong.

In our time one of the most radical versions of relativism is associated with studies in the first quarter of this century in theory of value, sometimes called *axiology*. Axiology designates the study of values in general, the general theory of value. Values fall—or appear to fall—into such different categories as moral, aesthetic, economic, etc. Primarily, the student of axiology examines their generic traits—what values in all categories have in common. If value *as such* is relative it must follow that its several varieties are relative and this, in fact, has been the position of those, sometimes called "subjectivists," who support what is generally known as the interest theory of value. The interest theory is at once a continuation of the hedonistic tradition in ethical theory and a response to the basic inadequacies of hedonism as a theory of conduct. A prior examination of hedonism, promised earlier in our discussion of Freud, is therefore in order.

We call that which we desire good and, since the object of all desire is pleasure, pleasure is the good and the good is pleasure. That, in essence, is the hedonist position. Belletrists have often said it better than philosophers. "Instead of founding a prize for the reward of virtue," wrote Gautier in the famous preface to an otherwise indifferent novel, "I would rather bestow a large reward on him who should invent a new pleasure; for to me enjoyment seems to be the end of life and the only useful thing on earth. God willed it to be so for he created women, perfumes, light, lovely flowers, good wine, spirited horses, lapdogs, and Angora cats."

Hedonism is proclaimed in Pope's *Essay on Man:*

Oh happiness! our being's end and aim!
Good, Pleasure, Ease, Content! What e'er thy name;

It is rockthrown in a posthumously issued recording of singer Janis Joplin (found dead of an overdose of heroin) called *Get It While You Can:*

We may not be here tomorrow,
 And if anybody should come along,
He gonna kill you with love and affection,
 I say, get it while you can, get it while you can.*

In some youth circles of the late 1960's and early 1970's— it is difficult to predict in an age when life styles change with startling rapidity what will happen by the late 1970's—one finds a kind of instant hedonism, associated with the drug subculture and sexual permissiveness, which dismisses calculations of consequences as part of a now démodé middle-class ethic. Such an attitude, expressed in the morally skeptical admonition, "Do your own thing," often combines incongruously with a high idealism which is, of course, the antithesis of hedonism. The paradox usually passes unnoticed.

The hedonist distinguishes, of course, between instrumental and final goods. A dentist's drill is painful and in itself bad, but as a means to the pleasure of freedom from a toothache, it is good. Whatever we call good is so, if not because it is pleasurable in itself, then because it is a means to pleasure. Moreover, pleasures vary in degree and lesser pleasures need not be permitted to interfere with greater ones. Few hedonists would counsel as did the early Greek Cyrenaics (or the late Miss Joplin) that we seek the enjoyment of the moment. The

* "Get It While You Can," words and music by Mort Shuman and Jerry Ragavoy. Copyright © 1967 by Hill and Range Songs, Inc. and Ragmar Music Corp. All rights administered by Hill and Range Songs, Inc. Used by permission.

more circumspect hedonist understands that some pleasures
are more enduring than others, are enjoyed at a disproportionate
cost in later pain, or seem more alluring prospectively than
they turn out to be in the having. There is nothing in the
hedonistic position that precludes the most careful calculations.
"No pleasure is a bad thing in itself," cautioned Epicurus, "but
the means which produce some pleasures bring with them disturbances many times greater than the pleasures."[1] An advocate
of the pleasure principle can without inconsistency heed such
cautions.

In modern times, Jeremy Bentham's is perhaps the best
known formulation of the hedonistic point of view. In a famous
passage he wrote:

Nature has placed mankind under the governance of two sovereign
masters, *pain* and *pleasure*. It is for them alone to point out what we
ought to do, as well as to determine what we shall do. On the one
hand, the standard of right and wrong, on the other, the chain of
causes and effects, are fastened to their throne. They govern us in all
we do, in all we say, in all we think . . .[2]

Bentham recognizes in the foregoing a distinction which he
thereupon promptly ignores, between what we ought to do and
what we must do. Everyone *ought* to seek pleasure, he says,
but also, everyone *seeks* pleasure. These express two different
views, *ethical hedonism* and *psychological hedonism,* and the
former is not derivable from the latter. It does not follow from
my seeking pleasure that I ought to; indeed, the reverse is more
consonant with the facts: I surely feel no "obligation," in the
sense in which that term is normally understood and used, to
do what I find pleasurable. And, in any case, as noted in our
earlier discussion of Freud's pleasure principle, "oughtness"
or obligatoriness is manifestly irrelevant to conduct that is
bound to take place anyhow. If I am so constituted in my very

nature that I *must* seek pleasure, it is surely pointless to say that I ought to, as nonsensical as saying I ought to breathe, or, if I slip off a cliff, that I ought to fall. Ethical as well as psychological hedonists commit this curious error, as when J. S. Mill declared that "the sole proof it is possible to produce that anything is desirable (i.e., *ought* to be desired) is that people do actually desire it."[3]

However, my concern at this point is not with hedonism as an ethical prescription but as a psychological generalization, and as such it suffers from a fatal flaw. For, quite simply, we do not *seek* pleasure, nor are the ends we seek means to an end beyond them which is pleasure or a pleasurable state. Pleasure is not the *cause* of desire. We have pleasure or satisfaction only because we first desire to possess objects or undergo experiences which, attained or undergone, give us pleasure or satisfaction. It is not some generalized feeling state called pleasure that we seek. In point of fact—we encounter here the well-known hedonistic paradox—if we seek pleasure we fail to find it, and we fail quite simply because pleasure is not an end in itself but is had only as a consequence of our having ends and being able to achieve them. The voluptuary, driven to invent artificial pleasures, is a pathetic figure doomed to defeat precisely because the implications of the hedonistic paradox elude him. If we had no ends or purposes we would find no pleasure. It is tennis I want to play and the game I want to win, and, if I play well and am able to win, I have pleasure or satisfaction. I like Beethoven sonatas: it is *these* I want to hear and, when I listen to them and they are played well, I have a feeling of satisfaction.

Professor B. F. Skinner was only repeating what pre-scientific philosophers, as he calls us, have been saying for a long time when he wrote in his most recent and much discussed book, *Beyond Freedom and Dignity,*

Men have generalized the feelings of good things and called them pleasure and the feelings of bad things and called them pain, but we do not give a man pleasure or pain, we give him things he feels as pleasant or painful. Men do not work to maximize pleasure and minimize pain, as the hedonists have insisted; they work to produce pleasant things and to avoid painful things.[4]

Whatever one may think of his extreme brand of behaviorism (see below, pp. 235–238), this view of psychological hedonism is quite unassailable.

Moreover, feelings of pleasure obviously differ, varying with the satisfaction derived from contemplating a beautiful landscape or embracing a beautiful woman or cultivating one's garden or teaching philosophy or eating a good dinner or helping striking farm workers. Some people derive satisfaction from joining holy orders and rejecting physical comforts, others— perversely, we say—from hoarding money and self-denial, still others whom we call flagellants, even more perversely, from whipping and scourging themselves. A few (perhaps most perversely) from writing books on ethics. To call the feeling states associated with all such experiences pleasure is to so dilute the meaning of the term as to render it useless: if pleasure embraces all the varied feeling states attendant on the attainment of our desires (even including the feeling of pain), it ceases to designate any feeling state and the statement that I seek pleasure reduces to the indisputable but utterly uninformative proposition that I desire whatever I happen to desire. The difficulty is not really lessened by substituting the term "satisfaction" for "pleasure" unless by satisfaction we mean, not a feeling state, but the fact that every desire impels in the direction of its consummation. ("Satisfaction," one should see, is ambiguous, referring, like pleasure, to a feeling state *or* to the completion of a process or fulfillment of a condition—e.g., "Their demands were satisfied"; "The requirement was satisfied.") But this is no more informative than saying that every event has a cause.

Much more is involved in all this than a mere verbal quibble. The assumption that we are moved by the desire for a kind of homogeneous feeling state called pleasure has led to a variety of pernicious consequences not the least of which is the contention that we are by nature inert, indolent, passive, requiring to be lured or bribed into activity by the promise of pleasure, or prodded by the threat of pain, when, in point of fact, the very life of healthy human organisms involves activity, directed or undirected.[5] Here we may indeed learn from Marx. The former view was more congenial to the ideology of a pecuniary society interested in stressing the need for incentives and rooting the profit motive in human nature. Clearly, the hedonistic view of human nature provided a welcome apology for capitalism. It is not surprising that, inconsistent though the pleasure principle might be with the thrift and work ethic of the "acquisitive society," hedonism found general favor among classical and neo-classical liberals from John Locke to the present day.

In the formulation given hedonism by Bentham there was additional reason for its ideological congeniality. His view of pleasure and pain as homogeneous feeling states leads easily to the conclusion that they can be broken down into units which, as commensurate magnitudes, can be added and subtracted, in brief, *calculated*, thus providing the basis for a genuine science of conduct. This is, indeed, what Bentham sought to accomplish in his well-known felicific calculus. Pleasure or pain varies, he noted, in (1) intensity, (2) duration, (3) certainty, (4) propinquity, and so on. Therefore: "Sum up all the values of all the *pleasures* on the one side, and those of all the pains on the other. The balance, if it be on the side of pleasure, will give the *good* tendency of the act upon the whole, with respect to the interests of that *individual* person; if on the side of pain, the *bad* tendency of it upon the whole."[6] Presumably it is in such careful calculations that men at the marketplace engage, and clearly no government bureaucrats should be permitted to meddle with such rational choices. To see that our feelings of satisfaction vary with the ends we seek, i.e., the kind of desire we try to consummate, is to recognize that they are *incommensurate* and no more to be added to or subtracted from each other than apples and bolts of cloth. Accordingly, assumptions like Bentham's did much to vitiate classical economics. The classical economists of the eighteenth and nineteenth centuries were lured by the prospect of translating the deliberations of *Homo economicus* as he calculates his profits and losses into a nice balancing of hedonistic magnitudes, but the qualitatively diverse feelings attendant on the gratification of our desires, whether at the marketplace or elsewhere, foil such calculations.

The interest theory of value possesses the virtues of the more venerable hedonistic theories without falling into some of the serious difficulties which brought discredit to hedonism. Like the hedonistic view, it has the great merit of requiring that the heretofore absolute claims of laws and codes be related to and tested against human needs and desires; like hedonism, it has a beguiling simplicity. But unlike hedonism, it recognizes the multiplicity and variety of the feeling states attendant on the gratification of our desires. And, unlike hedonism, it avoids treating such feeling states as the cause of interest or desire. As Professor S. C. Pepper points out, "The term 'interest' avoids most of the traditional criticisms to which 'pleasure' was subject, and retains most of the advantages which rendered the earlier hedonisms philosophically attractive."[7] Nevertheless, like many hypotheses which exercise a strong pedestrian appeal, the interest theory of value is in fact a sophisticated and complex doctrine which has failed to inspire unanimity of opinion even among its most vocal adherents.

It is interest as the pervasive character of the motor-affective life, the "state, act, attitude or disposition of favor or disfavor," which is "the original source and constant feature of all value," according to R. B. Perry.

That which is an object of interest is *eo ipso* invested with value. Any object, whatever it be, acquires value when any interest, whatever it be, is taken in it. . . .

The view may otherwise be formulated in the equation: X is valuable = interest is taken in X. . . .

This is value *simpliciter,*—value in the elementary, primordial and generic sense. It follows that any variation of interest or of its object will determine a variety of value; that any derivative of interest or its object will determine value in a derived sense; and that any condition of interest or its object will determine a conditional value. In short, interest being constitutive of value in the basic sense, theory of value will take this as its point of departure and centre of reference; and will classify and systemize values in terms of the different forms which interests and their objects may be found to assume.[8]

This is, perhaps, the classical statement of the interest theory of value. It is forthright and apparently unambiguous. We see at once that values are regarded as definable, as relative, and as constituted by motor-affective process.

Now when adherents of the interest theory of value identify the generic character of value with the motor-affective attitude of interest, they mean just that. Nothing is permitted to dilute the substance of pure liking as the sole and exhaustive ingredient of value. There may be some difference of opinion as to whether such liking is better characterized in terms of feeling or, more behavioristically, as motor processes designated as tendency, set, drive, or propensity, but on the issue that value is in essence irrational and that there is no other kind of value all exponents of the interest theory are at one. The consequence is a more or less sharp logical cleavage between values and the cognitive processes associated with them. That the association is intimate and complex is simply so much more reason for carefully distinguishing between them, Perry noted[9] and it is, Professor David Prall declared, the failure "to keep clear the distinction between cognitive judgment and motor-affective at-

titude" which is the root of the confusion he attributed to John
Dewey and the pragmatic or instrumentalist theory of value.[10]

How do the best known exponents of the interest theory
make out this distinction? There are, according to Professor
Perry, two possible relations of cognition to interest. We find
these relations expressed on the one hand in *value judgments,*
and on the other in *judgments of value.* A judgment of value
is one which notes, declares, or contemplates the presence of an
interest. Its relationship to interest or to the value which interest
confers or constitutes is as external as the relationship of any
judgment to any object or event. And, like any object or event,
a value remains a value, possessing such character as it has,
whether we express its occurrence in judgment or not. A judgment of value is simply a *post facto* description of a state of
affairs occurring independently of such a judgment. That this
state of affairs happens to be an interest does not in principle
differentiate its relationship to judgments about it from the relationship of sticks or stones or the nose on Cyrano's face to
judgments about them. The act of *cognizing* these states of
affairs has nothing to do with the acts or events which *constitute*
them. In a prolonged controversy extending through many issues
of the philosophical journals, advocates of the interest theory of
value disputed John Dewey's contention that values, though
related to feelings, are a product of what he called valuation
judgments. (See below, pp. 131–132.) To say that values are
known and created in the same act (as does Dewey) implies the
impossibility of knowing anything at all about them,[11] they argued.
In short, judgment, which is to say intelligence, presumably has
nothing to do with selection of our ends or ideals.[12]

Now judgments may be about anything, including themselves, or any pattern of things or events in which they play an
integral role. An interest is such a pattern of events. Whereas
there may be values without *ex post facto* judgments about
them, whereas, in other words, there may be interests without
judgments *of* or *about* interest, there can be no interest without

judgment. That is to say, every interest is mediated by judgment, and without such mediation there could be no interests. Such judgments are called interest or value judgments to distinguish them from judgments of value.

The point is simple. Interests appear at that level of organic activity distinguished by *prospicience;* they look forward. Hence, it is impossible to describe interests without a consideration of cognitive activities. Interest is not to be described merely by reference to organisms possessing accumulated energies and manifesting environmentally adapted propensities which are released when the organism is acted upon by a specific external situation. There is, besides, a differential factor which distinguishes action as purposive. *"The situation is construed by the agent in terms of something ulterior."*[13] Hence, one must go to psychological data, i.e., to a study of cognition, to supplement a biological account of interest. That is to say, interests are marked by a capacity to act in the light of expectation. Mere random effort does not account for the facts. Interest involves a reference to the future as in some sense governing the act. Accordingly, Perry concluded, "interest cannot exist without cognition." "Interest may . . . be said to be a product, derivative or *function* of cognition, in the sense that its satisfaction varies with the truth of the cognition which mediates it."[14] ". . . cognition and interest are interpenetrating . . . each may condition and partially constitute the other."[15]

On the other hand, interest is to be distinguished from expectation.

Expectation is an anticipatory response [which] . . . implies no disposition to bring its object into being, but only a readiness to deal with it when and if it occurs. Interest, on the other hand, promotes its object. To expect an event signifies only a disposition to act *on* it, while to be interested in an event signifies a disposition to act *for* it, or to provide an occasion for acting on it. This supplementary dynamic factor which distinguishes interest, lies in the governing propensity which renders the anticipatory set prepotent, and which gives a peculiar eligibility to any antecedent performance which affords promise of it. An expectation becomes an interest when the anticipatory response in which it consists, is *in demand*. The expectation sets the anticipatory response for a specific occasion; the interest provides subjective conditions which help to create the occasion, and so to facilitate the execution of the response.[16]

Thus, while he stressed the indispensibility of cognitive processes to interested activity, Perry was equally emphatic about distinguishing between interest and cognition and assigning the locus of value exclusively to the former. Although somewhat less decisive about the role of cognition in liking or interested activity, David Prall, an equally articulate exponent of the interest theory of value, shared this point of view. "Value," Prall wrote, "is precisely the term applied in common usage to objects which stand at the outer end of a relation called liking, the inner end of which is a human mind which likes."[17] The view has venerable precedents. In the seventeenth century Thomas Hobbes wrote: "Whatsoever is the object of any man's appetite or desire, that is it which he for his part calleth good."[18] The view of his great contemporary Spinoza is similar: "We endeavor, wish, desire, or long for nothing because we deem it good; but, on the other hand, we deem a thing good because we endeavor, wish for, or long for it."[19]

But what is there to be said about values once we have accepted Prall's or Perry's definition of value in terms of interest? Philosophers especially should always be prepared for the time when they may be confronted by an impertinent "So what?" There is, of course, a great deal to be said by way of identifying and describing the biological and psychological origins of values as thus defined, and not even their severest critics would charge that the exponents of the interest theory have failed to do this well. But those who defend this position appear to believe that there is much more to be said. They accept, to begin with, the conventional distinction between aesthetic and moral values. Since, later, we shall ourselves be interested in discovering the differentia which distinguish moral values, we may pause to see just what basis a motor-affective theory of value can supply for the distinction.

"What satisfies in sensuous perception is esthetically valuable; what satisfies as *conducive* to the good life in general has moral value. Moral value is thus *use-value, means rather than end*," Prall wrote.[20] But such an identification of moral value with instrumental value troubled Prall: ". . . the fact remains that Socrates act [his noble refusal to save himself from death] serves us in so definitely different a manner from that in which the typewriter serves us . . . as to be appropriately designated *absolutely* different." If, as he acknowledged, the former has ethical value and the latter does not, this is because "ethical value cannot be measured in terms of economic goods . . . It is valuable simply as being constituitive of the ultimately valuable . . . It is, in other words, not a means but an end."[21] Since this confronted Prall with the problem of distinguishing ethical from aesthetic values, he was immediately forced into this equivocation: "But even ethically valuable acts seem, too, to be means in a special way of their own . . ." The ethical is distinguished from the aesthetic "insofar [as it] is a means to an end." And yet elsewhere in this most protean of arguments it appears that, even if not quite so fully, ethical as well as aesthetic values belong to the realm of ends, and hence are *not* instrumental: "Esthetic value, in a fuller sense even than ethical value belongs to the realm of ends. *Both* are clearly enough distinguished from *utility* values, which are such only as they serve towards ends . . ."[22] (My Emphasis.) But the final verdict, however waveringly affirmed, is a reduction of ethical to aesthetic values—remembering that all felt satisfaction is "aesthetic" in this broad use of the term. This reduction becomes clear when after raising the question, "What sort of ends do we really wish realized?" he answered: "This is the most fundamental of practical questions. And it just *is* a matter of esthetic taste, of liking."[23]

Apart from the manifest failure to provide a basis for identifying moral values as distinguished from aesthetic values, the foregoing comment suggests another basic question. If, as Prall suggested, the most fundamental of practical questions concerns the sort of ends we really wish realized, how do tastes or likings become involved in such problems? How does it happen that interests become the objects of such critical examination? Is this not a circumstance connected with something outside of tastes or ends? It is of the nature of interests that they seek their satisfaction. The questioning of them must come from some other source. If such questions are fundamental to the study of values—and Prall seems to say so—then we must deal with more than interests; we must be concerned with more than the merely aesthetic to which Prall limits us. And since to question is to invite judgment would not such judgment be different in kind from the value judgments and judgments of value discussed above?

The problem is not solved by saying that the questioning of an interest is brought about by the impact of a more impelling interest. Such impact leaves us with no problem to solve on the purely interested level. As Perry pointed out, the degree of intensity of an interest which enables us to characterize it as more impelling can be identified only with the degree to which it has already acquired command of the body as a whole.[24] When Professor Prall suggests the centrality of the problem of what it is that we really wish realized, consistency with the interest theory of value restricts his meaning to what we ordinarily designate as a hedonistic calculus. We had better not, for example, drink too freely of scotch-and-soda, because the indulgence may have disastrous consequences the following day. But such a calculus does not bear on the kind of question Prall raised. The interest, or, in terms of our illustration, the aversion to an acute headache and other possible consequences is already given. There is no problem here of determining what we really wish. We may or may not have the strength of character to resist, but this is a problem in prudence which has no bearing on the direction of our interests. For Prall, as for any advocate of the interest theory of value, the sort of ends we really wish realized must be just the ones we have. However, he refers in many passages to ends of a "higher" order. What can this mean?

The interest theory of value makes the *having* of an interest absolute in its own right. As Professor Otto once observed, "In place of an eternal, immutable ethical truth we now have an indefinite number of impulses, aims, purposes, ideals, each absolute in its own right."[25] In the having of an interest, then, all questions of value are settled. In apparent consistency with this Professor Prall remarked that the "term 'higher' corresponds not to any difference in the nature of values (i.e., interests) as such . . ." To what, then, does it correspond? To ". . . the length or complexity of the various processes which precede such higher valuings."[26]

Prall unhesitatingly observed that length and complexity are not in themselves valuable, but that we always prefer those values which are preceded by these complex processes. But is this so? As a matter of fact, most people prefer simplicity to complexity and spontaneity and innocence to sophistication and subtlety. However much one may personally deplore the taste of the average reader, it is a fact that he prefers the Sunday supplement to the *Philosophical Review* and simple acts of bravery and honesty to the more complexly motivated behavior of the subtle moralist or self-conscious moral agent. Prall's answer is that individuals prefer those values which are conditioned by such techniques and skills as they may have achieved to values which in an earlier period were less complexly conditioned. Let us take his own illustration. Professor Prall found that he had enjoyed concerts which some years afterwards he regarded with actual aversion. "The concert as I heard it first had value, but that value was not so high as I perhaps judged it to be at the time."[27] Prall appeared to realize that he was here introducing a kind of error which is wholly incompatible with the interest theory of value. He remarked: ". . . I may seem to have introduced a new notion of value in saying that my first judgment as to the value of the concert was erroneous . . ."[28] This is indeed the case, since on the interest theory his early interest in the concert was as "right" as any other, provided he did actually have that interest and that this concert best satisfied his interest at that time. On the interest theory, one value has no more claim to validity than any other, and if the fact that the interest subsequently altered invalidated it, all interests would be in the same leaky boat. It will be best to continue with Prall's statement, however:

> I would of course admit that my later judgment is sometimes better than my earlier, or that a musician's criticism of a concert may express a more important judgment than that of one who is not a musician. But what does this mean? Simply . . . that I *find* that I actually do lay higher value on my present valuations than on my earlier ones. To say that my judgment of today is better than my judgment of ten years ago is merely recording the fact that towards my present judgment I have a motor-affective attitude of liking, whereas towards my judgment of ten years ago I am indifferent or even averse. To say that I value a musician's judgment of the concert is only to say that I *prefer* such a judgment to the judgment . . . of the musically illiterate.[29]

Clearly Professor Prall, like his great predecessor, J. S. Mill, was admitting through the rear door the very guest he rejected at the front. Mill's predicament is notorious. He affirmed the "Greatest Happiness Principle" as the basis of right and wrong, adding like a good hedonist that "By happiness is intended pleasure, and the absence of pain; by unhappiness, pain, and the privation of pleasure."[30] But, unlike Bentham, he did not agree that pleasures are alike, differing only in intensity and duration. In one of the most famous passages in the literature of ethics he wrote:

Few human creatures would consent to be changed into any of the lower animals, for a promise of the fullest allowance of a beast's pleasure; no intelligent human being would consent to be a fool, no instructed person would be an ignoramus, no person of feeling and conscience would be selfish and base, even though they should be persuaded that the fool, the dunce or the rascal is better satisfied with his lot than they are with theirs . . . It is better to be a human being dissatisfied than a pig satisfied; better to be a Socrates dissatisfied than a fool satisfied.[31]

But quite obviously, if pleasure is the sole criterion, one pleasure is as good as another, provided it is just as intense and, if intelligent people enjoy acting like fools—as is often the case— the hedonist is in no position to admonish them.

To return to Prall, there is an obvious and innocuous sense in which his statement might be construed as meaning that any interest now had is preferred to one had in the past. But Prall just as obviously did not mean to enunciate the platitude that the value I now have is higher simply because I now, in the temporal present, have it. My present appreciation represents *maturer, keener,* more exhaustive judgment. As we shall see later, this (always plus its immediate satisfactoriness, of course) constitutes its preferability or value, its claim to being higher. To be consistent, Prall would have to deny this. But if he does, then why introduce maturity and technical virtuosity at all? It is not merely the fact of the presence of the liking as present that makes it higher, but the greater *literacy* which it represents. In some sense which a subjectivist theory like Prall's cannot explain it is more *valid.* The theory provides a far more adequate psychological account of purposive behavior than the

traditional hedonisms. It fails to account for moral values and
the judgments of which they are an outcome.[32] It leaves us with
nothing but our prevailing tastes as the arbiter of what is
morally right or good.

Perry, like Prall, was, of course, aware of the main criticism
of his position. He conceded that the fact of desire is not viewed
as final in most judgments of value.

Objects of desire are held to be bad despite their being desired, and
desires themselves are held to be bad whether or no they are satisfied. Vicious appetites, vulgar taste, o'erweening ambition, are the
most notorious of evils. Indeed the general terms "desire" and
"interest" have acquired a specific flavor of moral disrepute. Must
we not conclude therefore that value, instead of flowing from interest,
is an independent, if not antagonistic, principle by which interests
and their objects are judged?[33]

Perry's answer was that desires may indeed in a *moral* context
be judged adversely, but only because they interfere with more
comprehensive desires or interests. And this is, of course, true.
But suppose they do not: are they then immune from judgment?
Or, put otherwise, is there no basis upon which our most comprehensive interests, our "life-purpose" to use one of Perry's
terms, may be subject to question? The interest theory provides
no such basis any more than it can provide an account of moral
conflict or of the sense of obligation which generates such
conflict and is central to our moral experience. Perry wrote of
morality as "man's endeavor to harmonize conflicting interests . . ." It is, he says, "the solution of the problem created by
conflict—conflict among the interests of the same or of different
persons." Conceived "as the harmonization of interests *for the
sake of the interests harmonized,*" morality can be described as
"a cult of freedom."

It does not force interests into a procrustean bed, but gives interests space and air in which to be more abundantly themselves. Its purpose is to provide room. And ideally the benefits of morality are extended to all interests. Hence moral progress takes the double form, of liberalizing the existing organizations and of extending it to interests hitherto excluded.[34]

Much of this is indisputable. But it is difficult if not impossible to see how on an interest theory of value it makes sense to speak of moral "conflict" where there can only be a mere test of strength in which a stronger interest displaces a weaker one. The mutation of interest no more argues a conflict than a change of color from red to blue evidences a conflict between two sense data.

So too with what Perry called moral progress. Interests can hardly be drives toward their transformation. It is difficult to find a place for moral progress leading to the enjoyment of interests hitherto excluded in a theory which, in the nature of the case, as Dewey pointed out, "holds down value to objects *antecedently* enjoyed."[35] We may indeed happen on new interests accidentally in the course of pursuing those we have, but it is surely not such inadvertencies to which Perry refers in the passage just quoted. As I shall stress later, progress is made when interests are *transcended* through the mediation of judgment, but as we have seen, such a role for reason is alien to the interest theory of value. Reason may not be the master of the passions, but neither need it be, as the interest theory requires us to conclude, their slave.

Chapter Five

Emotivism

Perhaps the most extreme and original case against the objectivity of ethical judgments is associated with one of the major variants of the so-called analytical movement stemming from the preoccupation of much twentieth-century philosophy, especially in the English-speaking world, with the analysis of language and the problem of meaning. It is not because value judgments are incorrigibly *biased* that the analytical philosophers, so-called, reject the cognitive claims made in such judgments, but because they are *meaningless.* Clearly, this is a more fundamental criticism. It will be found to differ basically from the interest theory just discussed.

Inspired by the protest of Bertrand Russell (e.g., his *Knowledge of the External World*) and G. E. Moore against the obscurantism of traditional metaphysics (and theology), the analytic movement received its greatest impetus from Russell's most famous student, a Viennese named Ludwig Wittgenstein who became for many, after the publication of his *Tractatus*

Logico-Philosophicus in 1919, the towering eminence of twentieth-century philosophy. The key to understanding the analytical movement is Wittgenstein's famous statement that philosophy "does not result in 'philosophical propositions,' but rather in the clarification of propositions."[1] In other words, philosophy can tell us nothing about the world. Whatever there is to *know* about the world is told to us by the scientist. If he can't tell us no one else can. There are no supra-scientific truths. There is no way of getting at truth except through the means used by scientists when they tell us about stars and galaxies and electrons and genes and chromosomes, etc. Talk about ultimate reality beyond what is disclosed by science is sheer obscurantism or pretension. How does it happen that philosophy has been afflicted with such infirmities? Wittgenstein's answer is simple, but it is extremely important and it is the key to understanding the course taken by much contemporary philosophy, including the philosophy of morals. "Our philosophical problems arise when language goes on holiday."[2] Once this is understood philosophy can assume its proper role and become *"a battle against the bewitchment of our intelligence by means of language."*[3] In amazing numbers the ablest philosophers of the English-speaking world have abandoned the historic interpretation of philosophy's role as the pursuit of wisdom, and, rejecting Plato's definition of the philosopher as the "spectator of all time and all existence," have obeyed Wittgenstein's injunction and gone out to do battle against the "bewitchment of our intelligence by . . . language." Almost in concert they have turned their attention to the analysis of language, convinced that if the philosopher cannot give us wisdom or truth, he can at least teach us to be clear.

Two major trends in linguistic analysis trace their lineage to Wittgenstein. One of these is *Logical Positivism* which, although now in semi-eclipse, has had a significant influence on the recent history of ethical theory. Its foundations were laid in Vienna before World War II by the so-called Vienna Circle, a group of brilliant philosophers who were also versed in science and mathematics. According to the logical positivists, all statements made in the domain of metaphysics (and theology) are *meaningless*. (This term is used by them descriptively, not pejoratively.) The words may be familiar and they may seem at first glance to look like a statement, but they are really *pseudo*-statements. Any language consists, it may be noted, of a *vocabulary* and a *syntax*, i.e., a set of words with meanings and a set of rules governing sentence formation. Therefore, as Rudolf Carnap, one of the major positivists pointed out, "there are two kinds of pseudo-statements: either they contain a word which is erroneously believed to have meaning, or the constituent words are meaningful, yet are put together in a counter-syntactical way, so that they do not yield a meaningful statement."[4]

Examples of metaphysical words which are said by Carnap to be without meaning are "the Absolute," "the Unconditioned," "the Idea," "the Infinite," "thing-in-itself," "absolute spirit," "non-being," and "God." However, not only words, but *sentences* may be meaningless even though composed of words which have meaning. Carnap gives two examples:

(1) "Caesar is and." That statement violates the rules of syntax so obviously that no one would use it. By the rules of syntax the sentence "Caesar is" must be completed not by a conjunction but by a noun or adjective (e.g., "Caesar is brave," or "Caesar is a general.")

(2) "Caesar is a prime number." This seems to be syntactically correct because "prime number" is a noun, but it is also meaningless because "prime number" cannot (by other syntactical rules) be affirmed of persons, only of numbers.

The foregoing examples of meaninglessness are easily identified. Many counter-syntactical statements in metaphysics are not and require more careful analysis. Carnap selects the following more detectable metaphysical example of what he calls nonsense from an article by Martin Heidegger, one of the important German existentialists:

What is to be investigated is being only and—*nothing* else; being alone and further—*nothing*. . . . What about this nothing? *Does the Nothing exist only because the Not, i.e. the Negation, exists?* Or is it the other way around? *Does the Negation and the Not exist only because the Nothing exists?* . . . We assert: *the Nothing is prior to the Not and the Negation*. Where do we seek the Nothing? How do we find the Nothing? . . . . *Anxiety reveals the Nothing.* . . . That for which and because of which we were anxious, was "really"—nothing. Indeed: the Nothing itself—as such—was present. *What about this Nothing?—The Nothing itself Nothings.*[5]

In fairness to Heidegger it must be said that "nothing" as he uses it is not to be confused with empty space or a vacuum. Even so, the analysts appear to have provocation when they denounce such a statement—or Hegel's statement that "pure Being and pure Nothing . . . are one and the same"—as meaningless.[6]

But *all* the statements of metaphysics, not just these, are meaningless, according to the logical positivist, and they are meaningless because they set an impossible task for themselves, that of trying, in Carnap's words, "to discover and formulate a kind of knowledge which is not accessible to empirical science."[7] They make statements which *are not verifiable and are therefore non-sense*. This brings us to the logical positivist's controversial *verifiability theory of meaning*.[8] Before commenting on this much discussed (and much amended) theory of meaning it will be useful to consider a list of statements. The following statements resemble each other in that they consist of words, are grammatically correct and, with two exceptions, make a truth claim. Those which make a truth claim differ from each other (apart from the fact that they contain different words and are of different length) in the manner and degree of their verifiability. (Before continuing with the comments which follow the reader should see if he can define these differences for himself.)

1. Reason is the Sovereign of the World; Reason is Substance, as well as *Infinite Power;* its own *Infinite Material* underlying all the natural and spiritual life which it originates, as also the *Infinite Form*—that which sets this Material in motion.

2. The addition of salt to water lowers its freezing point.

3. Official buildings, from the post office in the smallest town to the great structures in Washington itself, have been undistinguished and where fine buildings have survived from the past, they have often been damaged by tasteless additions or alterations.

4. Socrates was convicted and executed.

5. The unexamined life is not worth living.

6. The electromagnetic energy of an electron in an orbit depends on the diameter of the orbit. However, as long as an electron remains in any one orbit, its energy is constant and the atom emits no radiation.

7. If New York is larger than Los Angeles and Los Angeles is larger than San Francisco, New York is larger than San Francisco.

8. He is a married bachelor.

9. I promise.

10. Ban the Bomb.

Statement 1 is from the introduction to Hegel's *Philosophy of History.* Hegel (1770–1831) had an immense influence in the English-speaking world as well as in Germany, so we may assume that many people *thought* they understood what he meant by this statement and, of course, *he* must have believed he understood what he was saying unless he was perpetrating a huge joke. But language analysts find such words as "Infinite Material" and "Infinite Form" utterly opaque. We know what we mean when we talk about reason (sometimes) guiding human conduct; and we know what a substance like gold or salt is. But once we start speaking of reason as though it were a *substance* and then talk of it as the "Sovereign of the World," are we making sense or non-sense? The language analyst says the latter. Even if the *words* in this statement were clearer, the logical positivist would find statements such as this unverifiable and therefore meaningless. What are the operations by which we would go about confirming a statement like Hegel's? What difference would its acceptance or rejection make in the way we experience the world or guide our affairs?

Statements 2 and 6 both conform to the logical positivist's criterion of meaningfulness, that is to say, they are both verifiable and have indeed been verified, although they differ in that 2 is verifiable by *direct* observation and 6 only *indirectly* since no one has ever seen an electron, nor does an electron resemble anything that we have seen or heard or touched or smelled.

What about 4? Can it be verified? Yes, but obviously not in the way in which we verify 2 or 6. We can't reverse time to observe the conviction and execution of Socrates either directly as in 2 or indirectly as in 6. Confirmation comes about in other ways. We check with others besides Plato who refer to the trial (notably Xenophon in his *Memorabilia*). There might be a drawing on a vase, or a marble frieze might depict the event. (There is neither.) Socrates might have left us his memoirs. (He didn't.) Although the historicity of the trial of Socrates is not questioned by scholars (except as to details), clearly, since we are dealing with a unique and not a repeatable event, both the means of verification and its reliability are different. This would be true, of course, even for the report of a recent historical event such as that Roosevelt was president of the U.S.A. when Pearl Harbor was bombed. Just the same all such reports rely on observations, even though the observations were made in the past and not in the present (which on the instant becomes the past, to be sure.)

We come now to an important class of statements exemplified by 7 and 8. These statements are called *a priori* in contrast to, for example, 2 and 6 which are called *a posteriori*. They are also called *analytic* statements in contrast to 2 and 6, which are *synthetic* statements (although we have been warned by W. V. Quine and others against establishing sharp boundaries between them). These are basic distinctions which are indispensable to clear thinking. Even before giving these distinctions a second glance it will be noted at once that a quality of *certainty* attaches to the affirmation of statement 7 and the denial of 8 which does not characterize the other statements we have examined. Thus, it is clearly inconceivable that 8 could be true or 7 false, whereas the negatives of 2, 4, 6, 10 are quite conceivable.

We call 7 and 8 *a priori* because their truth or falsity is known prior to or apart from any specific experience. I need not have seen New York or Los Angeles or San Francisco or any city to know that New York is larger than San Francisco if it is larger than Los Angeles, and Los Angeles is larger than San Francisco. I could indeed substitute symbols for cities and say that, if A is larger than B and B larger than C, A is larger than C. Such statements, we say, are true by definition. Their truth or falsity is established by the rules of the language in which they are formulated. The truths of logic and mathematics are of this order. No one needs to have looked at circular objects, i.e., consulted any experience, to know that in Euclidean geometry the points on the circumference of a circle are equidistant from a point called the center. This *follows* from our definition of circularity. Similarly with the kind of deduction that occurs in a syllogism, as when we reason that, if all dogs are mammals and all setters are dogs, all setters are mammals. We need never have seen a dog or a mammal to derive this conclusion, just as we derive the conclusion that, if all A is B and all B is C, all A is C without experiencing anything—there obviously being nothing in the case of symbols to experience. This is, as we say, a truth of logic, just as it is a truth of logic not based on any observation that a Democrat will either be elected President of the U.S. or he will not. When we call this a truth of logic, and, as such, *a priori,* we mean (at the very least) that it follows from the rules of our language governing the use of such words as "or" and "not." And, as suggested, the same can be said for the truths of mathematics, which are derivable, it has been shown in recent years, from the truths of logic.

A *posteriori* statements, on the other hand, are derived from, and in that sense come after or are posterior to, experience. I can't know that heated objects expand or that the divorce rate is increasing without first making the appropriate observations. All the generalizations of science—that is, of the so-called *empirical* sciences (the natural and social sciences) as distinguished from the *formal* sciences of mathematics and logic— are of this order, i.e., *a posteriori.*

Corresponding to the polarity between *a priori* and *a posteriori* is the distinction between analytic and synthetic statements. Waiving discussion of the great controversies surrounding these distinctions, we may say that most contemporary philosophers (and all empiricists) would agree that all *a priori* statements or judgments are analytic—that is to say, in making them we analyze or derive the implications of what is already contained in them.[9] Ultimately they are reducible to a so-called *identical* proposition of the form that A is A. It would follow that the denial of an analytically true statement involves a *contradiction.* One can no more conceive of a married bachelor or of the falsity of 8 than one can conceive of a square circle.

Clearly analytical procedures of the kind referred to do not as such add to our knowledge of matters of fact, although they guide us to such knowledge by making explicit relationships of which we would otherwise not be aware. Synthetic statements, on the other hand, such as 2 and 6, do add to our knowledge of matters of fact. A synthetic judgment, as Kant (who was the first to make this distinction) argued, *is* informative in the sense that it tells us something *about* the subject.

And now consider statement 9. It is not at all like the statements thus far examined in that it does not purport to say anything true or false about an event or state of affairs, nor does it derive from the implications of a definition or premise. Clearly, in saying "I promise," I am not saying something that is true or false about what I am doing. The *saying* of it, the *act* of promising makes it a promise, so that "saying so makes it so" (provided that certain conditions are present that make it a genuine promise). Such statements have been called *performatives* and afford a good and often unidentified example of the *noncognitive* functions of language.

Statement 10 is an imperative, so-called, another example of the noncognitive use of language. It is quite different from a statement of the form "They shouted, 'Ban the Bomb,'" usually called an *indicative* sentence by grammarians. The latter statement makes a cognitive claim and can be confirmed or disconfirmed in the same way that we confirm or disconfirm Statements 2 and 6 or any statement referring to the occurrence or nonoccurrence of an event. Imperatives, on the other hand, although attempts have been made to reduce them to indicatives, have no cognitive status and are neither true or false. They are of special interest to the philosopher because, as will be seen later, attempts have been made to subsume all value statements under them.

Statements 3 and 5 differ in an important way from the others in that they are value judgments, the first about aesthetic values as reflected in such terms as "undistinguished" and "tasteless," the second about moral or ethical values as reflected in the term "worth." Clearly, they are distinguishable as a class from judgments about matters of fact such as 2. And here we have the makings of a great controversy which has occupied much of modern philosophy. Positivists contend that such statements are not susceptible of proof and are therefore without cognitive status. We are concerned here with what are called *normative* statements ("It is better to be a man dissatisfied than a pig satisfied"; "'Pop' art is an aesthetic abomination"), which often take the form of, or are by implication, prescriptive statements ("You ought not to live like a pig," "You ought not to like 'pop' art") in contrast to *positive* (a special use of this word) or *des*criptive statements such as we find in science. Such judgments of value are said (like performatives) to be examples of the noncognitive use of language; through them we may express our emotions or announce our preferences, or we may seek to convert others to our point of view. But, argues the positivist, there is no way of proving that living like a pig is morally objectionable if you mean by proof the kind of *a priori* demonstration used in formal logic and mathematics or the kind of procedures used in verifying the statement "Objects expand when heated." There is no way of proving that racism is evil if one means by this something other than "I don't like racism" or "I don't like racism and I want you to dislike it too." Therefore statements in which "good" and "evil" occur as predicates are meaningless. Since no observation can confirm or disconfirm them they have no cognitive status. Why, then, do we utter them? Surely not merely to announce that one has a liking or preference, although this may be the case, or partly the case, in some instances. We must see that language has uses other than the *cognitive* use, i.e., other than "usage of language for the purpose of expressing true statements."[10] There is also an *instrumental* use: "When we speak of *instrumental usage* of language," wrote Professor Hans Reichenbach, "we refer, in particular, to the aim of influencing the listener, or reader, for certain purposes intended by the speaker or writer." Such instrumental usage belongs to what he calls *"pragmatics."*[11] Language is used not only to state what is the case, i.e., to report. We may also wish to arouse attitudes in others, i.e., to get them, as in poetry, to feel certain emotions or to perform certain acts, as when I say "Ring the bell." When language is thus used instrumentally, the predicates "true" and "false" clearly do not apply; this is not, then, a *cognitive* use of language. And this, according to positivists, is the category into which all normative judgments fall.

Thus, "The presence of an ethical predicate in a proposition adds nothing to its factual meaning or content," A. J. Ayer insists in his much-discussed *Language, Truth and Logic.* Ethical concepts are "pseudo-concepts." ". . . if I say to someone, 'You acted wrongly in stealing that money,' I am not stating anything more than if I had simply said, 'You stole that money' . . . in a peculiar tone of horror." He goes on: ". . . in every case in which one would commonly be said to be making an ethical judgment, the function of the relevant ethical word is purely 'emotive' used either to express a feeling, or to arouse feeling in others sometimes to the point of having the effect of a command."[12]

Ayer distinguishes his admittedly radical subjectivism from the view of orthodox subjectivists like Prall and Perry who do not deny that ethical judgments express genuine propositions, namely, propositions about the speaker's feelings.

If this were so, ethical judgments clearly would be capable of being true or false. They would be true if the speaker had the relevant feelings, and false if he had not. And this is a matter which is, in principle, empirically verifiable. . . . On our theory . . . in saying that tolerance was a virtue, I should not be making any statement about my own feelings or about anything else. I should simply be evincing my feelings, which is not at all the same thing as saying that I have them.[13]

In other words, for Ayer a so-called ethical judgment is the *expression* of a feeling—as if one were to say "ugh" or "far out"—and not the *assertion* of a feeling.

Ayer modified his position slightly in later comments, placing more emphasis on the use of moral expressions to influence others (rather than as mere exclamations), and he tried to reckon with the more glaring shortcomings in his earlier statement. But his basic view that ethical judgments are neither true nor false and hence not really statements is retained. Since, in point of fact, we do give *reasons,* or surely think of ourselves as giving reasons, for our moral judgments, Ayer tries to reconcile this awkward circumstance with his noncognitivist position. The reasons we give, he says, provide no logical or scientific (factual) support for our judgments; the reasons are merely "expressive" or "influential."[14]

One may agree with Ayer that the reasons given do not constitute a scientific proof in the sense in which proof is supplied in the natural sciences, a concession which many— John Dewey, for example (cf. below, pp. 136–138)—would not make. What Ayer fails to reckon with is the possibility that reasons may support moral judgments in some other way. Professor A. P. Brogan, observes that what is needed is "a deeper consideration of the entire problem. . . . In everyday thought or language, we use methods of reflective inquiry and argument which may use deduction or induction as parts of the argument but which cannot be reduced to either one or both."[15] Quite so. In the sequel (cf. below, pp. 234–241) such a method will be suggested.

A more thoughtful formulation than Ayer's is provided by C. L. Stevenson, whose *Ethics and Language* has become the *locus classicus* of the emotivist, or noncognitivist, position, as this point of view has come to be known. Like Ayer, Stevenson rejects the conclusion attributable to all so-called interest theories of value, namely, that a moral judgment simply expresses the fact that the author of such a judgment has such-and-such a preference or feeling of approval and that, in so far, it simply gives *information* about his interests. Ethical statements are not simply *descriptive,* in this sense, although this may be an ingredient in them. "Their major use is not to indicate facts, but to *create an influence.*"[16] Their intent is not to announce that an interest exists, whether one's own or a group's, but to "recommend" and hence to alter interests.

When you tell a man he oughtn't to steal, your object isn't merely to
let him know that people disapprove of stealing. You are attempting,
rather, to get *him* to disapprove of it. Your ethical judgment has a
quasi-imperative force which, operating through suggestion, and in-
tensified by your tone of voice, readily permits you to *influence,* to
modify, his interests.[17]

Language, Stevenson notes, may be used for two general
purposes: to express beliefs (statements of fact); or to give
vent to our feelings (interjections), create moods (poetry), and
influence the attitudes and actions of others. He identifies the
latter as the *dynamic* in contrast to the descriptive use of language. When we engage in the dynamic use of language we use
words which have an emotive meaning. Borrowing from Ogden
and Richard's well-known work, *The Meaning of Meaning,*
Stevenson asserts that "The emotive meaning of a word is a
tendency of a word, arising through the history of its usage, to
produce . . . *affective* responses in people. It is the immediate
aura of feeling which hovers about a word." For example, "old-
maid" and "elderly spinster" may designate the same person but
the first obviously carries with it a freight of emotional meaning. And this is the significance of the word "good." It "has a
pleasing emotive meaning which fits it especially for the dynamic use of suggesting favorable interest."[18]

Thus, "good" is not merely an expression of interest or liking (A is good = I like or am interested in A). If this were the
case it would have little or no dynamic impact; to say "I approve of racial justice" or "Racial justice appeals to my interests" is hardly very moving. However, when I say "Racial
justice is good" I give it emotive meaning. Moral predicates are
thus rhetorical devices for influencing or persuading others.

There is, of course, another, *rational* way of effecting such
persuasion. I may cite facts, as when, in a dispute over publicly
supported low-cost housing, I try to show an opponent that the
cost of slum housing in terms of tax expenditures (for health,

fire, and police services, etc.) is higher than the cost of subsidizing adequate dwellings. Here I address myself to his *beliefs,* assuming that, when he knows the facts, he will no longer condemn public housing as an extravagance which hard-pressed taxpayers are unable to afford. But I may also address myself to his *attitudes,* taking him on a tour of slum areas to witness actual suffering, denouncing the injustice of a system that tolerates slums, appealing to my opponent's sense of social justice. Stevenson uses "attitude" as Perry and Prall use "interest"; it designates "any psychological disposition of being for or against something."[19] That is the role of all moral statements, according to Stevenson—to alter attitudes. They are thus essentially *non-cognitive* in character.

Stevenson fails to explain *why* such moral statements function more effectively in this way than simple announcements of one's own preferences ("I prefer adequate housing for all even if it means increased taxes"), a fatal hiatus in his account. And he neglects to distinguish between persuasion by means of moral statements or predicates and persuasion by divers other means, those methods so well known to the purveyors of cigarettes and deodorants, or to demagogues and rabble-rousers. If the methods of the latter are more effective than *moral* suasion in changing attitudes, as they often are, presumably it would be foolish to rely on moral suasion. After all, the hucksters too are attempting to change our attitudes. Moreover, emotivism curiously limits the use of moral predicates to contexts involving persuasion or the modification of the attitudes of others. There are clearly many notable occasions on which we make moral judgments affecting our own conduct which have nothing to do with influencing others—Stalin's daughter's decision to leave Russia, for example, and countless decisions like that one. And even where others are involved, we may simply want them to know where *we* stand without any hope of altering their attitude. Still, moral suasion does take place; the objection is that the way in which it is effected is surely vastly different (and, as will be seen later, much more complicated) than the mechanisms (pleasing associations, repetition, bandwagons) used by hucksters and by the emotivists who unwittingly play into their hands.

One need not linger over these probably decisive inadequacies. Situations in which moral suasion is intended *are* common and the emotivists must be credited with calling our attention to their importance. But, paradoxically, even if what they say about moral suasion were true, this would depend on our not knowing this truth. Once everyone knows the secret that Stevenson knows and discloses, albeit only in learned journals and books read mostly by students and scholars, the moral ploy will fail, if that is all it is—a ruse. Once we learn that moral predicates, appeals, for example, to our conscience or sense of obligation or justice, are based not on the moral *merits* of an issue, but are designed to manipulate us, the artifice can hardly work beyond such efficacy as it may derive from our suggestibility. (We know that hucksters and pitchmen don't believe what they say, and they know we know, but sponsors still spend billions of dollars on transparently mendacious advertisements, relying presumably on the power of pleasant association or suggestion through sheer repetition.) The use of emotion-laden words is bound to have less effect on us once we know what is going on.

It is here that we confront the naked skepticism of the emotivist in all its starkness since from his point of view it is nonsense to talk of the moral merit of a given course of conduct, as it is of *demonstrating* such merit. What one does is cash in on the common illusion (to use Freud's term) that there are such merits and demerits and that in some sense or other they *are* demonstrable. It must follow that, for the emotivist, moral predicates like "good" may be attached indifferently to any interest—as appropriately to a policy urging the torture of heretics as their tolerance, the enslavement of women as their liberation, the promotion of addictive drugs as their prohibition. Clearly,

goodness, like advertising and propaganda, is for the gullible—
a cynical and rather unsatisfactory teaching. One is reminded
of Plato's famous criticism of the Sophists in *Republic:*

It is as if the keeper of some huge and powerful creature should
make a study of its [the public's] moods and desires, how it may best
be approached and handled, when it is most savage or gentle and
what makes it so, the meaning of its various cries and the tones of
voice that will soothe or provoke its anger; and, having mastered all
this by long familiarity, should call it wisdom, reduce it to a system,
and set up a school. Not in the least knowing which of these humours
and desires is good or bad, right or wrong, he will fit all these terms
to the fancies of the great beast and call what it enjoys good and
what vexes it bad. He has no other account to give of their meaning;
for him any action will be "just" and "right" that is done under
necessity, since he is too blind to tell how great is the real difference
between what must be and what ought to be.[20]

Noncognitivists are undaunted by such implications of their
position. Thus, in a recent book, Professor Joseph Margolis, after
dismissing the possibility of objective moral appraisal, concludes that

It seems flatly impossible, by any conceptually defensible means,
utterly to disqualify, as being morally incoherent or morally objectionable, policies and commitments that deliberately advocate the
selective destruction of life and property. . . . repugnant as it may be,
there are absolutely no grounds on which policies of selective violence
and destruction of life and property can be shown to be conceptually
dubious or defective or inferior to policies that embody what are said
to be the most generous or altruistic or nonviolent or enlightened
values that the civilizations of the world have yet advanced.[21]

There is, if I may vary Alfred North Whitehead's famous
meteorological metaphor, a weather as well as a climate of
opinion. The philosophical weather has changed. Noncognitivism
is recently out of favor, but it still has articulate adherents.

Part Two

Abortive Escapes from Skepticism

Chapter Six

Intuitionism: Prichard, Ross, and Moore

Recently a runaway youth was locked up in a Miami jail cell with convicted felons and was found strangled to death several hours before he was to be released to his parents. He had been killed by the inmates, it was suspected after having been sexually assaulted. His was the second murder in a year in the Dade County Jail, a place of detention not untypical of jails throughout the country. The tragedy prompted the *Los Angeles Times* to editorialize as follows:

More than 25% of the nation's jails were built at least 50 years ago. About 6% are fully a century old. Most have inmate populations far in excess of what they were constructed to hold. There is nothing "correctional" about most of these facilities. They are too typically places of brutality, squalor and despair, and schoolhouses for recidivism.

Although difficulty might be encountered in placing blame, it requires no sensitive moral conscience to be revolted by the callousness which permits such conditions and the kinds of tragedies to which they lead. Nearly everyone recoils. And everyone understands what is meant when the conditions described in the *Times* editorial are denounced as evil—understands without the help of learned philosophers. Moral philosophy is thus confronted at the outset by a grand (and awkward) paradox: everyone understands moral judgments and, in some instances, nearly everyone concurs in them; and yet philosophers, although they have toiled endlessly at the task, have not been able to explain them to each other's satisfaction.

Fundamentally, it is this embarrassment to which *ethical intuitionism* is a response. Philosophers fail to explain what everyone understands because what they are trying to explain is essentially inexplicable. No reasons can or need be given for our sense of moral revulsion over the killing of a teen-age boy as a result of official irresponsibility and the indifference of Miami's citizens. We simply *know* that it was wrong; proof is not required. The certainty with which we render our verdict is quite undisturbed by the seeming inability of philosophers to agree about *why* it was wrong. To dismiss the sense of outrage we feel on occasions such as this as the reflection of a sense of guilt (in the Freudian sense) or of our group or class bias somehow affronts us. Perry's brand of subjectivism and emotivism are even worse, trivializing our deepest feelings. To say that our condemnation of the Dade County jail is merely the expression of one interest or desire among other interests or desires, including the interests or desires of those who are responsible for such prisons (maybe most of us!), and of the misfits, outcasts, and psychopaths who inhabit them, is to do violence to the nature of the moral experience. It is to explain the moral experience by talking it away. Ethical intuitionism is committed to preserving the integrity of this experience.

Long in eclipse, intuitionism was revived in the twentieth

century in part because of dissatisfaction with *teleological* ethics, so-called, and its reliance on consequences, whether in terms of one's pleasure or well-being (egoism) or the pleasure or well-being of the greatest number (utilitarianism), as the test of the rightness and wrongness of conduct. Plato, who sought in *Republic* to prove that the just man is happier than the unjust man, Butler, Paley, Bentham, Mill, all sought to justify moral conduct by a reference to consequences. H. A. Prichard's article, "Does Moral Philosophy Rest on a Mistake?" which appeared in 1912, did much to further the revival of intuitionism. He attributed the "mistake" to the assumption that obligation, for example, the obligation to humanize our barbarous jails and rehabilitate their inmates, is not self-evident and hence that it is necessary to give reasons, i.e., supply proof that such an action is right. Later I shall have my own quarrel with teleological ethics. (See below, pp. 164–168, 173, 178–179, 234.) Prichard's essential objection was that we do not come to appreciate an obligation by virtue of an argument, that is to say, by any kind of proof; we simply feel it, we have a *sense* of obligation.

Prichard urged, "the sense of obligation to do an action of a particular kind, or the sense of its rightness, is absolutely underivative, or immediate. . . . This apprehension is immediate, in precisely the sense in which a mathematical apprehension is immediate, e.g., the apprehension that a three-sided figure, in virtue of its being three-sided, must have three angles." Prichard contended that in both cases "insight into the nature of the subject directly leads us to recognize its possession of the predicate; and it is only stating this fact from the other side to say that in both cases the fact apprehended is self-evident."[1] If we have any question about whether there really is an obligation to tell the truth or repay a debt the answer is not to be found in citing reasons, i.e., "in any process of general thinking" but in "getting face to face" with the situation and then "directly appreciating" the obligation involved.[2] In *Moral Obligation* (published posthumously in 1937) Prichard's views are not substantially changed. Obligation, he insists is *sui generis* and therefore inexplicable except in its own terms and knowable, he again contends, entirely through immediate experience or intuition.

Prichard's intuitionism might never have spread beyond Oxford had not his renowned student, W. D. Ross,[3] rallied to the defense of the same view in two well-known works, *The Right and the Good* (1930) and *Foundations of Ethics* (1939). Like his teacher, Ross rejected the attempt of teleological ethics to base rightness on the "productivity of some sort of result." Ross observes that when an individual keeps a promise because he thinks he ought to do so, he is not thinking of the consequences of his action either to himself or others: "What makes him think it right to act in a certain way is the fact that he has promised to do so—that and, usually, nothing more."[4]

Motives as well as consequences are also excluded; rightness belongs to acts independently of motives. The result is a sharp distinction between *right* and *good*. The latter is an attribute of motives. Thus a right act can be done from a morally bad motive and inversely a wrong act can be done from a morally good motive.

Ross' intuitionism is somewhat less simplistic than Prichard's. He concedes that the obligatoriness of an action is linked with other features of it, and hence is not a kind of absolute and self-contained property; the rightness of a given act is dependent on its possession of other properties, though not to be identified with them. Thus, "even when we are under a special obligation the tendency of acts to promote general good is one of the main factors in determining whether they are right."[5] However, we are told nothing about the nature of the dependence—surely a crucial omission.

Also, Ross wrestles more forthrightly than Prichard with situations involving a conflict of duties when it is not always obvious which to heed. A useful distinction is made between *prima facie* duties, and *actual* duties. A *prima facie* duty would obligate us to act provided no greater obligation interfered. As such, for example, truth telling is a *prima facie* duty. However, if a would-be killer asked me for the location of a gun I had concealed my *actual* duty would be to lie to him. This does not mean that truth telling is any less an obligation. It is *always* that—in the abstract, but in particular situations it may have to be considered in relationship to and perhaps subordinated to other obligations, in this case my duty to protect others from violence when I can. Again, one may have promised to meet a friend for some trivial reason and feel justified in failing to meet him if a serious accident is thereby averted. But this is not because more good (i.e., a good or better consequence) is brought into existence. One has, Ross says, a *prima facie* duty to relieve distress as well as to keep a promise, and, in a given situation, it may be more of a duty than keeping one's word. But surely one may wonder why it happens to work out that way, why a duty to keep one's word, otherwise thought to be binding, somehow becomes subordinate to another duty when the latter involves avoidance of seriously adverse results. Ross appears to be using the very test of consequences he began by rejecting. In a curiously lame statement he concedes that although "promise-keeping . . . should come before benevolence, . . . when and only when the good to be produced by the benevolent act is very great and the promise comparatively trivial, the act of benevolence becomes our duty."[6] Surely this gives the intuitionist case away, especially when one wants to know the point at which the good produced *is* very great and the promise trivial. It may be assumed, for example, that our leaders promised the rulers of South Vietnam that we would come to their aid—no trivial pledge. Should it have been kept at the price of a prolonged war that decimated the population and ravaged the land of the country the pledge was intended to help? Intuitionism hardly helps in problems like these.

Ross explains the seemingly arbitrary priority he accords promise keeping over benevolence in the passage quoted above by urging that he is not only in a morally significant relation of benefactor to his fellows: "they may also stand to me in the relation of promisee to promiser, of creditor to debtor, of wife to husband, of child to parent, of friend to friend, of fellow-countryman to fellow-countryman . . . and each of these relations is the foundation of a *prima facie* duty . . ."[7] True, and this is, of course, the stuff of which moral problems are made. How does Ross advise us to proceed in such dilemmas?

"When I am in a situation, as perhaps I always am, in which more than one of these *prima facie* duties is incumbent on me, what I have to do is to study the situation as fully as I can until I form the considered opinion (it is never more) that in the circumstances one of them is more incumbent than any other . . ."[8] It would have been helpful had we been told what we do when we study the situation. Not only does the phrase suggest an absence of that self-evidence which the intuitionist has led us to expect, it means that at just the point where analysis might tell us most about how *prima facie* principles function in moral deliberation, and therefore about their real status, we are given a meaningless ambiguity. Had Ross used his formidable analytical powers to see what we do when we study the situation, he might have found that *prima facie* principles are not the mysteriously self-certifying absolutes to which he allowed himself to be driven in his flight from subjectivism but, as Dewey has noted, generalized points of view, embodying the cumulative experiences of the race, from which we view particular cases as they arise. (See below, pp. 163–164.) "They are thought of," Dewey writes, "as if they existed in and of themselves and as if it were simply a question of bringing action under them in order to determine what is right and good. Instead of being treated as aids and instruments in judging values as the latter actually arise, they are made superior to them."[9]

A different point of view, more in accord with Dewey's, will be suggested later. Meanwhile, grateful though we may be for his many subtle moral distinctions and keen insights, we must conclude that Ross is not much of an improvement on Prichard.

Well before the appearance of Prichard's article, a case for ethical intuitionism had been formulated by G. E. Moore, one of the most influential philosophers in the English-speaking world, whose *Principia Ethica* (1903) has perhaps been more widely discussed than any treatise on ethical theory written in this century. Moore, although aptly described as a philosopher's philosopher, had a disconcerting way of proposing dismayingly simple answers to complex philosophical problems. When philosophers contended with elaborate displays of logic that the material world is unreal, he purported to refute them by innocently holding up his two hands and insisting that these were real things—hardly the kind of artless argument one would expect from a Cambridge philosopher. Similarly, as philosophers debated endlessly over the meaning of goodness, he proposed to end the debate by announcing simply that good cannot be defined. In saying that good is indefinable, Moore hastens to explain, he is not concerned with definition as indicating the usage of a word—it is obviously possible to tell how the word is used —but with definition as indicating the property for which a word stands.

"If I am asked 'What is good?' my answer is that good is good, and that is the end of the matter. Or if I am asked 'How is good to be defined?' my answer is that it cannot be defined, and that is all I have to say about it."[10] Moore continues: "My point is that 'good' is a simple notion, just as 'yellow' is a simple notion; that, just as you cannot, by any manner of means, explain to any one who does not already know it, what yellow is, so you cannot explain what good is."[11] Definitions, it is explained, are possible only when the object or notion in question is complex. A horse can be defined because it has many different parts, properties and qualities. Not so with "good." Good is "that which ought to exist for its own sake."[12] But no evidence can be adduced for such a judgment; propositions of this kind, incapable as they are of proof or disproof, are intuitions, although Moore hastens to add that he does not thereby imply a special moral faculty which has the intuitions.

Moore is explicit about distinguishing intrinsic good, i.e., that which ought to exist for its own sake, from actions which ought to be performed because they lead to such good or goods, that is, from instrumental goods. Judgments concerning the latter, since they deal with causal relationships, do indeed admit of proof or disproof. Hence judgments concerning what kind of action one ought to perform depend on truths of two kinds: (a) causal truths concerning the results of the action, and (b) self-evident (intuited) truths concerning the good to which the action leads. Such good, as intrinsic, does not depend for its nature on its relations to anything else; it is an *objective* property possessed by an act or object completely independent of the act being willed or the object desired. When conduct does, in fact, lead to good in this sense, it is right. In the *Ethics* (1912) he notes that "the question whether an action is right or wrong *always* depends on its *actual* consequences."[13] Thus, unlike Ross, Moore regards right as a derivative moral predicate. For Moore rightness is not, therefore, self-evident, as Ross believed, but subject to proof or disproof on the basis of evidence, elusive though such evidence may be. In this respect Moore is close to the utilitarian (or teleological) view which Ross rejects. But, unlike the utilitarians, who would define good in terms of happiness or pleasure,[14] or the Aristotelians who would define it in terms of self-realization, Moore insists that it is none of these. If one asks *what* it is, he can only be answered that good is itself and not something else, to be known, as Ross believed right to be known, immediately, through intuition.

Moore's central point is that, although pleasure, self-realization, happiness, and the like may be goods, i.e., consequences of action of which goodness may be predicated, they do not define the nature of or constitute goodness itself. This is clearly shown, to take pleasure as an example, by the fact that some pleasures are judged to be bad, and are so judged without contradiction. The failure to see this and the corresponding identification of good with *other* properties of an object or action Moore calls the *naturalistic fallacy*. He regards this (confusingly named) fallacy as responsible for the errors which have plagued moral philosophy from the start. When one says that pleasure is the good, one means to say something about pleasure (in technical parlance, to make a synthetic judgment). Hence, as Plato pointed out long ago in *Philebus,* one cannot regard the good and pleasure as one and the same. Otherwise, it would be pointless to say that pleasure is the good since one would only be uttering the truism that pleasure is pleasure.

Those who defend the autonomy of ethics, and therefore reject an interpretation of moral predicates that would result in treating ethics as a branch of psychology or sociology, will be grateful for Moore's emphasis on the "naturalistic fallacy" (although *what* Moore means by calling good a "non-natural" property is completely unclear.)[15] In general the attempt by intuitionists to establish the objectivity of values, it will readily be conceded here, has the merit of repudiating the kind of easy acquiescence in the arbitrariness of value judgments associated with the views of Perry and Prall and the emotivists. We may well praise intuitionists for insisting that moral judgments, although not reducible to causal statements (the empirical statements of the sciences), are in *some sense* cognitive in character.

But mere assertion is not enough; the intuitionist fails us where we need him most. The presence of moral conflict belies the claim that duties or goods are self-evident. One suspects that intuitionist philosophies flourish among individuals so supremely confident of their values that they find it difficult to take alternative value schemes seriously enough to contemplate the possibility of genuine challenge and conflict. The self-assurance of Cantabrigians and Oxonians is notorious. Could intuitionism be a product of the serene and placid atmosphere of Cambridge and Oxford? However we answer this question, the important point concerns the obscurantism of the position under consideration. Moore, in drawing an analogy, as in the above quotation, between our experience of a sense datum like yellow and the immediate recognition of good, does not mean, of course, that we literally see good or know it through any other sensory organ. But the analogy is seriously misleading. We know about the perceptual mechanisms by means of which we see yellow but surely of no corresponding mechanism or faculty by means of which we discern good. Moore is too analytical to suggest that we are endowed with a moral faculty. Yet some kind of suprasensible observation is presumably indicated. It is clear, moreover, that the statement "This is yellow" ascribes a characteristic to something. It is highly dubious that "good" is the name for a characteristic in the same or any similar sense, although the statement "This is good" has the same grammatical form. When Moore says that the characteristic designated by the word "good" is unanalyzable he implies that it is a simple quality and not a relational property—related, for example, to the way in which conduct is willed—and the implication is made explicit by the analogy to one's experience of yellow, but he gives no reasons beyond the mere statement that it is so.

Thus, to escape relativism Moore isolates the moral sphere from the rest of human activity. Neither will, judgment, or feeling, nor any interaction of these, confers moral (or aesthetic) value on an act or object in the Mooreian axiology. Is good a kind of tertiary quality which just happens to grace such acts or objects (bad or evil dis-gracing them) as contingently as a secondary quality colors a canary? Hardly. But this is the strange conclusion to which Moore seems to lead us. We want to know above all *why* an act (or the avoidance of one) is obligatory, or *why* the outcome of an act should be called good or bad. Why *ought* we to do something about an inhuman penal system in which a teen-age boy is brutalized and killed—to recur to the tragedy with which this phase of our discussion began? Such questions are at the root of our moral dilemmas. But, crucial though they are, they are almost blandly ignored by intuitionists since *ex hypothesi* one does not question what is self-evident.[16] Earlier, it was suggested that intuitionism, whether it stresses good or right as the ultimate moral category, reflects in its reliance on self-evidence an assurance and confidence about moral principles peculiar to a stable culture. There are settled times when men guide themselves by principles inherited from the past which are so accepted as to be second nature. In such times principles take on a character of self-evidence. The Victorian–Edwardian era was such a stable time for England. Clearly the period during which the Greek Cynics, Cyrenaics, and Sophists flourished was not one of those times. Nor is ours.

The consequences of such complacency about values can be quite pernicious. R. M. Hare, to whose views I am about to turn, makes the following perceptive comment in criticism of the intuitionists:

Suppose that the people of a certain generation . . . have got very settled principles, inherited from their fathers. Suppose that they have become so settled as to become second nature, so that generally speaking people act on the principles without thinking, and their power of making considered decisions of principle becomes atrophied. They always act by the book, and come to no harm, because the state of the world in their time remains much the same as that for which the principles were thought out. But their sons, . . . as they grow up, find that conditions have changed . . . and the principles in which they have been brought up are no longer adequate. Since, in their education, much stress has been laid on observing principles, and very little on making the decisions on which these principles are ultimately based, their morality has no roots, and becomes completely unstable.[17]

This may well be what has happened to many of the young people of the second half of this century. In a world unsettled by wars, depressions, an endless succession of technological innovations, the power to exterminate humanity, to tamper with evolution and to transform experience with hallucinogens, this and future generations have burdens of decision for which the last generation, schooled in the observance of principles, cannot help them. The generation gap, so-called, is a periodic phenomenon. Ours has been broader, deeper, seemingly more painful. Perhaps the reason has just been given. For the few of this generation who turn for help to philosophers, intuitionism, with its emphasis on fixed principles instead of the choices and decisions leading to their revision, simply exacerbates the problem.

G. Warnock rightly characterizes intuitionism "as a confession of bewilderment got up to look like an answer."[18] That a book as barren of results as Moore's *Principia* could be regarded as one of the important works of this century is perhaps a measure of the desperate state of contemporary moral philosophy.

Chapter Seven

Prescriptivism: Hare

The failure of intuitionists to provide an escape from skepticism has spurred the quest for other solutions. Prescriptivism, in contrast to emotivism, is an attempt to impart a measure of rationality to moral discourse. At the same time it attempts to rescue moral predicates from the sheer triviality to which subjectivists like Prall and Perry would consign them, by stressing the role of such predicates in the *guidance* of conduct. According to R. M. Hare, its chief exponent, moral language (i.e., sentences containing words like "right," "ought," "good") is a variety of *prescriptive* language, by which he means that the office of moral principles is to guide conduct. Another obvious variety is the ordinary imperative as exemplified in a command like "Shut the door." Although the two are not the same, a careful examination of imperatives helps us understand the more complex logic of moral language, according to Hare, who has pioneered in the study of the speech acts we call imperatives.

Such an examination led Hare to deny that, as Ayer and

Carnap and others have claimed, imperatives or commands can be reduced to statements, or what grammarians call indicatives, although he concedes that it is difficult to explain the difference. A command, "Shut the door," is not the same as and does not mean the indicative, "I want you to shut the door"; the former is not, like the latter, about the speaker's attitude or state of mind, any more than are the instructions for making omelettes ("Take four eggs," etc.). Similarly, a moral statement such as "A is right" does not mean (except in a loose colloquial sense) "I approve of A."

Secondly, Hare rejects the emotivist thesis embraced by Ayer and Stevenson to explain why we couch what they too believed are imperatives in moral language—why, in other words, we say, "You ought to keep your word" instead of the simpler "Keep your word." Their explanation, it will be recalled, is that we want to influence others. He faults the emotivist explanation, among other reasons, because, as noted earlier, it reduces moral suasion to the level of mere propaganda and accordingly denies the rationality of moral discourse. He insists (rightly in my view) that a moral judgment must provide a *reason* for doing something. The answering of moral questions is not arbitrary but "is, or ought to be, a rational activity."[1] When someone asks, "What ought I to do?" it is surely farfetched to say, as the emotivist theory implies, that he is asking to be *influenced*. What he is obviously seeking is *guidance*, which is to say, reasons for pursuing one course rather than another. "The processes of *telling* someone to do something, and *getting* him to do it, are quite distinct, logically, from each other," just as, in the case of indicatives, "To tell someone that something is the case is logically distinct from getting (or trying to get) him to believe it."[2] If this is true of ordinary imperatives it is true of all prescriptive statements, including moral ones, Hare contends.

What does rational guidance consist of? It consists in the first place of indicating what, given one's principles, one must, in all consistency, *do*. Essentially statements containing terms such as "right" and "ought" are answers to the question "What ought I to do?" and the answer to that question is not merely an indicative or descriptive statement; it is prescriptive in the sense in which a command is prescriptive: one cannot logically accept a command without *acting* on it and, similarly, one cannot consistently affirm or accept a moral judgement without acting on it. In other words, one cannot consistently say, "You ought to oppose war" without implying the imperative "Oppose the war" and, indeed, "Oppose this war," *nor can one consistently accept such a moral judgment without committing himself to acting on it.* The former *entails* the latter. It is not a matter of being *"moved"* to do it, although that may incidentally be involved; one is committed by the *logic* of the situation.[3] If one doesn't act on the moral judgment, "You ought to oppose war," he hasn't really accepted it, any more than one can be said to accept a command such as "Shut the door" unless he acts on it. To this extent value judgments and imperatives are alike.

But obviously the task of rational moral discourse, i.e., of providing guidance to the morally perplexed, is more complicated than the simple reminder that if you believe all war is wrong you must logically oppose any given war. One may ask why is war always wrong? Hare rejects attempts, which have occupied much of the history of philosophy, to provide reasons for opposing war, or for any other moral position, by deducing the answer from allegedly self-evident principles. He argues quite decisively as follows:

Suppose that we were faced, for the first time, with the question "Shall I now say what is false?" and had no past decisions, either of our own or of other people, to guide us. How should we then decide the question? Not, surely, by inference from a self-evident general principle, "Never say what is false"; for if we could not decide even whether to say what was false in these particular circumstances, how could we possibly decide whether to say what was false in innumerable circumstances whose details were totally unknown to us, save in this respect, that they were all cases of saying what was false?[4]

But if there are no self-evident principles from which reasons can be derived, neither will mere factual assertions provide a guide to the really perplexed. If one doubts that war is always wrong, it will not be sufficient to urge—even if such facts were demonstrable—that war brutalizes people, or leads to dictatorship, or even that it leads to greater unhappiness than pacifism. Such statements do not prove that war is wrong—a prescriptive statement—unless, in conjunction with such factual (descriptive) assertions, one appeals to or accepts as a premise a moral (prescriptive) judgment, e.g., that it is *wrong* to brutalize people, or that dictatorships are *evil*, or that one *ought* to act in such a way as to maximize happiness. In other words, the *logic* of moral discourse is such that no moral *conclusion* can be derived from a set of premises unless one premise is a moral judgment. Hare agrees here with Hume—and Moore—that "is" propositions, i.e., statements about matter of fact, cannot yield "ought" propositions.[5] There can be no logical deduction of moral judgments from statements of fact.[6]

Hare's special way of formulating the position is this: "No imperative conclusion can be validly drawn from a set of premises which does not contain at least one imperative." This, he contends, is true of *all prescriptives, including moral* prescriptives.[7] The following syllogisms illustrate his point:

Invalid

Dictatorships suppress the rights of individuals	(descriptive-factual)
War causes dictatorships	(descriptive-factual)
War is evil	(prescriptive-moral)

Valid

Dictatorships, since they suppress the rights of individuals, are evil	(prescriptive-moral)
War causes dictatorships	(descriptive-factual)
War is evil	(prescriptive-moral)

Grant Hare's contention that logical relations between prescriptive judgments (even including commands) are possible and provide the basis for moral argument. But if this is so, what reason can be given for the moral premise from which the concluding prescription is derived? It may, of course, in turn be derived from a more ultimate prescription. But, ultimately, if one agrees with Hare, one must indulge in that very arbitrariness which he commendably says it is the task of moral discourse to avoid, namely a premise for which no reason can be given other than the statement that this is what one has chosen. At this point moral discourse stalls. Not only is justification unavailable, one premise and its implications ("War has the deep meaning that by it the ethical health of a nation is preserved. . . . War protects the people from the corruption which an everlasting peace would bring upon it.")[8] is on the same moral level as its opposite ("Let us ascend towards the principle that necessitates a perpetual peace.")[9] As Alisdair MacIntyre notes, nothing is left except assertion and counter-assertion.

However, Hare believes that this consequence is avoided by virtue of what he calls the *universalizability* of moral judgments, on which he laid increasing stress in a book, *Freedom and Reason* (1963), which followed his widely discussed *Language of Morals* (1952). Thus, although moral judgments resemble ordinary imperatives in that both are prescriptives, there is a fundamental sense in which they are different. Moral judgments (by virtue of having descriptive as well as prescriptive meaning)[10] are *universalizable*, Hare says. That is, such a judgment "commits the speaker to the further proposition that anything exactly like the subject of the first judgment, or like it in the relevant respects, possesses the property attributed to it in the first judgment."[11] On the other hand, imperatives, even when formulated as universals, are not universalizable: "It is, in fact, almost impossible to frame a proper universal in the imperative mood." Suppose, for example, one were to try to generalize the sentence "Do not ever smoke in this compartment."

First we eliminate the implicit "you" by writing "No one is ever to smoke in this compartment." We then have to eliminate the "this." A step towards this is taken by writing "No one is ever to smoke in any compartment of British Railways." But we still have left here the proper name "British Railways." We can only achieve a proper universal by excluding all proper names, for example, by writing "No one is ever to smoke in any railway compartment anywhere." This is a proper universal; but it is a sentence which no one could ever have occasion to utter. Commands are always addressed to someone or to some individual set . . . of people. It is not clear what could be meant by the sentence just quoted, unless it were a *moral* injunction or other value judgment.[12]

Thus the statement, "You ought not to smoke in this compartment," if used evaluatively, entails the true universal "No one ought to smoke in any compartment exactly like this one," which in turn entails the imperative "Do not smoke in any compartment exactly like this one." Hare is not saying that everyone *ought* always to adhere to universal rules. His is a logical rather than a moral thesis, i.e., it is a thesis about the meaning of words: "The meaning of the word 'ought' and other moral words is such that a person who uses them commits himself thereby to a universal rule."[13]

In sum, the rules of moral reasoning for Hare are two, corresponding to the two features of moral judgment: prescriptivity and universalizability.

When we are trying in a concrete case, to decide what we ought to do, what we are looking for . . . is an action to which we can commit ourselves (prescriptivity) but which we are at the same time prepared to accept as exemplifying a principle of action to be prescribed for others in like circumstances (universalizability).[14]

For example, if someone fails to pay me a debt and the law permits me (as it once did) to have him jailed, I cannot say he ought to be jailed, unless I am prepared to say that everyone ought to be jailed in similar circumstances and that I too ought to be jailed if in similar circumstances I am unable to pay a debt I owe. If I am unwilling to apply the same rule to myself (Which Hare believes would be the case in this instance) I cannot validly make the first judgment. Thus, the combination of prescriptivity and universalizability "is sufficient for establishing the rationality of morals," that is to say, of cogent moral argument, although it is "most fundamentally because moral judgments are universalizable that we can speak of moral thought as rational," i.e., "to universalize is to give the reason."[15]

Hare's skillfully elaborated position gave new vigor—at any rate, among philosophers—to discussions of moral theory. But it is clear that his preoccupation with imperatives, the meaning of which he has done much to clarify, has limited Hare's perspective on moral issues. Earlier we cited as an example of a moral judgment the statement "You ought to oppose war." Now "oppose" seems to be what might be called an "action oriented" word. (It really isn't always; it might simply be a feeling of being against.) Suppose the statement were: "War is wrong." Can one accept this proposition without committing himself to acting on it as in the case of responding to an ordinary imperative? May one just *believe* it? May one not, in fact, believe that war is wrong and do nothing about it, or announce that war is evil and still act contrariwise by accepting a draft? It would seem so. Indeed, we often make moral evaluations in contexts to which the guidance of conduct is clearly irrelevant, as when we say that Napoleon was inordinately ambitious, or Lincoln was a noble figure, or Churchill behaved like a knave in World War I and a knight in shining armor in World War II.

But this need not be one's main quarrel with prescriptivism. Hare rightly insists that moral discourse involves the giving of reasons for acting in one way rather than another. He is unable, as I am unable, to find any self-evident principles from which such reasons can be deduced. He also rejects naturalism, which he more aptly calls "descriptivism," agreeing, as we have seen, with Hume (and Moore) that "is" propositions, i.e., statements about matter of fact, do not yield "ought" propositions. But if, as Hare says again and again, moral discourse involves the giving of reasons, does prescriptivism provide a source of reasons, or a description of how we go about finding reasons, other than the reminder—useful, to be sure—that we should be consistent and sincere. Sincerity requires that *if* one judges war to be bad he ought to *oppose* war and manifest his opposition in some kind of *action;* and consistency requires that, if one condemns war, one ought to condemn this one. For similar reasons if you owe me money and accept the principle that you ought to pay your debts, you are committed to paying me, as must everyone in similar circumstances including the individual who offers such advice; you must in a sense as logically binding, we may even agree, as when, if you agree that all p is q, you must conclude that some q is p.[16] We may grant readily that if one makes a moral judgment in a given situation one cannot logically, i.e., reasonably make a different judgment on another occasion, unless it is different in some relevant respect or unless one retracts his first judgment, and that, tacitly or expressly, this principle is accepted when one makes a moral judgment. Sincerity and consistency are important traits to look for in someone who is giving us moral counsel—a point to which I shall return later.

But is the consistency implied by the universalizability on

which Hare places almost exclusive stress enough, especially since, from the point of view of one who differs with us, it may only mean—as Warnock points out[17]—that we are willing to make the same wrong judgment in every case? Are *these*—sincerity and consistency—the reasons of which we are in need in moral discourse? Do these reasons tell us *why* we ought to oppose war, or *why* we ought to repay a debt, or *why* (to recur to the example on which Hare elaborates in his second book) racial discrimination is wrong? Has Hare given us any reason for accepting the guidance of someone who disagrees with us? Why should his course be preferred to the course dictated by our prevailing preferences? At best Hare gives us *some* of the identifying characteristics of moral discourse and *some* of the ways in which we go about finding reasons for our moral judgments. But surely moral deliberation—whether or not expressed in actual discourse—involves much more. Clearly moral discourse affects conduct—one's own or the conduct of others. Hare tells us about *one* of the ways in which it affects conduct when it takes the form of a prescription. But to dwell exclusively on moral prescriptions is to omit a great deal, including what we need most (and what Hare has told us ethics must lead us to), namely, how we go about supporting our moral judgments and making our moral choices and decisions.

We may agree with Hare that ethics is morally neutral and that attempts to provide an ethical theory that will indicate or decree a particular set of values is bound to run afoul of the criticism of one or other of the relativists. If the quest for objectivity is not to be chimerical it must not attempt to certify this or that value, or line of conduct, or way of life. This is the course that convicts us, as the relativists have properly warned, of cultural chauvinism, dogmatism, absolutism. Objectivity must be found then not in the *content* of moral judgment, not (as Moore and the intuitionsists suppose) in that which moral judgment finally vindicates as good, desirable, laudable, but in the *manner* in which we judge, the *way* in which we will one or other course of conduct, the *form* (as distinguished from the content) of our choices and decisions. This (as will be seen) was Kant's great and abiding insight (cf. below, p. 234). And this Hare understands. But the method of universalization, whether Hare's or Kant's, only reflects the perception that an undogmatic escape from skepticism requires a formalistic ethic; it provides no program for such an ethic. We must look elsewhere.

Chapter Eight

Instrumentalism: Dewey

Fame is fleeting even among those who, like philosophers, are thought to deal in eternal verities. A generation ago it would have been gratuitous to remind readers of John Dewey's pre-eminence among twentieth—century philosophers. Today such a reminder may be needed, even for graduate students. With tireless perseverence Dewey sought to defend the objectivity of value judgments while shunning metaphysical and theological dogmas and rejecting the kind of obscurantist intuitionism championed by Ross and Moore. Since both the accomplishments and limitations of that effort were dictated by the instrumentalist philosophy from which Dewey takes his start, some reference to his more general philosophical orientation will be helpful.

"Instrumentalism" is Dewey's name—he preferred it to "pragmatism"—for his view concerning the nature of knowing. Instrumentalism starts with the lesson learned from Darwin that man is an organism derived from and continuous with other species of organisms. Instrumentalism is therefore biologically oriented: "Suppose we take seriously the contribution made to our idea of experience by biology," Dewey proposes. If we do, the basic relationship in terms of which to understand man must be the "intercourse of a living being with its physical and social environment."[1] Elsewhere he writes: ". . . the interaction of organism and environment, resulting in some adaptation which secures utilization of the latter, is the primary fact, the basic category. . . . Knowledge is not something separate and self-sufficing, but is involved in the process by which life is sustained and evolved."[2] Accordingly, knowing is not the activity of some occult agency called a rational faculty to which a world of external objects is inexplicably revealed. There is no spectator-like mind which somehow looks out upon or views an ulterior reality. The very words usually used to express the cognitive relationship—"reflect," "grasp," "view," "apprehend" (Latin: *prehendere,* to seize)—are highly metaphorical and quite misleading to the extent that they suggest that mind is a kind of mirror that reflects or duplicates an antecedently given reality or perhaps a light that illuminates it.

Thinking is not, then, a gratuitous activity that just happens. It is not a supernatural or extra-natural phenomenon marking a break between man and nature, as the seventeenth-century Cartesians (and our own conventional wisdom) would have it. Instead it is a complex and highly effective way, continuous with and derivative from other ways, of enabling man—inferior to other organisms in mobility, armor, and natural armament— to cope with his physical and social environment. Originating in confusion, uncertainty, trouble, when the balance between the human organism and its environment is disturbed, thinking serves the practical purpose of restoring equilibrium. It is, Dewey says, a mode of "directed over action" and ideas are "anticipatory plans"[3] designed to resolve difficulties or solve problems. Ideas are hypotheses to be tested by reference to their success in removing the difficulty which generated them. As such they are tools, instruments—hence "instrumentalism"— and their validity is determined by reference to whether or not they work.

If ideas, meanings, conceptions, notions, theories, systems are instrumental to an active reorganization of the given environment, to a removal of some specific trouble and perplexity, then the test of their validity and value lies in accomplishing this work. . . . Now an idea or conception is a claim . . . or plan to *act* in a certain way as the way to arrive at the clearing up of a specific situation. When the claim or pretension or plan is acted upon *it guides us truly or falsely;* it leads to our end or away from it. Its active, dynamic function is the all-important thing about it, and in the quality of activity induced by it lies all its truth and falsity. The hypothesis that works is the *true* one.[4]

Dewey cites the procedures of modern experimental science as confirming this view. The scientific manner of thinking does not disclose the independent reality of things any more than does any other way of thinking. It is simply a more carefully contrived and more versatile way of *dealing* with things.

Central to Dewey's position is his denial that the immediately felt or perceived content of experience, i.e., sense data or configurations of sense data, have cognitive status. The objects of knowledge are not such antecedent existences; these are, he says, the "subject matter *for* knowledge."[5] The object of knowledge emerges as the outcome or end-product of a process involving the performance of operations of inquiry providing "knowledge of relations between changes which enable us to connect things as antecedents and consequences."[6] Experimental science is simply such inquiry at its best, but genuine science, we are reminded, "is impossible so long as the object esteemed for its own intrinsic qualities is taken as the object of knowledge."[7] Knowledge "is an affair of *making* sure, not of grasping antecedently given sureties."[8] In other words, "the found rather than the given is the proper subject matter of science."[9]

The notorious problems raised by Dewey's account of knowing and the extent to which his account is idealistic, realistic, or a Kantian blend of the two are not of concern here. Attention is called to it in order to point out that two aspects of his instrumentalism have a direct bearing on Dewey's treatment of value judgments: his linking of inquiry to problematic situations and their resolution; his emphasis on the creative role of intelligence in constituting the object of knowledge out of the material of our raw experience.

In an extended debate with Prall, Perry, and other advocates of the interest theory of value that flared recurrently in the professional journals over a period of about fifteen years, Dewey contended that the judgment "I desire *A*" is not the same as the judgment "*A* is desirable." The former describes a fact in quite the same sense that the statement "I drove my car to work" describe a fact (or set of facts); the latter is a judgment of value declaring that *A ought* to be desired. Dewey was convinced that such judgments of value can be demonstrated, which is to say, that reasons can be given to support them, and that they are therefore cognitive in character. That is what he meant by calling them objective.

Dewey first distinguishes "immediate" goods in their "immediacy or isolation." Such immediate goods are, he notes, "an intellectual abstraction for any grown-up person."[10] They involve judgment of a kind—as Prall and Perry note (see above, p. 77), all interests or desires are mediated by judgments, which is to say they are not just blind tropisms; we have before us an *idea* of what it is we like or desire. But at this level the good or value, if we choose to call it that, derives, not from the judging, but from the affective or feeling factor—the brute (though not necessarily brutish) liking.

But we not only *have* desires or interests, we also ask if they are worthwhile. This occurs, Dewey notes, when we are compelled to choose between them and other incompatible desires or interests. One then asks of any object of desire whether it really is so desirable. *Is* it a good thing? Thereupon valuation takes place. "Enjoyment ceases to be a datum and becomes a problem."[11] An interest or desire acted upon, or an act or object approved, after such evaluation is different from what it was before such evaluation occurred. It is now validated, warranted. The value involved is, Dewey would say, value of an irreducibly different kind, value found to be such *"in consequence* of judgment."[12] Judgment has obviously played a different role here than in the first case where it focuses on the object of interest, concerning itself only with the attainment of that object. Judgment is now concerned not with the object of interest, but with the interest itself, its real as well as merely apparent nature, its relations to one's other interests and to the whole complex of interests which constitute one's way of life. Judgment is not now merely serving an interest but transforming it and thereby playing a creative role. The value that emerges is not something merely reflected in judgment, but *constituted* by judgment. Valuation judgments, as Dewey calls them, are concerned "with estimating values not in existence and with bringing them into existence."[13] The class of values thus identified are not, to be sure, divorced from affective content, i.e., from our feelings. But they are, he says, values of a *plus* sort. There is a difference, he writes,

Between valuation as judgment . . . and valuing as a direct emotional and practical act. There is a difference between esteem and estimation, between prizing and appraising. To esteem is to prize, hold dear, admire, approve; to estimate is to measure in intellectual fashion. One is direct, spontaneous; the other is . . . reflective. We esteem before we estimate, and estimation comes in to consider whether and to what extent something is *worthy* of esteem.[14]

Dewey unfortunately employs the term value for mere likings simply *as had,* prior to their having been subjected to a critical examination as a result of which they *become* values. But his intent is clear enough. Values are not merely stated (as in *post facto* judgments about them), they are instated. "To judge value is to engage in instituting a determinate value where none is given."[15] ". . . . I do not conceive that propositions *about* values already given *as* values are valuation judgments at all . . ."[16] Thus, the judgment that an object of liking is valuable is not the mere declaration over again that it *is* an object of liking; it marks an operation in which the object is determined as *worthy* of being liked. A judgment of value does not merely declare that an object is desired or admired, but that an object thus desired or admired is desir-*able* or admir-*able,* that is, that conduct is warranted on such occasions when the mere incitement of a liking is not deemed a sufficient warrant.[17]

So far so good. Dewey saves judgments of value from the triviality to which by implication advocates of the interest theory reduce them. They are not mere judgments about facts. "To say that something is enjoyed is to make a statement about a fact, something already in existence; it is not to judge the value of that fact. There is no difference between such a proposition and one that says that something is sweet or sour, red or black. It is just correct or incorrect *and that is the end of the matter.*" On the other hand, a judgment about what is *to be* desired and enjoyed is ". . . a claim on future action; it possesses *de jure* and not merely *de facto* quality."[18]

Dewey's general theory concerning the nature of knowing and its inception in problematic situations led him to concentrate, as did few of his critics, on the kind of problematic situation that precipitates such evaluation. There are, he noted:

two differing types of conduct; two differing ways in which activity is induced and guided by ideas of valuable results. In one case the end presents itself directly as desirable, and the question is only as to the steps or means of achieving this end. . . . Such is the condition of things *wherever one end is taken for granted by itself without any consideration of its relationship to other ends.* It is then a technical rather than a moral affair. It is a question of taste and of skill.

In such situations the moral issue does not arise. However,

But let the value of one proposed end be felt to be really incompatible with that of another, let it be so opposed as to appeal to a different kind of interest and choice, in other words to different kinds of disposition and agency, and we have a moral situation. . . . We have alternative ends so heterogeneous that choice has to be made; an end has to be developed out of conflict. The problem now becomes what [end] *is* really valuable. It is the *nature* of the valuable, of the desirable, that the individual has to pass upon.[19]

What is the nature of the evaluative process on which Dewey rightly insisted? In such situations "When ends are genuinely incompatible, no common denominator can be found," Dewey observes perceptively. The tribute is appropriate because the point rarely receives sufficient stress, and, as will be noted in detail later (see below, pp. 178–179), is fatal to the traditional versions of teleological ethics, which is to say, to much of the main corpus of ethical theory. Unfortunately, Dewey himself ignores the point when he addresses himself to the nature of evaluation. Such evaluation turns out to be an inquiry into the "causes and consequences" of the alternatives in a problematic situation, so that we end up with a new version of utilitarianism, albeit purged of the hedonism with which Bentham and Mill afflicted it in the nineteenth century. "After all we are only pleading," Dewey writes in *Reconstruction in Philosophy,* "for the adoption in moral reflection of the logic that has been proved to make for security, stringency and fertility in passing judgments upon physical phenomena."[20] And again: "Inquiry, discovery take the same place in morals they have come to occupy in the sciences of nature. Validation, demonstration become experimental, a matter of consequences."[21] Having done this we are no longer acting arbitrarily; we now have *reasons* for acting as we do.

But what standards are we to use for evaluating those causes and consequences? They do not speak for themselves. We should surely learn as thoroughly as we may what the causes and consequences of conduct are, and the knowledge thereby gleaned may well persuade us that a given end is not as attractive as it promised to be on first inspection. But what if distrust of the standards by which causes and consequences are evaluated is of the essence of a moral dilemma, as Dewey has wisely told us it is? When "the value of one proposed end [is] felt to be really incompatible with that of another," Dewey says in the passage quoted above (p. 133), "no common denominator can be found." But there is no problem of lack of a *common denominator* if we allow the weight or intensity of our interests or desires to control the situation. The problem is only one of deferring choice or decision until the facts about our interests or desires are in, or resisting the temptation of immediate gratifications when they threaten more highly prized long-range interests. Such problems are not inconsiderable, given human frailty. Dr. H. Hartmann, a well-known psychoanalyst, tells us that "Most men know almost nothing about the genetic aspect of their morality, and not too much about the structure and hierarchy of the values that they actually stand for in their thinking and actions."[22] However, once the facts are ascertained and strength of character triumphs over temptation (if it does), stronger interests automatically take over. We have no *real* problem in the moral sense, that is to say, no lack of a common denominator. If there is such a lack this must be because we are *unwilling to rely* on the strength of our prevailing preferences, however enlightened and informed by careful inquiry, and require a different kind of guidance than a full factual account of the conflicting alternatives. Unfortunately, Dewey suggests no other way.[23]

In a true moral dilemma the facts, so far as we can determine them, may all be in and make their contribution to weakening or reinforcing our prevailing preferences, as the case may be. Does doubt end there? Sometimes, and perhaps most of the time. But do we not on critical occasions question our judgment? The inquiry is made and the evidence is at hand. We respond to such data according to our prevailing preferences and tendencies. But may we not ask if our present preferences and tendencies are to be trusted and can *such* a question —here regarded as the truly ethical one—be answered by a mere marshaling of facts as before? "The good man not only measures his acts by a standard," Dewey wrote in his early *Ethics* (1908), "but is concerned to revise his standard. . . ."[24] But Dewey fails to enlighten us in this critical area. In the final analysis, for him, a moral or ethical problem calls for no different kind of deliberation or judgment than any other problem; it is no different from the technical problem of finding the means that most effectively serve our ends. Such inquiry falls within the province of the behavioral sciences and ethics is left with little more than the counsel—surely meager and commonplace in this context—that we look before we leap. This our mothers could have told us with no prior initiation in the mysteries of philosophy. But ethics, the sequel will seek to show, is much more than this.

It is not enough to find the most efficient means for effecting our purposes; it is important as well that we learn as much as possible about their bearing on each other. Such knowledge is greatly advanced by use of that same experimental method which has served science so well. Moreover, such knowledge no doubt leads, as Dewey says, to a revision of our purposes even though this is not the objective of our inquiry. I like to smoke and then learn from medical science that smoking threatens a more important value (viz., avoidance of a lingering death from cancer). I support public policies designed to curb inflation because it harms persons on fixed incomes. I learn from economists that the policies used to curb inflation lead to mass unemployment, a causal relationship of which (let us assume) I was previously unaware. If avoidance of mass unemployment is more important to me than avoiding the penalties which inflation inflicts on people with fixed incomes my opposition to inflationary policies (e.g., government spending) will be modified. On the other hand, mass unemployment may not be regarded by me as such a dire consequence. It may force labor to be more efficient, to make fewer "unreasonable" demands, etc., etc. Once again science—this time not economic science—may enter in to tell me that mass unemployment generates social strains and tensions which can lead to revolution or (as is more likely) dictatorship, and I may find this evidence persuasive. Thanks to the power of habit and the tendency of short-run gains to blind us to long-term benefits, we are not easily persuaded, as Dewey was of course aware. We tend to ignore unpleasant facts. We are often imprudent. We often succumb to temptation. But all this concerns the intelligent realization of our prevailing purposes whether these be social objectives or our personal advantage. It says nothing about their intelligent and deliberate *reconstruction* (as distinguished from change that is mere happenstance), which is what is involved, as Dewey has taught us, in the ethical situation. That too calls for experimental undertakings, but, as will be seen later, in a sense unique to the ethical experience.

". . . escape from the defects of transcendental absolutism is not to be had by setting up as values enjoyments that happen anyhow, but in defining value by enjoyments which are the consequences of intelligent action."[25] Dewey's unswerving commitment to the methods of the experimental sciences prevented him from seeing that there are other methods of intelligent action. Mankind's great hope, he believed, is in the "transfer of experimental method from the technical field of physical experience [science?] to the wider field of human life." He often deplored the fact that while "we trust the method in forming our beliefs about things not directly connected with human life . . . we distrust it in moral, political and economic affairs,"[26] and he consistently condemned the tendency of moralists to "draw a sharp line between the field of the natural sciences and the conduct that is regarded as moral."[27] It did not occur to him that such distrust might be inspired by the limited relevance of experimental science to an authentic moral dilemma.

Dewey more than almost anyone else tells us about the true nature of moral dilemmas. As noted earlier, the pragmatic (or instrumentalist) epistemology which led him to regard all inquiry as problem-solving, whatever its merits in general, enabled him to see more easily than others that, if we are to understand moral deliberation, we must focus attention on the problematic situations which prompt such deliberation. But Dewey believed that the opposite to reliance on the experimental techniques of the natural sciences for the solution of such moral problems is either blind subservience to custom and authority masquerading as absolutist dogma or surrender to arbitrary choice. These are not the alternatives, as he might have recognized has he not been so completely under the spell of experimental science and given it so great a monopoly over the "ways of knowing."

He himself points the way. Well before it became fashionable in some quarters to credit existentialists with a monopoly of insight into the human condition, Dewey anticipated them by noting that

value is technical, . . . economic, etc., as long as one thinks of it as something which one can aim at and attain by way of having, *possessing;* as something to be got at or missed. Precisely the same object will have a moral value when it is thought of as making a difference in the *self,* as determining what one will *be,* instead of merely what one will *have.*[28]

We should be grateful for this insight. But if in a moral conflict the question at issue is the kind of self one shall become, one is beyond the point of considering a given end in its relationship to his other ends and engaging in that inquiry into causes and consequences which informs him about the full nature of the relationship. One is, to say it otherwise, beyond the help of the experimental sciences and the method they employ. It may well be, as Professor George Geiger has persuasively urged, that Dewey's "experimentalism" is not confined to any one pattern of investigation and that for him "all areas of experience are equally real and have their own unique problems and therefore their own unique modes of solution."[29] But, close as he comes to it, Dewey does not tell us what, in the case of an ethical problem, the unique mode of solution is. Quite the contrary. "Where will regulation come from if we surrender familiar and traditionally prized values as our directive standards?" Dewey asks. "Very largely," he answers, "from the findings of the natural sciences."[30] However, our problem, when it is ethical, concerns how we treat the ends and consequences once we learn what they are, once, that is to say, we have exhausted the resources of experimental inquiry in the sense in which it is employed in the sciences. What are we to do when the problem concerns not *what* an end is in the fullness of its consequences so far as we can ascertain them, but whether to seek it after the facts are in?

As this is written the newspapers report that a Los Angeles judge who abhors the death penalty has just pronounced it against Charles Watson, chief executioner in the seven gruesome killings known as the Tate-La Bianca murders committed at the direction of cult leader Charles Manson. The judge was moved by some of the psychiatric testimony. However, he concluded that he would be remiss in his duty if he were to upset the decision of a jury that had "agonized" so conscientiously over its verdict. "I, too, have agonized over those verdicts because I know ultimately it is my function to either set them aside, let them stand or reduce them," the judge said. "I abhor the death penalty as much as anyone does," he added, "but the death penalty is on our books and on this level[31] we are compelled to follow the law as it is on our books."

Surely the judge knew all the causes and consequences of the options open to him. What then was he "agonizing" about? That is to say, what did his agonizing consist of? This is the critical question that Dewey in the end leaves unanswered despite insights, of which the sequel will take note, that do much to further our understanding of the moral experience.

Part Three

An Alternative to Skepticism

Chapter Nine

The Task of Ethics

From the beginning man has been like so much driftwood buffeted about on a sea of desires, moved by forces which he has had no part in shaping. He is born with imperious creature needs—for food, shelter, sex—and the multitudinous ways in which these and other less urgent needs are gratified are normally determined for him by the conditions of his physical and social environment. His routine duties, his goals, his interpersonal relationships, his view of the world (whether or not articulated) are predefined for him. If the complex system of rules regulating the gratification of his wants and needs, basic or other, and the value judgments associated with them, have changed through the ages, the causes of such change have been external and fortuitous from the point of view of the individual —stemming from natural disasters, from war and conquest, from the impact of new tools and weapons. In brief, man has been almost wholly "other-directed," whether by the law, custom, and authority prevalent in his culture, or by the simple and inexorable requirements of physical survival in an often inhospitable world. As Tawney once remarked, most generations walk in a path they neither make nor discover.

It was this way for everyone during most of the history of the race until circumstances made possible a liberation of the individual—some individuals—from complete subservience to the group and complete absorption in a struggle for bare survival. It is still this way for anonymous millions dominated overwhelmingly by hunger, disease, and the rigid institutions of a closed society. But it is no longer so for *all*. Some have been able, deliberately, *on their own initiative,* to revise or reconstruct their values and, at least at certain critical junctures, to alter their course and guide their own development. They have been able to achieve what we sometimes refer to as *self-determination,* to exercise "free will" in what, I shall later contend, is the only meaningful sense of that difficult term. This occurs at those moments of moral perplexity when one finds the goals one has sought or the standards to which one has adhered somehow inadequate and asks: "What ought I to do?"—when one feels *obligated* to find out, when one suspends the principles by which one has heretofore been guided, re-examines them, modifies and even abandons them. This involves a process of validation which consists of finding *reasons* for our likings or preferences and, in so doing, of giving *objective* status to what would otherwise remain at the level of brute liking or *subjective* preference, of finding them "good" or "bad." Although they are often misinterpreted, experience surely attests to such occasions. They are, in fact, central to our moral experience and I take it to be the main task of ethics, and a task unique to it, to consider such experiences, to examine the conditions under which they take place, and to describe the *procedure* involved in evaluation in a way that reckons with their distinctive character.

It should be emphasized that, as noted earlier, the conditions indispensable to such deliberation are relatively recent developments when viewed in the perspective of man's long history. For moral consciousness as thus adumbrated is not an original endowment; it is an achievement, a product of social evolution and personal development. The kind of moral reflection that manifests itself in doubt, suspended judgment, and choice or decision hardly lies within the powers of a child; and neither could it be encompassed by our aboriginal ancestors or, for that matter, by those in any society, literate or pre-literate, for whom everything is fixed and decreed by inviolate law and custom or the sheer exigencies of survival.

Oddly enough, students of ethics have rarely started from such situations of moral doubt, challenge, and choice. *Particular* moral dilemmas are the stuff of which great novels and dramas are made (or were once made), but philosophers have all too often been content to leave the examination of such dilemmas to novelists and playwrights (who nowadays also often fail us) and have neglected to extract generalizations from them that might throw light on the moral life. If one wonders why, the not too flattering answer may be that they have often been primarily concerned with providing an apologetic for one or other system of values or way of life and hence have taken for granted one or other prevailing moral code or ideal to the neglect of the situations in which moral codes are reformulated and new ideals actually chosen. This is not intended as an indictment. After all, philosophers did not, until recently, have the benefit of the insights made available by cultural anthropology, psychoanalysis, and the sociology of knowledge; although they might indeed have been more self-critical had they given more heed to the perceptive skeptics in their midst.

The point will be returned to later. Here I wish to stress that what has been said thus far, little though it is, suggests the *autonomy*, that is to say, the *irreducibility* of ethics. Heavily as ethics must rely on psychology and anthropology, it is not a branch of either. It has its own distinctive subject matter, for it is not primarily a study of *what* men have praised or prized, nor of the psychological or sociopsychological conditions which have led them to praise or prize one alternative over another. As will be seen later, the inescapable implication of some ethical theories is the reduction of ethics to psychology or social psychology, much as this was the case in a different context with Freud. But such a reduction, I shall contend, must ignore a new dimension of human nature and, in this lapse, a new manifestation of nature itself, as novel as life was once novel in a world that had not yet harbored it, as different as man himself was different among primates. This is the dimension in which, through moral deliberation and choice, *we* determine and if need be reconstruct our values instead of having them determined and changed for us. It will be seen that psychology as it is conventionally understood does not investigate this dimension.

If ethics is autonomous, having its own subject matter, may it still be called a science? I recur to a question initially raised in the introduction to this inquiry. It may or may not depending on what we understand by "science." Ethics is a science when it approaches moral phenomena, the data of the moral life, on the assumption, which is made here, that these are natural phenomena occurring within the system of nature and wholly explicable without reference to supernatural or extra-natural forces. It is a science, also, in the sense that it endeavors to understand such data in terms of general principles. It is a science, finally, in the sense that it is concerned with description, that is to say, with providing an account of man's experience when he is asking the question "What ought I to do?" or is acting from a sense of obligation, or calling upon others to be morally responsible and praising or condemning them for succeeding or failing to be so.

But the *sense* of duty or obligation, whatever else it turns out to be—and this, of course, has yet to be examined—is, as the term "sense" implies, private; and whether an individual before acting has been morally responsible and first asked himself what he *ought* to do cannot be determined merely from an inspection of his overt behavior. Thus ethics is not a *behavioral* science in the conventional sense of that term, and for this reason might better be said to be concerned with *conduct* rather than behavior (a distinction which seems to me useful and which I shall define more carefully later). If, in other words, the social sciences cannot concern themselves with essentially private deliberations—I avoid the term "feeling states" as misleading—or with the *meaning* that behavior has to the individual engaging in it, if a datum of science must be public in the sense that it can be *directly* experienced by others, then ethics is not a science.[1] I regard this as a narrow interpretation of science, at any rate, of the science of man. For the life of man includes the phenomenon of meaning, including the meaning of his action to him, and this must be reckoned with if the study of man is to include his most distinctive trait and, in the case of the data of ethics, his most distinctive *achievement*. Whether or not ethics is called science becomes a verbal question, provided one recognizes that in either case we must reckon with the fact that the *same* overt pattern of behavior may or may not be the outcome of ethical deliberation and choice, and that, if we limit ourselves to observing behavior, we cannot know. And to say this is to say that behavioralists cannot know what sensitive and perceptive individuals—at any rate since the time of the pre-Socratics and the Hebrew prophets—have found most significant in their experience.

What has been said implies the separation of ethics from homiletics and from morals in the usual sense of the latter term. As ethicists—I now venture to adopt this virtually unused and rather contrived and stilted term since "moralist" has acquired precisely the connotation I wish to avoid—we do not engage in moralizing; We are not interested in *what* is found right or wrong, good or evil, and in persuading people to act right and do good (or the reverse), except inadvertently or incidentally. Rather our interest lies in describing what transpires when they make such distinctions, that is to say, how these distinctions, when they occur in an ethical context, come to be made. The ethicist may have strong views about the use of heroin, Jack the Ripper, conscientious objectors, the papal encyclical on birth control, the sex habits of hippies, the profit system, or the control of the arts in the U.S.S.R. But these will be peripheral to his main concern, which is what it means to judge an action good or bad and why such a judgment is properly called ethical in one context and not in another.

In the discussion which follows it will be assumed, in sum, that an adequate ethical theory will reckon:

(1) with the belief or conviction in certain circumstances that we *ought* to act in one way rather than another, that is, with the *sense of obligation* with which we elect one course of conduct in preference to others, often in response to a sense of *duty* or what we call the *dictates* of *conscience;*

(2) with the conviction that in these circumstances we make such choices as *free* agents in some meaningful sense of the term "free" and thereby change ourselves into something other than we are—that is, transcend ourselves;

(3) with our adverse judgment of egoists and the corresponding view that one's conduct to be truly ethical must exhibit concern for others even to the point of acting contrary to one's interests;

(4) with the respect for law which clearly plays an important role in moral deliberation;

(5) with the reference in *some* sense to interests, preferences, wants, satisfactions, and our judging some of these as good and some bad.[2] This not arbitrarily, but for *reasons* which thereby provide an *objective,* cognitive, basis for characterizing such judgments[3] as *justified* or *unjustified,* even though they may not be confirmed or disconfirmed as are true or false descriptive statements about matters of fact;[4]

(6) with the difference in kind between such *evaluative* judgments—which, since we ought to do what is good and not do what is bad, are often loosely and ambiguously called "prescriptive"—and the descriptive judgments of matters of

fact which comprise the corpus of science as science is conventionally understood;

(7) with the fact that in some way or other moral suasion occurs, in the course of which values are changed, and that much discourse assumes the possibility of such suasion.

If it appears strange to a reader not familiar with the literature that such a formal enumeration as the foregoing (obvious as much, though perhaps not all, of it must seem to him) should have been found necessary, the answer must be that an astonishing number of recent theories either ignore many or most of these requirements or deal with them in ways that are disconcertingly sterile. What has seemed most meaningful and important to thoughtful and sensitive persons universally admired for their sense of moral responsibility has been dismissed or oversimplified by many contemporary philosophers; this, possibly because they have become too wary of the *culs de sac* in which their predecessors became lost, or squeamish to the point of dullness about clarity, or so dominated by explanatory theories fashioned for other purposes that they have inevitably misunderstood man's actual moral experience. G. J. Warnock has good reason to conclude, after an examination of recent theories of ethics, that "much recent moral theory has been misguided in its aims and unrewarding in its results."[5]

There is, to be sure, an easier way, than by such a tedious inventory, of underscoring the requirements of an adequate ethical theory. In 1968, shortly after Warsaw Pact troops moved into Prague to crush the freedom spontaneously emerging there after years of Communist repression, a group of students gathered at the St. Wenceslas monument and hurled bitter defiance quite literally into the barrels of the guns of the advancing troops. Previously, some who had fought the tanks with sticks and stones and their bare hands had been shot down. On this day shots were fired over their heads and, momentarily at least, they were spared. Simultaneously, in Moscow's Red Square a small number of Russians, one of them the son of Litvinov, another the wife of an imprisoned poet, publicly denounced the Russian action as the brutal aggression it in fact was. An adequate theory of ethics must somehow make sense of such action, of the admiration it aroused even, one suspects, among the Russian aggressors, of the condemnation provoked almost everywhere by the Kremlin's actions, of the conflicting impulses and loyalties which must have preceded these bold acts of defiance.

There are, of course, examples closer to home. Some years ago, when McCarthyism threatened to engulf America in an ugly wave of witch-hunting and the House Un-American Activities Committee (HUAC) was using its powers more to punish unpopular dissent than to find facts that might provide a basis for legislation, one of America's most distinguished playwrights, Arthur Miller, was hailed before the Committee. He was, with one exception, what in those days was called a "co-operative" witness: he did not invoke the Fifth Amendment to avoid testifying, and he confessed freely that at one time he had been a member of the Communist Party. Like many others he had been drawn to the party in the 1930's when the American "system" was anything but viable, and had later, after a bitter taste of it, rejected communism. But Miller refused one Committee request: to divulge the name of those he had known as fellow-Communists, most of whom, like himself, had since repudiated communism (and all of whom were doubtless known to the Committee). "I must live with myself," he said.[6] In consequence, Miller was cited by Congress for contempt, a citation calling for a year in jail and a fine. Happily, the citation was subsequently thrown out by the U.S. Supreme Court. Although the reader will quickly have discerned where the writer's sympathies lie, this is a case on which, unlike the more recent Kremlin action, opinion will be divided. Nevertheless here, as before in innumerable other instances, an adequate ethical theory must explain why an individual risks great damage to himself to protect people whom he hardly knows, and it *must see if there is an objective way of evaluating Mr. Miller's conduct without reference to one's own feelings concerning what he did.*

The task of ethical theory is complicated at the outset by a confusion of the several uses of "good" and "right" and "ought." In ordinary discourse we generally fail to distinguish between the ethical and non-ethical uses of these terms and to a surprising extent this failure has affected the deliberations of moral philosophers. There are some uses of "good" and "right" and "ought" with which we need not be concerned. For example, we say that Laver is a good tennis player, this Tiepolo is a good example of the Venetian school, that was a bad (though never an "evil") move in chess, this is a bad blade. In every case the objects or acts satisfy or fail to satisfy certain criteria by reference to which the predicate is applied. A good tennis player is one who wins (or exhibits a certain grace or pace in hitting the ball), the attributes of the Venetian school are well known to art historians, a move in chess is bad if it leads to loss of the game, a blade is bad (usually) if it is dull. The predicates good and bad are applicable even though we have no interest in tennis, painting, chess, or shaving, although it is clear that others must have been interested, else no criteria would have been set up in the first place. We might, like Plato, say of any particular thing that it is a good or bad (though never perfect) example of the kind or class of which it is a member, just as we say that any circles we draw varyingly approximate the idea (or definition) of circularity. C. A. Baylis reminds us that when we apply the label "good" to something we often mean that it is a "good thing of a certain kind" without committing ourselves to saying that the kind itself is good in any normative sense.[7] Thus we might refer to a good poison gas, a good Nazi or Stalinist, etc. Similarly, uses of "ought" and "right" can be cited which are irrelevant or only remotely relevant to moral discourse.

It is possible, in these days of preoccupation with language analysis among professional philosophers, to become so lost in exploration of such usages that we forget the salutary reminder of Professor Alexander Sesonske when he warns that "Those who take the primary task of ethical theory to be that of defining particular terms tend to become involved in an endless and rather fruitless unraveling of different 'senses' of these terms, almost to the point of losing the theory in a maze of subtle distinctions."[8] I shall try to avoid this pitfall and be concerned here with value predicates in four different an often undiscriminated or confused contexts labeled respectively the aesthetic, prudential, jurisprudential or moral, and ethical. The first task of ethical theory is carefully to distinguish these four uses.

Chapter Ten

The Aesthetic
and Prudential
Uses of "Good,"
"Right," and "Ought"

"Prior to anything which may be called choice in the sense of deliberate decision come spontaneous selections or preferences. . . . We are so constructed that both by original temperament and by acquired habit we move toward some objects rather than others." At the level thus described by Dewey,[1] when we call the object of any preference good we mean that we desire it, it *is* preferred. What we prize may of course vary indefinitely from such elementary goods as food, adequate shelter, relief from pain and illness, or sexual gratification to great wealth, rare paintings, a game of chess, improving the living conditions of the

people of Appalachia. It may turn out that because of its consequences or the means needed to attain it, i.e., because of the relations it sustains to other interests or preferences, a desired object or experience is discovered not to be good. But this does not
detract from the fact that, *in itself,* i.e., *as had,* and apart from
such relations, it is good just because it is desired or, as Perry has
said, *is* an object of interest or, as others have said, is a state of
satisfaction or enjoyment.[2] The flame itself is pleasing even though
it may turn out not to have been worth the candle.

Considered thus, one desire or gratification has no more worth
than another. Dewey's comment again clearly applies:

In isolation one enjoyment cannot be said to be higher or lower than
another. There is nothing intrinsically higher in the enjoyment of a
picture or an instructive book than there is in that of food—that is,
when the satisfaction is taken apart from the bearings and relationships of the object in life as a connected whole.[3]

At this level pushpin *is,* to recur to Bentham, as good as poetry.

"Good" when used in such a context is not a moral or ethical
predicate at all. It may more appropriately be called an *aesthetic* predicate, not indeed in sense of attributing beauty to an
act or object, but in the more literal and more general sense of
declaring that an object or act is enjoyed, that we have a favorable feeling about it, that a sense of satisfaction, gratification,
even elation is attendant on our experiencing or the anticipation
of experiencing it. David Prall's words are appropriate:

Esthetic objects [i.e., the objects which fulfill interests] are valuable
in themselves, simply as such objects, and whenever an object becomes valuable simply as an object—out of all other relations but
that of its *objectivity*—it is esthetic value that it possesses. If there
is one mark of the esthetic consciousness that is definite and pronounced, it is the intrinsic or isolated nature of the experience.[4]

The aesthetic consciousness, Prall remarks elsewhere, is a "resting in itself."[5] It may be added that any interest, as such, is marked by complete absorption in its object. In its hypothetically purest state it represents an engrossment so complete that, without the intrusion of other factors, the very partiality that gives it its distinctive quality is not recognized as such. To be sure, intellect, at its behest, selects among objects, rejecting some and appropriating others, but in such a way as though there were no other basis or principle except that supplied by the present interest for making these allotments.

It requires the talent of an artist to so involve us in enjoyments that we treat them as self-contained, oblivious of ulterior consequences and unconcerned with economic issues about other possible uses of the means on which such enjoyments depend. One becomes lost in contemplating the ceiling of the Sistine Chapel (when the chapel is not swarming with tourists), in listening to the *Moonlight Sonata,* in attending to a great performance of *Hamlet,* so that one is not diverted by extraneous economic calculations concerning the alternative uses of scarce means, (e.g., should the resources spent on building Lincoln Center or the cathedral at Chartres have been used to help the poor?), or by moral deliberation relating these enjoyments or their objects to ends or purposes which they may serve or subvert (e.g., does the poetry of Ezra Pound—assuming it is good—encourage anti-Semitism?). Ideally, when we view an object aesthetically, whether this be a natural object such as a rainbow or a work of art, we are concentrating on *it,* not on its external relations to the artisan or artist (if it is an artifact), to us, or to its causal antecedents or social consequences."[6]

Interests, then, are preoccupied *exclusively* with, or involve drives exclusively toward, a *specific* object or condition of equilibrium or state of feeling. They are distinguished by singleness of purpose. They might be described as intolerant. They are in an important sense self-enclosed. However, objects or experiences, including works of art, cannot be enjoyed in complete isolation, except perhaps in rare moments of bliss or ecstasy. The very fact that our desires vary in intensity prompts us to *prefer* one satisfaction over another, which means that they have been compared and, to that extent, related to each other. The gratification of any interest invariably entails some adverse consequences. It costs something. If we enjoy one thing we cannot enjoy another. Even if, as an old Irving Berlin song reminds us, the best things in life are free (monetarily), they monopolize attention and take time which might be spent on something else. Notoriously, experiences that are intensely pleasurable can have painful consequences and goals that seemed attractive from a distance leave us feeling unrequited when we attain them; and (not to be pessimistic) the converse may, of course, be the case. In short, we learn to treat interests not in isolation, but as they bear on our other interests and ultimately on our whole scale of values. We learn, as Dewey says, to judge our desires and their satisfactions "as elements in a larger whole of conduct and character"[7] and to suspend judgment and refrain from action pending careful reflection. We look before we leap. It is a hallmark of maturity to substitute reflection for spontaneous action in this way.

Such conduct is called rational. The rational individual knows what he wants, selects the means (within the limits of his knowledge) that are most likely to get him what he wants, and does not allow a lesser want to get in the way of a greater one. Obviously, rationality in this sense is only partially attainable. I am not concerned here with the conditions under which crude, rule-of-thumb, intuitive calculations give way to the more refined computations made possible when alternatives are quantified; nor with the extent to which the utilities or disutilities involved can be expressed mathematically in such a way as to maximize expected satisfaction; nor, finally, with recent work in decision theory (including game theory) which has outmoded earlier, simplistic ideas and ideals of rationality. For ideological reasons that need not be explored here[8] the classical liberals of the eighteenth and nineteenth centuries enormously exaggerated the extent to which such rationality ("maximizing expectable utility") prevails, especially at the marketplace, and almost completely ignored the role of the non-rational and irrational in conduct. Nevertheless, calculation of this kind obviously plays a large part in conduct, so large a part that it is often regarded as the essence of morality and provides the matrix for such virtues as prudence, forethought, discretion, providence, care, reasonableness.

"Good" when used in the context under discussion means consistent with our prevailing pattern of preferences or liking or interest. In contrast to the *aesthetic*, this use of good may be called *prudential* or, in the broadest sense of the term, *economic*. Professor Sidney Zink makes the distinction especially clear in a discussion of the conflict he finds between the demands of morality and the demands of art:

Morality insists upon the interconnectedness of experiences; art insists upon the self-containedness of each particular experience. The moral man scrutinizes the given action for its relations to other actions; the aesthetic man absorbs himself in the immediate experience. Morality insists upon the inviolability of the man, art upon the inviolability of the experience. Morality recognizes the fact of dimensionality in life; art stresses the fact of qualitativeness. The first would make life consistent; the second would make it intense. Morality speaks in the interest of the whole, art in the interest of the part.[9]

All this can be epitomized by saying that at the prudential level the judgment of any particular interest is mediated by the notion of a *self*, a self which transcends any *particular* interest—a self representing and for our present purpose describable as the totality of our interests.

Clearly judgment functions differently at the prudential level than when it operates at the service of an immediate desire. In a limited sense it performs the creative role assigned to it by John Dewey (see above, pp. 130–131), since as he stressed, any given interest or preference may well undergo change when examined for its bearing on our other interests or preferences. One may want very much to enter politics and seek public office and refrain when one realizes on reflection how much will have to be given up in terms of family life, privacy, opportunities for unhurried reflection, freedom to express oneself frankly, and so on.

But in such situations our prevailing standards of value or preference are not themselves in question. Reflection is still their servant even though it may result in the modification of a *particular* desire. Its office is to make sure that we are doing what we really want to do. The comparative attractiveness of the alternatives in the foregoing illustration need not be at issue. One knows that he prefers his family life, privacy, independence; the problem is to learn if a political career excludes one's enjoyment of these values. The solution may well prove difficult, but finding it is a matter of learning the *facts* about what is required for election to office: the hours of campaigning before election and of socializing after election, the way in which office-holders must compromise or conceal their beliefs to conciliate constituents, etc., etc. In the case of aesthetic goods one's problem is limited to choosing the means most likely to further the desired end. Here the problem is one of relating our ends to each other, of finding out how one bears on another. If moral deliberation were limited to this kind of problem its concern would be with descriptive generalizations that fall within one or other of the sciences, and ethics, if it were limited to an account of such situations, would be no more than an adjunct of psychology or social psychology. Those who would explain ethics on such a model may be called *reductionists* meaning, as used here, that they support the reduction of ethics to one or other of the behavioral (descriptive, positive) sciences. They would not agree with Kant that "it is quite a different thing to make a prosperous man and a good man, or to make one prudent and sharp-sighted for his own interests, and to make him virtuous . . ."[10] An adequate theory, it is assumed here, will provide for the autonomy of ethics, that is to say, will not explain it away. Reductionists, as thus identified, fail to reckon with the central phenomenon of our moral experience, the *sense of obligation* to which the discussion must now turn.

What can be said preliminarily about the sense of obligation? It must be clear at the outset that, when conduct is regarded as obligatory, we are *not* prompted by our prevailing inclinations, desires or interests, and usually, in such instances, are acting contrary to them. Indeed (as Kant suggested), it is only in the latter case that we can be really certain that we are acting from a sense of obligation. We surely feel no moral obligation to do what we want to do. If one likes to play the piano, his playing the piano is hardly likely to be thought of as obligatory or expressed in the judgment, "I ought to play the piano." His liking takes care of it without the intervention of moral imperatives. When, in a loose sense one says, "I ought to practice," surely "ought" in this context has hardly more ethical import than in the statement that one ought to use reinforced concrete to make a structure more earthquake-proof.

When, then, is obligation felt in the moral sense, if not when we are acting in response to our interests or desires, or choosing those among competing alternatives that are most consistent with our prevailing scale of values? Does it, in fact, make sense to say that we *can* act contrary to our interests? If so, when are we impelled to go contrary to our interests under conditions *that cannot be described simply as the impingement of a stronger interest?*

Apart from parental injunctions, the most prominent of such

impulsions, antedating such others as there may be, issue from
law, whether in the form of rules laid down by custom and
embodied in the *mores,* law sometimes designated as "natural,"
or law written out in legal codes and commandments—provided,
of course, that obedience to such dictates is from motives other
than a fear of punishment, since in the latter case obedience
would be based on a prudential calculation of interests. At this
point conduct takes on another dimension.

Chapter Eleven

Good and Right as Jurisprudential or Moral

We have now to deal with a third use of the term "good": good in what may be called the *jural*, or, more appropriately (since, as will be seen, it cannot be divorced from *some* reference to consequences), the *juris-prudential* sense. Conduct is called good in this sense not because it serves a desire, satisfies an individual or social need or interest, or, after reflection, is found to be in accord with our prevailing schedule of preferences, but because it accords with *law* or with accepted standards of morality. I shall call this use of "good" *moral* as well as jurisprudential in deference to common usage, but I must warn in advance that common usage neglects a profoundly important difference between two uses of the term "moral," one of which will later be carefully distinguished as "ethical."

Conduct is called good in the present context, not because of its consequences, but because it is *right*. Right is the basic moral predicate to which good as thus far defined is irrelevant or from which good is derivative. Although right and good are often used interchangeably, to say that conduct is right in the distinctive sense is to say that a given act is in accord with a law or principle which we have a *duty* to obey or *ought* to obey from a feeling of *respect* for law, even though we are thereby required to repress desire or go contrary to interest. Much conformity is no doubt habitual and routine or coerced, and hence devoid of moral implication, at least from the point of view of the individual involved. But generally speaking the most important rules or laws, whether at the reflective or pre-reflective level, are invested with a special aura designed to inculcate reverence for the law and awe of its author, as our own sacred texts abundantly suggest. We are not only *obliged,* but *obligated* to obey.[1] The law is not merely a rule to be obeyed, but a rule which ought to be obeyed so that action in accord with it is not merely right in the sense of being correct (e.g., "That was the right road to take to get to Paris") but in a *moral* sense which we have now to explore.

The gratification of our interests is, of course, frustrated in countless ways by our limited abilities and our disabilities and by a world that is more often hostile than hospitable. It is with the problems thereby posed that we deal in a prudential context. But, beyond such limitations, our interests are enmeshed in a complex web of social restraints and requirements. The world consists not only of recalcitrant things which we confront with limited capacities, but of persons or groups of persons who are not, like things, dumb and inarticulate. They have their interests and demands as we have ours; and theirs and ours must somehow mesh. This has not been left to chance or choice.

In the vital areas institutions provide appropriate mechanisms for sifting out or selecting those demands that are "legitimate," as the demands of a spoiled child, for example, are not; and by virtue of our involvement in such institutions we have *duties* and *responsibilities* and others have *rights* which by common understanding and consent transcend our interests as individuals.

In many instances "duty" and "responsibility" are too specific or suggest too structured a relationship to convey what is involved, the sense of which is better expressed by saying that conduct is guided by respect for the integrity or inviolability of human personality or by a tacit commitment to the Kantian dictum that we treat others as ends, not as means.[2] Thus, we abhor torture and refrain from it as we do from the gratuitous taking of human life, but it seems artificial to designate this as a duty or obligation as in the case of repayment of a debt or a father's support of his children. Clearly condemnation of torture is better characterized as reflecting respect for the sanctity of the human person, vague though this may be, than as dictated by a sense of duty or a feeling of obligation.[3] But the dynamics are the same: *in either case we subordinate our interests as individuals to a "higher" or, better, a "larger" wisdom, whether this be the wisdom of God, of a departed ancestor or folk hero, or—at a more sophisticated level—simply of law itself as the funded "wisdom of the ages."*

In any event it is important to see that at least some such limitations are not viewed as restraints to be opposed or obstacles to be overcome, but, initially at least, as requirements to be acknowledged and accepted so that even when, moved by temptation or passion, we breach them, we feel a sense of guilt.

One is not then simply a bundle of interests pressing for gratification, one recognizes others as *persons*[4] and becomes a person in being so recognized by them. As such, one is involved in countless relationships: as a spouse, a parent, a citizen; as a teacher or student, an employer or employee, a buyer or seller; as an individual who promises or is promised, who borrows or lends. In every case our several roles invest us with rights and involve us in obligations which are often at least as urgent as our creature needs and interests, or our convenience as we may at any moment see it. Such obligations become standardized and formalized and, where performance is of special importance to society—or to groups or individuals within society wielding sufficient power—are promulgated in laws. Normally we accept these obligations as a matter of course, at the outset by virtue of having been indoctrinated from infancy—from the moment a child learns, for example, that it does not take what it wants without the permission of a parent and, as it grows older, without reference to the wants of at least some others. In brief, what we encounter are not mere forces and objects, but *claims* and *rules,* the rightness of which, in the absence of important complicating factors yet to be noted, we learn to *respect*—much as we learn our mother tongue.

Whatever incidental reference may be made to consequences and whatever regard for consequences may have inspired a given moral law, it presents itself as appropriate and right *in itself,* i.e., as superior to any test of consequences. It may do so by claiming divine origin or self-evidence of one kind or another, but a functional justification in empirical terms is readily available. *If the law were not independent of such utilitarian tests, whatever enduring values it embodies, i.e., whatever its "larger wisdom" or ultimately beneficent consequences might be, would be lost upon partisans calculating their interests and, in the absence of other imperatives, using judgment inevitably chained to the service of such interests and handicapped by limited experience.*

It is all too easy to parody the Kantian version of truth telling—always tell the truth without reference to consequences —by showing the preposterous result of telling the truth in some situations, for example, telling a would-be robber where you have concealed your wallet. But the need for reference to other considerations than a calculation of consequences will be seen in better perspective if we take as an example the use of torture. The Inquisition used torture to extract confessions from heretics, the Nazis tortured Frenchmen during the German occupation to combat the French resistance, Frenchmen tortured Algerians in the early 1960's to get information that would help them suppress a rebellion. There are reliable reports that Americans have used or condoned torture in Vietnam. All did so presumably to bring about consequences they regarded as desirable. Such practices, it so happens, are repugnant to all decent men. They are outlawed by national statute and international protocol. Few of us could bear to witness them even as fiction on the screen and fewer would contemplate perpetrating them. But if there were *only* the test of consequences, as utilitarians contend, would not examples like the foregoing inevitably multiply since such a test would free us to exact information by torture whenever our needs were sufficiently exigent? Suppose our purposes nobler than the objectives of Germans in occupied France, Frenchmen in Algeria, or Americans in Vietnam, and our outlook broader than Inquisitors punishing heretics. Suppose innocent lives could be saved in a situation in which the intended victim could escape torture if he gave the required information. One individual's pain—avoidable if he cooperates—against the lives of one or ten or a hundred others? Should we assent? The verdict of utilitarians, who would guide public policy by reference to the goal of maximizing the satisfaction of the largest number of people,[5] would have to be in the affirmative. From the point of view of utilitarianism, as Professor Rawls points out, "there is no reason in principle why the greater gains of some should not compensate for the lesser losses of others; or more importantly why the violation of the liberty of a few might not be made right by the greater good shared by many."[6] In his widely acclaimed *The Theory of Justice* he rightly contends that utilitarianism,

for all its plausibility, often offends our sense of justice and
flouts our common moral intuitions.

To say that torture is monstrously wrong, even in the circumstances cited above, is not, of course, to say that the consequences obtainable by torture are morally irrelevant, but *that
the values involved are too important to trust to judgments
reflecting our interests, however humane such interests might
seem to us to be; or, that the circumstances are such that we
are unable to weigh all the values involved.* Presumably the
Inquisitors and the Nazi, French and American torturers (unless
they were sadists, which they could have been) all judged that
they were saving lives or serving ideals for which lives were
worth risking.[7] After all, torture was not always as despised as
it is now. It would take a morbid interest in the forms of man's
inhumanity to man to endure descriptions of devices by means
of which physical torture has been used until relatively recently
to convict and punish the wicked.

Today such practices are banned, for example, by Amendment VIII of the American Constitution which forbids "cruel
and unusual punishments" and the Geneva Convention of 1949
which, among other things, outlaws all forms of "mental and
physical duress" in eliciting intelligence information from
prisoners of war. Such bans are in accord with the conscience
of all civilized persons. The bans are not qualified or conditional.
They do not provide exceptions permitting torture to save
innocent lives or, in the case of those who have committed
heinous crimes, to serve as a deterrent to others. They declare
categorically that torture is wrong. For most of mankind this
has become a moral *law*. And to say this is to say that the worth
of the practice is not subject to debate, at any rate to any kind
of debate *the terms of which would be dictated by our convenience or prevailing standards or interests.* There would remain then, only (although often formidably) the jurisprudential
problem of determining whether a given practice, for example,
capital punishment or solitary confinement or prolonged incar-

ceration in any one of our prisons as presently operated, is a breach of this law.

Attitudes toward capital punishment afford another interesting example. The U.S. Supreme Court has held in *Furman v. Georgia* (1972) that a capital sentence is unconstitutional in cases where the jury or the court has discretion to impose a lesser sentence. Earlier, in a more sweeping decision, the California Supreme Court had outlawed capital punishment under the "cruel and unusual punishment" clause of the state constitution, despite Governor Ronald Reagan's protest that "there's cruelty when you execute a chicken to have a Sunday afternoon dinner." Presumably Governor Reagan and the great majority of Californians who voted in 1972 to amend their state constitution so as to restore the stricken statutes and to declare that these statutes "shall not be deemed to be, or constitute infliction of cruel or unusual punishments within meaning of [the] California Constitution," believe that capital punishment is needed as a deterrent. However, it is significant that those who defend capital punishment as a deterrent do not advocate torture for the same reason, although in all consistency they should. It is also significant that hardly anyone, including most opponents of abolition of the death penalty, proposes the experimental revival of capital punishment for those found guilty of particularly offensive crimes such as the "pushing" of addictive drugs, *even if capital punishment were shown to reduce traffic in harmful drugs.* Why not? The average person will answer in such vague terms as "the sanctity of human life" and argue that capital punishment would not be right even though the life at stake was that of no more than a contemptible scoundrel. Implicit in such a statement, I contend, is the important recognition that there are some values which our necessarily limited experience may preclude us from knowing, values that may be too important to be left to the verdict of our prevailing biases. We therefore feel under obligation to resist the test of consequences even though the consequences (e.g., deterring traffic

in heroin) might come out as predicted. If there were not such
a sense of obligation we might promptly revert to the day when,
as in England as late as the nineteenth century, over two
hundred crimes, including horse and sheep stealing, were punishable by death.[8]

Reinforcing such attitudes is the perception shared by most
wise men that in human affairs consequences are notoriously
difficult to predict—as the architects of major revolutions who
find themselves facing the firing squads of their successors have
discovered. There are, in brief, good empirical reasons for not
staking everything on our ability to forecast the future, as
Danton, Robespierre, Trotsky and Zinoviev, and legions of ro-
mantic revolutionaries in our time failed to see. Such caveats
are, of course, favored by the conservative who urges that we
not forsake a known present for a precarious future. If, all too
often, this degenerates among the well-situated and smugly-
satisfied into a timidity about all social change—best summarized as a willingness to let ill enough alone—it nevertheless
contains a sound warning.

Thus far "law" has been used ambiguously. For Susan
Anthony, famous suffragette, the moral law, as she understood
it, decreed that women be granted suffrage, but in her time
that was neither in the mores or written into the law of the
land, and she was promptly arrested when she tried to vote in
the election of 1872. Neo-Thomists, who believe in natural law
think of it as a higher law rooted in human nature and com-
manding the assent of all rational men. For them man-made
law is actually nullified if in conflict with natural law.[9] Such
appeal to natural law or to a higher law is the usual recourse of
those who defend standards of morality inconsistent with the
prevailing mores and with statutory law. Established moral
principles, the mores, so-called, or the dictates of natural law
may or may not be embodied in formal statutes expressing the
will of a sovereign authority able to enlist coercion to enforce

it. I shall therefore reserve the term "rules of law" for the latter
and designate the former as "standards of morality,"[10] but not
venture at this point into an exploration of the complex and controversial relationship between the two.[11] Even if, with Jeremy
Bentham, John Austin, and legal positivists in general, we
warn against blurring the distinction between standards of
morality (what ought to be) and rules of law (what is), there
clearly is, as H. L. A. Hart urges, an intimate connection between law and morals. Rules of law always claim to reflect or
embody the right moral principles, and they resemble moral
principles in relying for conformity at least in part on reasons
other than a fear of punishment. (See below pp. 172–174.) To
be sure, fear of punishment is the factor that gets stressed in
simplistic approaches to the authority of law, as in Glaucon's
famous appeal to the fable about the shepherd Gyges who,
finding himself in possession of a ring that made him invisible
and hence safe from detection and punishment, seduced the
queen and killed the king.[12] But we are not all, or at any rate
not always, Lydian shepherds; the law may be obeyed from
respect for a particular moral principle embodied in it or, at a
more sophisticated level, as by Socrates in the *Crito*, out of respect
for law in general, i.e., for lawfulness per se. It is also clear, on
the other hand, that we may conform to moral principles or
codes, as distinguished from law, not from a sense of their
rightness, but from a fear of the consequences of nonconforming
quite analogous to fear of the sanctions formally invoked against
those who violate statutory law—fear, for example, of punishment in an afterlife meted out by a sovereign divinity if not an
earthly sovereign. And, of course, both kinds of motive may
ride in tandem. Except for the fire-and-brimstone morality of
certain religious sects, it is a safe generalization to say that
conformity to moral rules and codes tends to be secured by
other than physical and economic sanctions, i.e., by praise and
blame, approval and disapproval, admiration and ridicule, and

above all the internalization of these through early indoctrina-
tion as the "voice of conscience"; whereas enacted or statutory
law no doubt relies more on what Max Weber called a "coercive
apparatus." I am simply noting that the difference often gets
exaggerated and that *respect* for rules of law is at the least a
significant factor in their acceptance. As Philip Selznick observes,
"The key word in the discussion of law is *authority*, not coercion."[13] Implicit in such respect, it is important to emphasize, is
an "understanding" that the rules of law or standards of morality
accepted as binding in a given situation would apply similarly
to others in a like situation, but I shall have more to say about
this later. (See below, pp. 197–198.)

Whether conduct which conforms to a moral standard or
rule of law is inspired by fear of the consequences and is hence
the outcome of a prudential calculation, or by respect for the
law and hence by a sense of obligation can be determined only
by taking what H. L. A. Hart calls the "internal" point of view.[14]
For example, in the so-called counter-culture, "ripping off" the
Establishment is completely permissible, since for these neo-
Proudhonistes (Proudhon: "Property is theft") the private enterprise system is itself a way of institutionalizing theft. Having
adopted larceny as part of his new life style, an Abbie Hoffman
(author of *Steal This Book*) may avoid stealing from fear of
detection and punishment. His reticence is hardly comparable,
however, to the restraint of a law-abiding citizen who cherishes
the same merchandise but regards shoplifting as morally repre-
hensible, although the visible behavior pattern is the same.
Similarly, a member of the Mafia may avoid profitable traffic in
heroin for reasons quite different from those which deter the
average entrepreneur although, again, the immediate result is
the same. Surely moral theory must reckon with the difference,
even though the overt behavior patterns and consequences are
the same, between a commitment to honesty and careful driving
on the ground that dishonesty and jeopardizing the lives of

others is wrong, and a calculation expressed as "Honesty is the best policy" and "Drive carefully, the life you save may be your own." To an observer relying solely on external evidence there is no difference between the instances cited, and this would also have to be the position of the doctrinaire behavioralist in the social sciences. But the difference is decisive to many philosophers (utilitarians excepted) and is surely reflected not only in our moral appraisals but in judicial decisions.

Waiving consideration here of the difficult methodological and even metaphysical issues involved in making this distinction between internal and external points of view—they come to a focus in controversies over the so-called method of *Verstehen* ("understanding" is the best English equivalent), with which Professor Hart does not himself reckon[15]—it is my assumption that the distinction between the prudential and jurisprudential is important for an understanding of the data of ethics, even though, as will shartly be argued, it is only preliminary to a full understanding. A jurisprudential problem has to do with situations requiring the subsumption of particular cases under general rules which we acknowledge an obligation to obey. It need not be contended that judgments in such cases are exercises in pure reason and we shall not concern ourselves here with whether such decisions are or are not the outcome of wholly logical operations. Probably this was not the case when California's Republican attorney general ruled in 1971 that the law required newly enfranchised college students, most of whom have a bias in favor of the Democratic Party, to register at the residence of their parents and hence cope with the complications of an absentee ballot. More likely it was in the case of the state's Supreme Court, which unanimously reversed this ruling. In any event, the jurisprudential problem can be quite complex. As H. L. A. Hart points out, even in the case of carefully composed statutes, although judges may speak as if their decisions were "necessary consequences of predetermined rules whose meaning is fixed and clear," in most cases that are litigated "neither statutes nor precedents in which the rules are allegedly contained allow of only one result."[16]

However, at this point I must return to the phenomenon of obligation. The concept is notoriously elusive for those who are empirically oriented but, as suggested in the foregoing discussion, not inexplicable. When we acknowledge an obligation or act from a sense of obligation our conduct[17] is not nearly as mysterious as theists invoking supernatural agencies or intuitionists postulating special moral faculties would have us believe. They have acknowledged defeat in the quest for understanding, but we need not. In sum, when conduct in conformity with a law or standard is prompted by a sense of obligation it is more than mere habitual action *and more than blind acceptance.*[18] Implicit in such conduct, I have contended, is a reason perhaps only rarely articulated. It is suggested in the decision to subordinate one's interests or convenience to an obligation, for example, to keep a promise. This means that one refuses to judge the action required by the rule from the point of view dictated by his interests. And this in turn suggests a tacit recognition that there is a wisdom superior to one's own, which is to say, an acknowledgment of the limitations of one's own judgment and of the possibility of undiscerned values that transcend one's present power or competence to judge. "It is the function and service of any institution, in matters belonging to its province, to lead the individual beyond such limits of belief or conduct as his own reason may be able at the time to suggest or approve."[19]

This is the basis of that respect for laws and rules which eludes theories that reduce moral deliberation to a prudential calculation of interests or consequences. Such respect, it must be emphasized, is not another interest competing with other interests. It has, I have sought to show, its own dynamic. Kant's comment concerning his own reliance on this concept, although only a footnote in his magisterial *Fundamental Principles of the*

Metaphysic of Morals, is quite decisive. "It might be here objected," he wrote, "that I take refuge behind the word *respect* in an obscure feeling . . ." But:

Although respect is a feeling, it is not a feeling *received* through [outer] influence, but is *self-wrought* by a rational concept, and, therefore, is specifically distinct from all feelings of the former kind, which may be referred either to inclination or fear. What I recognize immediately as a law for me, I recognize with respect. This merely signifies the consciousness that my will is *subordinate* to a law, without the intervention of other influences on my sense.[20]

To be sure, rules are accepted as obligatory at least in part because they are believed, in Professor Hart's words, "to be necessary to the maintenance of social life or some highly prized feature of it."[21] The sense of obligation may assume, in other words, that the law reckons with consequences and that action in accord with it is right on that account. This is, in fact, the major reason for our finding "juris-*prudential*" more descriptive in this context than simply "jural." But the assumption that law takes account of consequences and must ultimately be vindicated by its consequences does not require that *we* know or that we be able at the moment of decision to *appraise* these consequences ourselves; indeed, *it assumes that we cannot appraise or do not trust ourselves to appraise them.*

This is the point generally missed by utilitarians, past and present. They have gone to great effort to show that obligatory action to be justified must have *some* good consequence. If it is said that in a moral situation one does not refer to consequences they mistakenly take this to be the same as saying that consequences are without import. This is not so, and failure to see it explains the notorious difficulties encountered by utilitarians in attempting to account for obligation.[22] The point is also missed by G. E. Moore when he urges that " 'right' does and can mean nothing but cause of a 'good result' . . . and . . . no action which is not justified by its results can be right . . ."[23] It does not follow that right is synonymous with *instrumental* good (means) as this term is conventionally used. The point missed by Moore is that, when we act from a sense of obligation and are acting "rightly," that is, in accord with the moral law, we are not calculating or appraising these good results ourselves; we are refusing to make the determination.

The point also escaped Hume when he wrote in *On the Passions* that "Humility is a dissatisfaction with ourselves, on account of some defect or infirmity."[24] If we strip away the symbolism, ignore the myths and rituals—the Sinaic legend, the priestly liturgies, the judicial wig and ermine—which reinforce this attitude and supplement the personal experiences that may have persuaded us of our limitations, we find the sense of obligation imbedded in a core of simple humility, the Socratic wisdom that knows that one does not know; that is what is asked of us when we are enjoined in the Old Testament to "walk humbly with thy God." This, provided we discount the complete self-abnegation demanded by such as Calvin, is the deeper import of the Christian emphasis on humility: "Blessed are the meek: for they shall inherit the earth," an insight bearing on the "transvaluation of values" to which Nietzsche was quite blind when he stormed that "Christianity is the revolt of all things that crawl on their bellies against everything that is lofty. . . ."[25]

A final point must be made. Because the sense of obligation as thus far described is first felt in connection with our relations to others it has often been limited to other-regarding conduct. This is an error. I may recognize a duty to myself (e.g., to avoid addictive drugs or even physically harmless but debilitating euphoriants), and my conduct may be characterized as morally right or wrong even though no one else is affected. Moreover, paradoxical though it may seem, such a sense of duty to oneself is not the same as what we conventionally understand by "self-interest"; we speak of self-respect as well as self-interest, and the same dynamics are involved as in other manifestations of obligation. The point will be clarified as we proceed. Here it need simply be noted that such a sense of obligation to oneself is a social derivative; we acquire or learn it (unlike self-interest) by virtue of first having acted from a sense of obligation in our relations with others. Once I regard others as persons and they regard me as a person it is almost assured that I shall come to regard myself as such in the sense described above.

Chapter Twelve

Good as Ethical

As yet no reference has been made to the great difference between respect for law at the level of *customary* morality, where the authority of the law is taken for granted, and respect for law at the level of *reflective* morality. The fundamental difference, as we shall later see in detail, is that in the case of customary morality the law is regarded as beyond challenge and hence is accorded priority over other promptings or incentives to action. At the level of reflective morality, probably first achieved by the philosophers of the Greek Enlightenment in the fifth century B.C. and some of the Hebrew prophets, law assumes a different role and "good" and "ought" take on the meaning that identifies them as distinctively ethical predicates.

I shall shortly consider this fourth use of good—good used as an ethical predicate—which it will be the task of the remainder of this volume to examine. Here it may be noted preliminarily that the very term "reflective morality," and the prospect that law may be viewed as subject to challenge, suggest (1) not merely

176

respect for law but an explicit awareness of the *role* of law in moral deliberation, (2) a *self*-awareness either negligible or absent at the level of customary morality, an awareness marked in part by the advent of *conscience as an arbiter of conduct,* so that what presents itself at the pre-reflective level as the "word of God" or some such *external* constraint is now internalized as one's own moral intuitions speaking as the "voice of conscience";[1] (3) an expansion of the sense of obligation to include obligation to oneself; (4) an awareness of oneself as a free agent able to direct the course of one's own development, i.e., as *self*-determined. All this is implicit in what might be called the sense of individuality. "I must live with myself," Arthur Miller said, in refusing to answer the House Un-American Activities Committee. (See above, pp. 150–151.) For him, as for all whose conduct is morally responsible, a sense of self-integrity or self-respect had priority not only over the threatened consequences[2] to him of such a refusal, but over the *law* which endowed a congressional committee with authority to require an answer.

Whatever the complex social changes connected with the emergence of such a sense of individuality at the level of reflective morality, it is clear that, at the least, it is associated with an awareness of the diversity of moral standards and rules of law and of their frequently changing and conflicting dictates, a sophistication about the sources of standards and laws, a discovery of their often spurious claim to impartiality and their sometime obsolescence and, above all, a recognition of the importance of other promptings and obligations.

We have now to see what such promptings and obligations might be. Are there, to recur to the question with which this phase of our discussion began (see p. 144), other circumstances in which we feel impelled or obliged to go contrary to our prevailing values or interests under conditions which cannot properly be described as the intrusion of another stronger interest? And, if so, will this require us, as suggested, to reckon with another kind of value predicate involving an *ethical,* as

distinguished from an aesthetic, prudential (economic), or jurisprudential (moral) use of the term good? We must now note
that:

(a) Individuals whom we regard as authorities may counsel us
    not to obey a law or custom or to go contrary to our pres-
    ent conception of our interest.
(b) Others appeal to us for help in circumstances that require
    action violating a rule of law or some accepted moral stan-
    dard or involving a sacrifice of what we are now enjoying.
(c) We may be so aroused by an injustice that to "right" it
    we jeopardize everything we have heretofore valued.
(d) Some deep feeling of loyalty or friendship or love may
    prompt us to defer acting on our desires, to ignore our
    convenience, and to question standards of value which we
    have heretofore taken for granted.
(e) Our natural impulses call upon us to challenge or reject
    the rigid restraints often imposed by habit, law, custom,
    and to recognize not merely the health hazards of excessive
    repression but the role of the impulses as a source of in-
    vigoration and renewal for life as a whole.[3]

In such instances we have a conflict of ends, not a conflict of
alternative means or of different ruling; or interpretations of the
law. What one *ought* to do now poses a wholly different *kind*
of problem in that, by contrast to situations in which we can
resort to prudential calculations and jurisprudential judgments,
*there is now no end or standard or law to which we can refer
for a solution,* since by definition our accepted ends or standards
or laws are in question. We may avoid such occasions by
promptly rejecting a proposed course of conduct just because it
is incompatible with our prevailing standards or with accepted
law. Some will say, as did the German underlings who sought to
extenuate their complicity in genocide, *"Ein Befehl ist ein Befehl,"* an order is an order; the law decrees obedience to one's

superiors. But if we *refuse* to reject a course at variance with the one we have been following, and acknowledge a rivalry, no appeal to an established or heretofore accepted law or to an inclusive end whether of "happiness" (Mill) or "self-realization" (Aristotle) or (in the phrase of a recent writer) to a "way of life"[4] will help. No doubt we want happiness whatever way we decide. And no doubt we want to realize ourselves. The trouble is that the ways of life or the kinds of happiness promised are *different* and *opposed* and each rival alternative promises that we shall find more fulfillment by acting on it.

Failure to realize this vitiates the teleological tradition which has occupied so much of the history of ethics from Plato to Mill. Teleological ethics refers us for the solution of such moral problems to the consequences of the alternatives and their contribution to an end which in Aristotle's words is "that for the sake of which everything else is done."[5] There should, of course, be a reference to the consequences by way of more fully defining the nature of the alternatives before us. But there can be no reference to the consequences for a *solution to the problem* as thus defined, since no standard is available for evaluating them. As noted in our earlier examination of Dewey's position, teleological ethics, with its stress on an inclusive end by reference to which moral problems can be settled, reduces all such problems to the prudential level.

Why *should* we suspend our prevailing standards and recognize the appeal of rival alternatives? Since few questions have been more neglected in the history of ethical theory, it may be well at this point to consider a typical ethical problem and thereafter, in more detail, some of the several kinds of promptings out of the conflict of which such problems emerge. We shall find, I hope, that the decisions made when we have such conflicts need not be arbitrary or subjective and that reasons can be given which will be *respected* by others with different values and hence be regarded as objective. We may find an answer that appears to have eluded subjectivists and intuitionists and some of their recent critics.

A celebrated historical example of a typical ethical problem will serve as well as any other. It has the advantage of enabling us to exercise a measure of license in our interpretation, not, indeed, of the facts of the case, which are well known, but of what may have transpired in the mind of one of the chief actors. It may fairly be claimed that there are good *prima facie* reasons for the inferences I draw, even though it is always hazardous to read other people's minds.

On October 15, 1894 Alfred Dreyfus, a captain in the French army, was arrested and accused by his superiors of transmitting military secrets to the German Embassy. Although he protested his innocence he was found guilty on the basis of an alleged resemblance between his handwriting and the handwriting on the incriminating document and sentenced to life imprisonment on remote Devil's Island. His outraged family, convinced of his innocence, was unable, in the absence of new evidence, to secure a review. Although no motives for treason could be found—Dreyfus had been an exemplary officer, he had no bad habits and possessed an independent income—there was a leak of the kind of information to which he had access (the leak awkwardly continued after his incarceration) and his colleagues were for the most part relieved that the traitor was not a typical French officer. Dreyfus was a Jew.

As readers of history know, Captain Dreyfus was eventually found innocent, but it took twelve long years to exonerate him. Attempts to vindicate Drefus were denounced as a Jewish conspiracy to discredit the Army or a Jewish–German plot to weaken France. A wave of anti-Semitism swept over the French people. Differences over the question of Dreyfus's guilt escalated into a broad ideological struggle in which clericalism, a militaristic and authoritarian nationalism, and monarchism were aligned against humanism, rationalism, and republicanism. Before the truth finally prevailed France was shaken to its foundations. War ministers resigned. Frenchmen rioted. Governments fell. The General Staff threatened to resign *en bloc*. It seemed for a while as though truth had ceased to matter among men who professed to venerate it. The nation which by tradition is said to worship reason succumbed to a prolonged fit of irrationality verging on hysteria.

A few courageous men such as Clemenceau, Zola, and Scheurer-Kestner rallied to the Dreyfus cause, but in this strange historical drama it was an Army officer who first broke the case. Lieutenant Colonel Georges Picquart, newly installed as head of the Second Bureau, the military agency responsible for counterintelligence, came into possession of information which definitely established the guilt of another officer and exonerated Dreyfus. He reported to his superiors and was promptly advised to ignore what he had found. "The Dreyfus case is closed," he was told.

By any normal expectation Picquart should have acquiesced; officers with his kind of training obey superiors—they are not usually crusaders. (He may well have shared the general dislike among French officers for the handful of arriviste Jews in their midst. He did have a distaste for Dreyfus.) But Picquart refused. He was subsequently shipped off to a remote post, subjected to virulent character assassination, and finally imprisoned. Bitterly denounced by his superiors and fellow officers as a traitor to the Army which to him had been "mother, father, wife, and children," his response was, "I will not carry this secret with me to my grave."[6]

Except for his ability and this one deviation, Picquart was apparently a typical Army officer, indoctrinated in its ways, devoted to its ideals, sharing many of its prejudices. Nothing—at any rate nothing until the Dreyfus Affair came along—was so important to him as a successful military career. He is said to have been on his way to becoming the youngest general in the French army. Good officer that he was, he did not at first release the information, hoping that his military superiors would take the initiative. Instead, despite the indications that Dreyfus was innocent, stubborn officers at the highest echelon, having persuaded themselves of his guilt and anxious to avoid embarrassment to the Army, tampered with the documents to strengthen their case and dispel doubts.

As the Army became increasingly compromised those who pressed the Dreyfus cause posed a threat to its very integrity. Which is more important, Picquart was asked, the fate of one man—and a Jew at that—or the reputation of the Army, that same army which, others added, was the shield of the Republic and the one hope of avenging France's humiliating defeat in the Franco–Prussian war? Had Picquart no sense of loyalty, if not to the Army, at least to his country? Such pressures, combined with the threat to his career and eventually to his personal freedom and safety, must have been almost overwhelming. Opposed to lifelong loyalties and commitments, a brilliant career, the esteem of his fellow officers, was a belief in justice and a sense of obligation to speak the truth. Perhaps also a sense of moral indignation and a feeling of compassion for an innocent man condemned for life to Devil's Island and for his family.

Picquart's decision may have been instantaneous and unwavering. His may have been a strictly jurisprudential problem, as such problems have been defined here. But, given the kind of forces playing on him, we may fairly assume that, unlike Zola or Anatole France, a man of the colonel's background did not arrive at his decision easily. It would require the talents of a novelist or playwright to probe the mind of Picquart and expose the diverse values that must have been weighed in his deliberations, the hesitations and misgivings, the soul-searching, and the basis on which he arrived at a decision.[7] We may fairly surmise, however, that he felt called upon to abandon or reconsider precious values which he had always taken for granted, to view them in a new light, perhaps to find new *reasons* for them. We may infer that moral codes, standards, and judgments of value he had always taken for granted no longer seemed adequate in the new situation. No doubt such standards had always included honesty and the belief that an innocent man should not be punished, the principles by which he ultimately guided his conduct. But they had never been tested in a situation where they were in opposition to such cherished values—his career and an opportunity to serve his country, the prestige and honor of the Army, and, as the case assumed critical proportions, the internal peace and tranquility of France itself. Picquart's feelings of loyalty and commitment to the Army were formed before its complicity in a cruel miscarriage of justice. The value he found in a military career did not involve his envisaging a time when he would be required to suppress the truth. Here, surely, was a situation in which one could not act *merely* from respect for a given moral law; the law was in conflict with other laws. Nor could one appeal to inclusive ends such as happiness or self-realization; clearly one had the problem because one's previous or prevailing views of happiness or self-realization were not adequate to the situation. The trouble was that different *kinds* of happiness, different ways of realizing oneself were opposed and in conflict.

How are problems of this kind solved? How do we justify our choices in situations such as this? As Nowell-Smith quite correctly notes, when "someone says . . . 'I ought to do *x*' he lays himself open to a request for reasons and he must be prepared with an answer."[8] What *reasons* can be found in an ethical problem for taking one course rather than another, given (as I am contending) the unavailability of those empirical reasons or tests of consistency which are used respectively in prudential and jurisprudential problems? Before attempting to answer these questions, there are prior questions that must be raised to which some attention has already been given: Why are we in certain instances aroused by injustice; why do we on critical occasions respond to an appeal to our sympathy, or the counsel of an authority, or the promptings of loyalty and love, or the sense of duty or of obligation to a higher law, though we are thereby required to sacrifice or risk the sacrifice of everything we hold dear? Much as moral subjectivists and skeptics may dismiss or ignore such occasions or talk them away, Colonel Picquart's moral courage, although possibly too rare, is hardly unique, as we are reminded by a Russian poet (Sinyavsky) sentenced to five years of hard labor for protesting suppression of the arts in the USSR, or by Vesalius, founder of the modern science of anatomy, risking the wrath of the Inquisition to steal corpses for his anatomical studies, or a thrice-decorated American colonel, graduate of West Point and veteran of the heaviest fighting of the Vietnam war, applying for dismissal from the army as a conscientious objector. Everyone will have his favorite examples. How are we to account for them, especially since, as I contend, the experience involved cannot be described, without ignoring relevant and decisive differences, as the displacement of a weaker interest by a stronger one? The answer must be that we recognize such promptings as providing standpoints enabling us to escape the isolation and confinement of our given interests or patterns of interest so as to regard them from a different point of view. We do not indeed abandon our prevailing preferences. We *suspend* them with a view to testing them against alternatives not envisaged when we first adopted them. We declare that they will not be permitted to determine conduct until other possibilities have been adequately probed.

However, the kind of suspension of one's prevailing interests exemplified in the case of Colonel Picquart or Arthur Miller would hardly be considered if one did not have a conception of the self as transcending the *totality* of one's *prevailing* interests or standards of value. In the earlier discussion of prudential problems reference was made to the conception of a self transcending any *particular* interest or preference and representing the totality of our interests. Let us call this one the *enjoyed* self, identified as it is with our prevailing preferences. We have now to see that there is also what for lack of a better term may be called a *transcendent* self able to disassociate itself from the enjoyed self because, having first identified itself with others (or other standpoints), it is able to see the enjoyed self from another point of view. As already suggested, such points of view may be brought to attention and invite consideration in quite different ways: through an arousal of our sense of injustice; through direct appeals to us for sympathy, leading us to identify ourselves with the needs of the appellant; through personal ties of love and friendship; through general rules of law and standards of morality (as discussed above); through the counsel of an authority. All ethical judgments in the distinctive sense of that term are mediated by such a transcendent self—it could as well, perhaps, be called the ethical self—just as all prudential judgments are mediated by the enjoyed self. Since the transcendent self is identified with the interests of others, it is quite in accord with the interpretation of obligation thus far made to speak of it as a self to which we can have a sense of obligation quite distinguishable from self-interest (without in any way straining the meaning of obligation) and make sense of the common reference to self "respect," as a prudential (utilitarian) ethic cannot.

The transcendent self is not a Cartesian "I"—a thing—any more than is the enjoyed self. It is not suggested that it is an entity or a substance. It is not Freud's repressive superego, although Freud's comment in *The New Introductory Lectures* that the ego "can take itself as an object, . . . observe itself, criticize itself, and do Heaven knows what besides with itself"[9] is surely suggestive. Nor is there any mystery about it: it has its natural history emerging, although only to be sure under appropriate social conditions (see below, pp. 242–243), from the most universal and elementary experience. We acquire new interests and discover new values in the course of pursuing old ones, since such pursuit, involving us as it does in a quest for means, inevitably expands experience. The loss of one's fortune, the defeat of one's country in a disastrous war, serious illness or physical disability, a thousand different happenings may involve us in experiences generating new interests and new preferences. Failure at one enterprise may drive us into another. We modify our goals as we learn their relationship to each other. It hardly requires great acumen to infer from such basic experiences that there are all kinds of ends or purposes of which we are at any given time wholly unaware that might, if we came to know them, engage us and even be found preferable to our prevailing ends and purposes. The transcendent self emerges when this awareness becomes explicit, and *new preferences are an outcome not merely of chance or accident but of a deliberate and purposeful reexamination of one's prevailing values.* The Socratic quest for self-knowledge can be advanced only in this way, as his dictum that "an unexamined life is not worth living"[10] reminds us.

The transcendent self manifests itself, in other words, in a kind of awareness kindled by moral crises, an awareness that the enjoyed self could be other than it is; it marks recognition of the possibility of our becoming something different from what we are[11] and it expresses itself operationally by identifying itself with other standpoints so that a comparison can take place. The enjoyed self is other-directed; the transcendent self as thus defined is inner-directed or, to use Kant's term, *autonomous.* Since *ex hypothesi* the enjoyed self is identified with our prevailing preferences, we may say that the process of evaluation is a kind of "conversation"[12] between the two selves (or the two roles of the same self) in the course of which the right and the good are pitted against each other and finally come to terms. The appeal of the transcendent self is and must initially be to right, of the enjoyed self to good. In one of his most suggestive comments John Dewey wrote:

The essence of the claim which Right puts forth is that even if the thing exacted does not appeal as his good to the one to whom it is addressed, he *should* voluntarily take it to be a good; that, in short, it should *become* his good, even if he does not so judge it at the time. This element of the "should" or "ought" is what differentiates the idea of Right from that of Good.

But, Dewey goes on, "it does not cut the idea wholly loose from that of Good, for what 'should be' is that an individual should *find* the required conduct good."[13] This is a typically ethical as distinguished from a prudential, jurisprudential, and aesthetic predication of good. "Good" is that which has been found good, but *only* as the outcome of testing it against alternatives in an ethical dilemma. As some have suggested, it would be more apt to use "better than" since such a locution more clearly suggests reference to the situation that gives it meaning. "Good" as thus used is, in the sense defined by Paul Taylor, a "ranking" rather than a "grading" word, indicating as it does that an act or course of conduct is found better than or worse than the alternative(s) with which it has been compared rather than good or bad by reference to some ideal or absolute standard.[14]

At the outset of this chapter it was noted that the emergence of reflective morality (ethicality) from customary or conventional morality is associated (among other things) with the advent of conscience as an *arbiter* of conduct. I place the stress where it is to emphasize that conscience at this level is not the servile executor of authoritarian moral decree, the stern and undiscriminating monitor of our adherence to established morality; on the contrary, it voices in the morally sensitive (conscientious) individual his refusal to be bound by standards and principles in new situations for which they were not envisaged. As such (as Freud failed to see) conscience is not the agent of rigid conformity, but an expression of the will to be free. It takes us *beyond right and wrong*. It is manifest not in the guilt sense that haunts and punishes us for our transgressions, but in the sense of self-possession we feel when we are in charge of our own lives.

Hopefully, it will not labor the example to urge that Picquart himself had to *recognize* a problem in the new circumstances, as his fellow officers did not. He had to be a man of good conscience, to have a sense of *responsibility*, that is to say, a certain awareness of himself as an active agent capable of altering the course of events and making his *own* decisions, of knowing, as we say, that it was "up to him." In Kant's suggestive phrase, the will at such junctures must become the "author of its own principles."[15] Such cases call for a conception of a larger self than the self identified with this or that standard of conduct, a feeling that such a self might be diminished by insensitiveness to the possibilities latent in a new situation. Picquart had to be willing to project himself into points of view other than that dictated by his former conception of his interests, into Dreyfus's point of view, the point of view dictated by the time-honored principle that innocent persons should not be punished. "Willing" is used here advisedly; it suggests an act of will as well as a disposition or state of mind. It is in this way that we exercise free will in the only meaningful sense of that term—which cannot imply in the empirical point of view from which this is written that such conduct is not causally conditioned, only that oneself as thus conceived may be or become one of the conditions of conduct.

A similar emphasis will be found in the works of the Existentialists and of existential psychiatry, in which a person is viewed as the sum of his choices, or what Sartre calls his "projections." However, although we may be grateful to the Existentialists for recognizing this power of man to choose his own course of action and in effect to be the "novelist" of his own character, and for giving this recognition practical and dramatic impact, it should be noted that the theoretical grasp of such an interpretation of freedom is no Existentialist monopoly and antedated the Existentialist vogue of the 1940's and 1950's.[16] In any case, we may agree that not all men are subject to history, especially many of those who have played a large part in making it.

A final point. Zola's is the role in the Dreyfus affair which has attracted most attention. His "J'accuse" finally made the position of the anti-Dreyfusards untenable; he had to seek refuge in England to escape the consequences. There is no intent here to detract from the noble part he played, and yet there is an important sense in which, as the drama is unfolded to us, we admire Picquart more. Zola's actions were *in character:* we expect this of Zola. *He was being himself.* His great protest was consistent with deeply rooted beliefs, a lifetime orientation. Not so, Picquart. We sense that he had to transform himself—to make himself something other than what he was. His was, one may say, an exercise of ethical judgment in the distinctive sense.

Chapter Thirteen

The Role of Authority

The basic question raised earlier (p. 183) now requires an answer: how are ethical problems as thus described to be solved? If there is no end to which we can refer, if there is no moral "faculty" which informs us, if there is no quality of rightness inhering in action or of good inhering in objects intuitively manifest to us or self-evident to reason, if there is no supreme authority for one course of conduct rather than another—and this, empirically oriented as I am, has been my assumption— are we left with nothing but arbitrary choices, that is to say, decisions for which no reasons can be given? To answer affirmatively would be to assert that the problems we have identified as distinctively ethical are not problems after all; they are only, as the logical positivists were fond of saying, pseudo-problems, since it is of the nature of an ethical problem that we seek reasons for acting in one way rather than another. There is a more adequate answer. It will be found if we look more carefully at the promptings that move us in a typically ethical situation and the manner in which we act on them.

Earliest in the development of the individual and simplest as a model of how promptings other than our prevailing preferences function in moral deliberation, are those which fall under the rubric of authority. Authority may manifest itself in the impersonal dictates of law, the internalization of these in conscience, the externalization of conscience in God, and in the example and counsel of persons whom we respect and admire. Concern at this point is with the last of these.

Let us assume that one whom I respect and admire—and we do admire and respect a great many persons with whom we are not in agreement—suggests that I act in a way which would go counter to my prevailing preferences. Any consideration of the merit of his proposal to the extent that this involved a specific judgment of preference would *ex hypothesi* be unfavorable. Do we ever entertain suggestions of this kind—do we ever, that is, suspend our value judgments and, refusing to be governed by them, act upon such a prompting? Action need not be overt, of course; all that is required is that we project ourselves into the proposed point of view and enact in imagination—Dewey called it "dramatic rehearsal"—the indicated course of conduct.

A denial of the possibility of such action makes it difficult to understand how moral suasion takes place at all. To be sure, we often persuade others to change their views by calling their attention to facts of which they were unaware. One might change another's attitude toward capital punishment, for example, by pointing out that the repeal of capital punishment has or has not been followed by an increase of the crimes punishable by death; or someone's views concerning legalizing abortion by pointing out the number of pregnant women whose lives have been lost in consequence of their resorting to medically unqualified abortionists; or views on public housing by showing that it is cheaper for government to subsidize adequate

housing for low income groups than to pay for the costs of
crime, fire, and sickness caused by slums. One may also raise
questions of consistency, possibly modifying attitudes by pointing out the vast discrepancies between precept and practice in
sex conduct, for example, or in the Federal government's requiring that packages of cigarettes carry a health hazard warning while it subsidizes tobacco crops. In all such cases, persuasion is effected and agreement secured within the framework of
a common set of values. Often, however, the facts do not prevail and considerations of consistency become hopelessly obscured. When this happens one may conclude that the conflict
lies deeper and involves values themselves. It is here, in disputes
over values, that our differences are crucial. Can such differences
be reconciled?

The question concerns the possibility of moral suasion in the
true sense. If we did not at times act on the suggestions of an
authority simply because he was an authority and not because
of our judgment concerning the merit of his proposal, such
moral suasion would not take place. In such cases we look
forward, to be sure, to possible enjoyments or satisfactions, but
they are of a kind the nature or quality of which we are not on
the basis of our present standard of judgment able to envisage
or anticipate. We do believe, in other words, that when placed
in the position to which the action recommended by an authority would lead, we may be admitted to experiences of satisfaction, appreciation, or well-being of which we could not partake
without suspending the value judgments which involve disapproval of such action. Otherwise, there would be no warrant
at all for our action. To say that the ethical situation involves
the transcendence of interest implies only the interests engaging
the agent at the time of his finding himself in this situation.
Thus, the essence of reliance upon authority in an ethical
situation consists of a willingness to accept the dictates or suggestions of authority not directly because of *what* is proposed,

but because of a belief in the integrity and insight of the authority himself. If we are responsive to his suggestions, it is not
the merit of the proposal which we consider but the merit of the
authority.

In some quarters, to be sure, reliance on authority has for
many reasons become suspect. Authority speaks first and most
commonly in the role of parent. Given the long period of childhood dependency parental authority starts out with a built-in
bias in its favor. But that role has in recent times undergone a
notable weakening reflected in what we are now accustomed
to call the "generation gap." Filial rebellion is, of course, nothing
new, but it has assumed new proportions in our day. This may
be, as indicated earlier (see above, p. 116), because this generation of parents has burdens of choice and decision which cannot be eased by appeal to the established principles on which
earlier generations relied. Bereft of the guidelines on which
their parents relied, parents today are bewildered and baffled
and understandably inadequate in situations that defy the
powers of professional counselors, not to mention untutored
fathers and mothers. The result is not necessarily or even usually
rebellion. As Kenneth Keniston has written, "The real token
of generational discontinuity is . . . a vision of parents and those
of their generation as irrelevant, as merely old-fashioned or as
'square'."[1] He goes on.

Increasing numbers of young Americans find themselves so distant
from their parents that they can neither evaluate nor rebel against
them. Instead, they 'understand' them. . . . Many young Americans
feel toward their parents a sympathy, a compassion, and a pity that
most of us can feel only toward that from which we feel ultimately
detached; and with this sympathy goes a strong sense—an implicit
realization—on the part of both parents and children that the two
generations face such different life situations that the way parents
conducted their lives may be neither good nor bad for their children,
but simply irrelevant.[2]

It is not entirely, one may add, that the rules and times have changed. That has happened before during migrations, wars, and assorted disasters, although not so rapidly. The problem is that rules of *any* kind are now often unavailable and the *ad hoc* decisions of parents in complex situations fail to fill the gap, leaving fathers and mothers discredited and often rejected. The consequences can be disastrous:

from his parents a child has traditionally learned the meaning of adulthood, of maleness and femaleness, of work, play, and social membership. By identifying with his parents, by internalizing their ways of doing things, by imitating their behavior, he has known how to become an adult. . . . With no exemplars, no objects of identification, and an obdurate refusal to accept them, the result is often that perplexity, self-fragmentation and confusion we see in many alienated young men.[3]

Other authority than the parental is, of course, available: psychoanalysts for the well-to-do, teachers, in declining number—clergymen, and, among older people, more or less successful members of one's own peer group. All too often, however, the the consequence among the young has been a rejection of all authority,[4] rationalized by an identification of reliance on authority with authoritarianism. But the difference is crucial and at this point must be underscored.

In the authoritarian situation recourse to authority is generally not a matter of choice or discretion, although criticism may be eschewed voluntarily, even to the point of ignoring contradictions or assuming that there is some inscrutable explanation for them, by the communicants of a hierarchical church or the faithful in a totalitarian society. In any event, submission is unquestioning. Disobedience is punished. The authority is infallible and hence resists tests of his adequacy; his verdict is final. Moreover, the authority insists on a monopoly of the qualities on which he bases his claim to superior wisdom. Accordingly his status is not to be attained by others. The relationship between the authoritarian and his clients is based on preserving a fundamental inequality and efforts to close the gap are forbidden. Authoritarianism thwarts ethical deliberation; reliance on authority, on the other hand, is a factor in making it possible.[5]

Recourse to authority in ethical situations is voluntary, tentative, and experimental. The authority is not an oracle, does not claim infallibility and is not regarded as infallible; on the contrary, authority is subject to tests concerning his trustworthiness. And, these failed, we may well ask of him what God asked of Job: "Who is this that darkeneth counsel by words without knowledge?" It is, indeed, to such tests that I would at last direct attention because they provide the *reasons* for moving in one direction rather than another. Given what has been said, it must follow that they are *formal* tests. To call them formal is to say that they can be applied *without reference to the content of the proposal*. They are thus tests—tests of *reliability*—to which all parties can agree regardless of their differences over standards or values. They are commonplace enough: Does the authority have an extended and varied experience? Is he informed? Has he consistently exhibited concern for and interest in others? Does he generally give careless or thoughtful advice? Does he take advice from others? Has he been rigid or flexible in the way he has lived his own life? (Mark Twain once said: "I hate to take advice from some people when I see how bad *they* need it.") Is he patronizing and condescending? Is he vain? Is he candid and honest? Is he consistent in the kind of advice he gives? Other similar tests will occur to the reader. Admittedly it is not always possible to apply such tests without bias, but this is only to say that honesty to oneself is difficult of achievement. We are often guilty of bad faith. The important point is that *the reasons cited*

*for heeding an authority do not involve prejudgment of the
values at issue and hence do not arrest moral growth but encourage it.*

The dictates of law also fall under the rubric of authority,
as noted earlier (p. 191). Since the differing roles of law at
the jurisprudential and ethical levels have already been noted,
I may limit myself here to the tests to which in the ethical context law may be submitted. As Phillip Selznick observes, "The
obligation to obey the law should be closely tied to the defensi-
bility of the rules themselves and of the official decisions that
enforce them."[6] If law is not the "gunman situation writ large,"[7]
if, contrary to Austin and the positivists, law is not merely what
the sovereign commands and enforces, but derives much of its
efficacy from its success in enlisting our assent concerning its
rightness, it becomes relevant to specify the conditions under
which assent should be given or withheld. Here, as in the case of
reliance on personal authority, criticism and defense of the
law's dictates need not be a prejudging from one's own prevailing point of view of the consequences of adherence. *Formal*
tests are available, formal, again, in the sense that they do not
require us to pass on the indicated course of conduct and will
be agreed upon both by those who approve and disapprove of
that course.

In the first place, the law must be true to itself. There is
what Professor Lon L. Fuller calls—perhaps not too felicitously
—the "internal morality of the law."[8] That is to say, the law is
not such simply because it is the edict of a sovereign (whether
people or *roi de soleil*) capable of enforcing it. If for no reason
other than the caprice of the sovereign it applies sometimes on
Mondays, Wednesdays, and Fridays and sometimes on Tuesdays,
Thursdays, and Saturdays (and never on Sundays); or if, again,
at the whim of the sovereign, it applies to citizens *A, B, C,* and
not citizens *X, Y, Z,* it is not law—at any rate it is not, by common consent, a law that commands our *respect* even though it

may command, i.e., coerce us. The law must at least provide for like treatment of like cases. If the sovereign is able to say "The law is what I say it is," this is no law at all.

Again, the law may be ambiguous and, as such, a mere disguise for the arbitrary will of the sovereign. In the United States the conspiracy law, loosely applied and almost routinely used against political militants (e.g., the Harrisburg Seven, the Chicago Seven, and labor organizers in the early days of the trade union movement), is so ambiguous that it prompted Francis B. Sayre, one-time director of the Harvard Institute of Criminal Law, to warn in 1922 of the "transcendent importance that judges and legal scholars . . . reach some common and definite understanding of the true nature and precise limits of the elusive law of criminal conspiracy," and Judge Learned Hand to call conspiracy laws a "prosecutor's darling." In the USSR, Article 70 of the Russian Republic's criminal code, under which writer Vladimir Bukovsky was sentenced to twelve years imprisonment and Soviet historian Pyotr Yakir is now being prosecuted (July 1972), is at least as ambiguous; it proscribes "defaming the Soviet political and social system."

In sum, the minimal claim that law makes is that it provides for order and regularity in human affairs. The Duke of Wellington saw the point when, after defining military law as the "will of the general who commands the army," he added, "in fact . . . no law at all." I do not yet speak of good or bad order—the order may be that of a jail—I do not even claim that bad order is better than anarchy or no order at all; only that law without order is a contradiction in terms. What has been said implies the exclusion of retroactive law and bills of attainder.[9] In brief, regardless of our view of the *content* of a law, we can all agree that law *as such* must conform to such basic requirements. A system of laws which *arbitrarily* excludes members of society from sharing in the amenities of civil life, as the Jews were excluded under Hitler or blacks have been excluded in the deep South, fails to satisfy such requirements. It is the arbitrariness of such exclusion that is crucial. There must be some point or meaning to the exclusion—if only that natural harmony of interests which rationalized the brutal exploitation of workers during the raw youth of industrial capitalism. To be sure the point may be lost on the victims, as it must have been on the women who heard the U.S. Supreme Court declare in 1872 that "the natural and proper timidity and delicacy which belongs to the female sex unfits it for many of the occupations of civil life." The court was sustaining their exclusion from the practice of law.

Other formal tests are relevant, even if less likely to evoke a consensus and, in most cases, more susceptible of bias in their application. Does the law ignore or frustrate virtually universal needs and aspirations? Is it out of accord with long established social practice? Does it rest on a broad or narrow basis of consent? Was the law an outcome of prolonged consideration or a mere reflection of what Burke called "the vulgar practice of the hour"? Has the law survived reasoned criticism or has it been held immune to reexamination? Does the law as interpreted and enforced serve the purpose for which it was intended or some irrelevant purpose, as in the case of the due process clause of the Fourteenth Amendment which, adopted to protect the rights of blacks, became a device by means of which for a long time private corporations achieved immunity from regulation? Does the law attempt to regulate those activities of individuals which have negligible social consequences, that is, do not affect anyone except themselves (e.g., miscegenation, the sex relations of consenting adults) and therefore call less exigently—not to mention less properly—for public regulation?

Finally (at least as far as this enumeration is concerned), we may ask whether the law does indeed serve all, and thereby justice, or is the servant of special interests. The test can be applied beyond such manifestly biased laws as those which imposed a property qualification on the exercise of suffrage[10] or excluded women from voting. For example, a law imposing conscription for military service during time of war may present draftees with a variety of now all too familiar problems. One may, of course, comply readily or reluctantly, resolving such problems as there are at the prudential or jurisprudential levels. On the other hand, one may consider resisting the law either on the basis of principle (if one objects to this war or all war), or because it unfairly curtails one's earnings (e.g., if one's necessarily short career as a successful professional athlete is interrupted). The law on its side counters with appeal to one's loyalty to country and sense of duty, as well as with threats of punishing draft-resisters. The point to be stressed here is that, independently of one's judgment concerning the value or disvalue of compulsory military service, without reference, that is, to the *content* of the law, it may be subjected to purely *formal* tests. In particular: does the law favor one class to the detriment of another; is the machinery for administering the law such as to carry out its stated purposes; does the need that resulted in conscription still prevail? For example, during the Civil War, under the North's Draft Act of 1863 a draftee could be exempted if he furnished a substitute or paid $300.[11] In the South exemptions (one overseer for each plantation with fifteen or more slaves, etc.) provoked the charge that it was "a rich man's war and a poor man's fight." If "universal" military service now appears to exclude such brazen economic favoritism, it is often argued that the draft law is still biased against ethnic minorities and those who are too poor to pay for the services of a skilled draft counsel.

The questions raised above may be directed at our tax laws. The law purports to tax individuals according to their income and yet in 1970 after passage in 1969 of the largest tax reform act in our history, there were still 3,314 persons with incomes above $30,000 who paid no tax, including 394 with incomes over $100,000. The National Committee for an Effective Congress refers to this and to increasing reliance on regressive taxation (the social security tax, which is the most regressive of all federal taxes, has tripled in the last 10 years) as "a moral issue", which, of course, it is. One might avail himself happily of all the loopholes and enjoy all the tax savings thereby made possible, one might even oppose income taxes as such and still agree that the present income tax law (1972) fails to satisfy the formal criteria cited above: clearly it does not accomplish its avowed purpose and it manifestly favors one class over another. When,

> The law locks up the man and woman
> Who steal the goose from off the common,
> And lets the greater felon loose
> Who steals the common from the goose,

we hardly need the sardonic humor of that old quatrain to remind us that such a law has lost its moral claim on us. We need not agree with Thrasymachus that "in every case the laws are made by the ruling party in its own interest . . . so . . . that what is 'right' is the same everywhere: the interest of the stronger party,"[12] nor with the wholesale charge of Marx and Engels in the *Communist Manifesto* that "your law (*Recht*) is but the will of your class exalted into statutes (*Gesetz*),"[13] to see that much law *is* dictated by the rich and powerful or heavily biased in their favor and, to that extent, without claim to our respect.[14]

Surely it may be asked of the laws protecting private property: does the system of property relations, and derivatively the laws which preserve it, proportion reward to merit or otherwise distribute benefits by generally acknowledged standards of fairness,[15] a test which the laws protecting the French aristocracy, for example, failed glaringly to pass in 1789; does it frustrate or further purposes to which all parties subscribe, such as occupational freedom of choice and consumer freedom; does it promote the fullest realization of productive potentialities with minimum harm to the environment, minimum loss of irreplacable resources, and optimum provision for leisure? No doubt in making all such determinations subjective interest will parade as objective judgment, but not inevitably and not without inviting exposure.

In the *Crito* Socrates personifies the laws of Athens which his friends, aiming to save his life, beg him to disobey, and enters into a celebrated dialogue with them.[16] Following that precedent the laws might engage us in a somewhat different kind of colloquy:

"We do not command because of our power alone," the laws say, "but because of our rightness; it is not mere submission we seek, but respect."

To which those to whom the laws apply (henceforth call them the "governed") respond, "You are wise not to rely on coercion—at any rate, exclusively—because the balance of forces shifts. Force will be met with force. Your genius is that you give us something better than the law of the jungle.

"Agreed," say the laws with appropriate pride.

"But if it is *respect* you want and not mere acquiescence in the use of brute force," say the governed, "that is to say, if you want our voluntary submission to your decrees without reference to our interests, or our judgment of our interests, you must show us that *you* are not the servant of *their* interests. Do you acknowledge such a responsibility?"

"That seems like simple reciprocity," say the laws, uneasily pretending not to be sure about who "they" are to whom "their" refers. "We have no choice now that our divine origin carries so little weight in this secular world."

"Very well, will you agree that you are unable to make such a showing of impartiality unless, when goods that we all want are distributed unevenly, you can give reasons for such disparity, *reasons that commend themselves to the disadvantaged* as well as the advantaged?"

"What might such reasons be?" ask the laws.

"Let us see what such reasons would not be," respond the governed warily. "Two of your arguments in favor of the prevailing system of property relationships are specious moral arguments, one of which only the most gullible would buy."

"What argument is that?" ask the laws.

"That property is a 'natural' right and that one may not be deprived of it, regardless of what kind of property it is and how one came by it."

"Granted," say the laws. "The appeal to natural law is too transparent. We've given it up."

"The second so-called moral argument is much more plausible, although it's only a sneaky version of the first one."

"What's that?" ask the laws.

"It's the argument that everyone has a right to the fruit of his effort and if he is talented and energetic enough to produce a great deal of wealth, he has a right to keep it."

"Surely that's generally conceded," say the laws. "If you had read John Locke's *Treatise of Civil Government* you would know that property is 'whatever he [man] hath mixed his labor with,' or Adam Smith who found that 'The property which every man has in his own labor . . . is the original foundation of all property,' or Jeremy Bentham from whom we learned that 'It is this right that has overcome the natural aversion to labor.' "

"But all that doesn't make it right. The implication of your argument is that someone with great talent *deserves* what he makes, and that isn't at all self-evident, any more than it's self-evident that someone who has inherited wealth has a natural right to keep it. In both cases you present us with a mere assumption. You haven't given any reasons, at any rate of the kind that would be found persuasive by anyone except the beneficiary. Having abandoned the appeal to natural law, you no longer defend inherited wealth that way. Why invoke it in the case of wealth produced by the talented? After all, isn't talent inherited? Doesn't an athlete inherit his physique, a singer her voice, John S. Mill—child prodigy that he was—his intelligence? We know that athletes, singers and the like train endlessly and that genius has been described as a capacity for taking infinite pains, but isn't it also a matter of luck—the good fortune to have the right parents, or to have been born at the right time and place? Why should that be rewarded? And, even if it weren't luck, even if by virtue of diligence and other excellent traits of character one made the best use of his inherited or natural gifts, why *ought* that to be rewarded?"

"Because," say the laws, "there's a functional relationship between talent and wealth; and wealth (whether in the form of an athletic performance, a concert, a book, or a steel mill) wouldn't have been created if the talent that went into making it had not been rewarded. That was the point Bentham was making."

"Hold on," say some of the governed, at any rate those of them who are moderately sophisticated. "That's no longer an 'ought' or moral argument. That is a psychological generalization involving questions of fact about human nature, questions about what is and is not needed to provide an incentive to effort. And that varies with different cultures; it is not, as you assume, a constant. No doubt the inhuman conditions under which work was carried on during Bentham's time called for a good deal of incentive. To settle such questions we should call in economists and social psychologists. However, since you have chosen to invade their province, we as laymen may be pardoned if we recall totally dedicated persons who labored endlessly and made enormous contributions to society without thinking of rewards in the form of wealth—people like Galileo and Michelangelo and Einstein and legions of lesser people. But let's skip that. Let's suppose you are correct about the need for pecuniary incentives, at least as regards most people in our society. Are you, then, prepared to say that you withdraw your protection from the possession of wealth that has no justification other than the interest of its owners in keeping it, and that you will protect wealth only if such protection serves the interests of those who do not have it? Do you agree with the Harvard professor who says that a society to be just must through its laws and institutions distribute all social values—liberty and opportunity, income and wealth—equally, 'unless an unequal distribution of any, or all, of these values is to everyone's advantage'?[17] That surely is the implication of your argument that the reward of merit is functionally justifiable."

"We probably must if we are to base our authority on more than our command of brute force," the laws answer, as they stir uneasily.

"Let's get specific by way of testing the sincerity of your professions, since you are so often accused of double-talk. There are, of course, many kinds of property. One of these, to take an example, is ownership of sub-surface resources. If the owner of the land under which valuable minerals lie performs no function in connection with finding them, extracting them, or marketing them, why should society pay tribute to him, as you now require—with special tax benefits thrown in?"

"To be consistent, we would have to say because he has the power to get us to exact that tribute," concede the laws after a long silence. "We are his servant, to be honest with you."

"You may get obedience from us but you hardly deserve respect in that event—at least as far as your protection of *that* kind of property is concerned. But let's go on. What explanation have you for the protection you give to inherited wealth, beyond, perhaps, a humane minimum to provide for modest established expectations? Demonstrate your impartiality here if you want our respect. We are not challenging all categories of property, mind you, so don't get alarmed. And, as far as our *interests* are concerned, those of us who are fortunate enough to inherit property want as much as we can get. Moreover, we haven't thought through the economic consequences of a steep increase in inheritance taxes. We simply find it impossible to discover a plausible functional justification for inherited wealth (or wealth received in the form of gifts) that obligates us to *respect* the law that protects it. We may have to obey such a law for other reasons. It may even be that the strains and tensions and disruptions attendant on changing such a law would cancel out the benefits, but in that event we could at least agree that the basis of consent was political and not moral."

It is not recorded that the laws answered, although a *sotto voce* comment was overheard on the need for large disparities in wealth and income to sustain the arts and other refinements of civilization, and one law is said to have whispered furtively of the need for large pools of capital for the expansion of production.

Such are the tests to which laws may be submitted. Formal though they are, it must be agreed that they have broad implications for the guidance of public policy, as they have for the choices we make in guiding our personal conduct.

Chapter Fourteen

Sympathy and the
Sense of Injustice

Of all the promptings to action sympathy and the sense of injustice are most closely associated in every day discourse with ethical conduct. And yet, taken for granted as such promptings are, their proper understanding has proven elusive. Both, when acted upon, led to other-regarding conduct. But obviously not all other-regarding conduct, for example, a physician's concern for his patient's recovery, or a professor's desire that he be understood by his students, is an outcome of sympathy or a sense of injustice. (To simplify the discussion I will leave further reference to the sense of injustice until later.)

It will avoid some of the confusion that has beset discussions of benevolence if I recur to my earlier categorization and note that other-regarding conduct occurs at the aesthetic, prudential, jurisprudential, and ethical levels. The difficulty often encountered by philosophers stems from regarding one or the other of these as all-inclusive, which is to say from confusing one

variety of other-regarding conduct with the others. I shall deal
with each of these in turn, but we must first be clear about our
terms. *Sympathy* in the most general sense denotes, as C. H.
Cooley said, "the sharing of any mental state that can be com-
municated."[1] I am concerned here with sympathy in the narrower sense defined as "the capacity to apprehend the pain,
suffering, or signs of negative emotions in man or animals and
to respond to these with appropriate negative feelings." Sympathy is distinguished from *empathy* by the same writer: "The
connotations of empathy are emotionally neutral. . . . In empathy
one attends to the feelings of another; in sympathy one attends
to the suffering of another, but the feelings are one's own. In
empathy I try to feel your pain. In sympathy I know you are in
pain, and I sympathize with you, but I feel my sympathy and my
pain, not your anguish and your pain."[2] It should be made clear, as
the foregoing comment does not, that empathy may involve the
duplication or mimicry of "positive" feelings such as joy, exulta-
tion, hope, as well as feelings of distress produced by pain,
frustration, fear, despair. By contrast, sympathy in the narrower
sense used here is aroused only by need or distress. Empathy poses
difficult epistemological problems of which sympathy as a phenomenon is free.[3] The natural history of the latter is, indeed,
familiar enough.

Powerful psychological and social forces render members of
primary groups immediately responsive to each other's needs.
No doubt, as evolutionists have pointed out, such mutual re-
sponsiveness is directly related to its enormous survival value.
True, the Darwinian idea of a competition for survival and a
consequent view of nature as "red in tooth and claw"—the
words were Tennyson's, not Darwin's—tended to encourage
emphasis in discussions of human nature on a dog-eat-dog
aggressiveness and, in the early twentieth century, the doctrine
of Social Darwinism provided a pseudoscientific basis for the
kind of jungle ethic recently revived in the writings of Ayn
Rand. But Kropotkin was closer to the truth when he contended

that survival comes about not by virtue of superior aggressiveness but because of mutual aid,[4] and contemporary evolutionists have agreed.[5] Indeed, mutual aid is so prevalent among animals that Darwin himself imputed human sentiments to them, egregiously perpetrating the pathetic fallacy, so-called;[6] and it is clear that biological factors, notably the long period of dependency of the human infant and the more durable family tie encouraged by the uninterrupted sexual availability of the human female, enormously expand mutual aid among humans.

Apart from primary group loyalties and attachments, we tend to be distressed at the suffering of others, even of animals. Such distress may be felt even though one may not be disposed to offer help and even though, surrounded by endemic suffering, we tend to become calloused. In many instances, of which the paradigm case would be the anguish felt by a mother over the suffering of her child, the mechanism at work is what in the literature of psychoanalysis is called "introjection," an unconscious psychic process in which one person "lives" another's experience. The psychodynamics of such feelings need not detain us here. The point is that when the help rendered is spontaneous, unreflective, immediate—as in many, if not most, cases of parents' concern for their children or the action of a soldier in risking death to save a wounded comrade—this is other-regarding conduct at the aesthetic level, as I earlier called it, *i.e.*, at the level of interest, a level marked by complete engrossment in the end to be attained without attention to relations, causes, consequences. Strictly speaking, such conduct is other-regarding only retrospectively or from the point of view of an external observer; from the point of view of the individual giving help the distinction between self and other dissolves in the immediacy of the response. If sympathy, as has been suggested, involves helping others with full awareness of the difference between self and other, then the spontaneous aid given a needy child by its parent, suggesting complete identification of the self with the other, does not fall under this rubric. This is confirmed by ordinary usage in which it would be odd to refer to the "sympathy" displayed by a mother risking her life to shield her child from immanent danger or to the "altruism" of which the child was thereby a beneficiary.

The case is quite different at the *prudential* level. There is a conscious polarization of self and other or of "them" and "us"; others are treated as means and the self as end, and help or service is rendered only if it furthers the self. Obviously, a great deal of help given others is inspired by such calculated self-interest, whether it be America's foreign aid program justified often not in the name of common humanity but as serving our national interest, or a bequest inspired by the tax benefits and public honor it brings the donor. Such prudential action is other-regarding, but not inspired by sympathy or compassion and hence not properly called altruism. There is, indeed, as in sympathy, an awareness of distress, but no concern over removing it except as a means to furthering one's own interests.

During the eighteenth and nineteenth centuries, finding their model of human nature at the marketplace where—whether it be labor, money, or commodities—men presumably strive to buy for the least and sell for the most, the reigning ideologues concluded that *all* conduct is similarly motivated. Man can act from no other motive than a selfish one even when he purports to do otherwise. A century earlier Hobbes had expounded this view in his famous "selfish system" according to which altruism, so-called, is nothing but disguised self-interest. The view dominated the nascent social sciences and even invaded theology so that Abraham Tucker (1705-1774) could declare that the "perfect Wise-man or Christian Sage, acting always invariably for the Glory of God" must have "a thorough conviction . . . that acting for the divine Glory is acting most for his own benefit;"[7] and the great Blackstone, digressing from jurisprudence into theology could find that "the Creator . . . has been pleased so to contrive the constitution and frame of humanity that we should want no other prompter to enquire after . . . but only our self-love, that universal principle of action."[8] As might be expected egoism received its greatest impetus from the political economists. The founder of the modern science of political economy, describing the motives of the individual in an exchange economy, asserts:

He generally, indeed, neither intends to promote the public interest, nor knows how much he is promoting it . . . By . . . directing . . . industry in such a manner as its produce may be of the greatest value, he intends only his own gain, and he is in this, as in many other cases, led by an invisible hand to promote an end which was no part of his intention. Nor is it always the worse for the society that it was no part of it. By pursuing his own interest he frequently promotes that of the society more effectually than when he really intends to promote it. I have never known much good done by those who affected to trade for the public good. It is an affectation, indeed, not very common among merchants, and very few words need be employed in dissuading them from it.[9]

Again:

It is not from the benevolence of the butcher, the brewer, or the baker, that we expect our dinner, but from their regard to their own interest. We address ourselves, not to their humanity but to their self-love, and never talk to them of our own necessities but of their advantages."[10]

Whether Adam Smith had abandoned or modified the position taken in his earlier *Theory of the Moral Sentiments,* where sympathy is not reduced to self-interest and is regarded as central to moral conduct, or was limiting egoism to the motives prevalent at the marketplace, the "selfish system," as Hobbes had bluntly formulated it a century earlier in the *Leviathan,* now took over. Bernard de Mandeville summarized the then prevalent and still commonly held view when he wrote of "Private vices, public benefits." The "friendly qualities" and "kind affections," are not the foundations of society; on the contrary "What we call evil [i.e., egoism] in this world . . . is the grand principle that makes us sociable creatures."[11]

Granted that much other-regarding conduct is of the prudential kind in which we heed Herbert Spencer's advice that we ought to help others because they in turn help us, the assumption—encouraged by the prominence of *Homo economicus* during the high noon of capitalism—that *all* conduct, including all altruistic conduct, must be explained in terms of enlightened self-interest has bred prolific confusion. It is difficult in the first place to understand what that self would be which, separate and apart, is set up over against other selves in relationship to which it as an entity may be either benevolent or selfish. Referring to that "strange affectation in many people [the Epicureans, Hobbes] of explaining away all particular affections, and representing the whole of life as nothing but one continued exercise of self-love," Bishop Joseph Butler (1692–1752), in the remarkably acute preface to his celebrated *Sermons,* wrote: "It is not because we love ourselves that we find delight in such and such objects, but because we have particular affections toward them. Take away these affections, and you leave self-love absolutely nothing to employ itself about; no end, or object, for it to pursue. . . ."[12] Egoism as conventionally expounded is impaled on this point.

The coup de grace to notions of the self such as those taken for granted by egoists was delivered by William James in a memorable passage:

But what is this abstract numerical principle of identity, this "Number One" within me, for which, according to proverbial philosophy, I am supposed to keep so constant a "lookout"? Is it the inner nucleus of my spiritual self. . . ? Or is it perhaps the concrete stream of my thought in its entirety, or some one section of the same? . . . Or, finally, can it be the mere pronoun I? Surely it is none of these things that self for which I feel such hot regard. . . . To have a self that I can *care* for, nature must first present me with some *object* interesting enough to make me instinctively wish to appropriate it for its *own* sake, and out of it to manufacture one of those material, social, or spiritual selves, which we have already passed in review. . . . *The words ME, then, and SELF, so far as they arouse feeling and connote emotional worth, are OBJECTIVE designations, meaning ALL THE THINGS which have the power to produce in a stream of consciousness excitement of a certain peculiar sort . . .*

To sum up . . . we see no reason to suppose that self-love is primarily, or secondarily, or ever, love for one's mere principle of conscious identity. It is always love for something which, as compared with that principle, is superficial, transient, liable to be taken up or dropped at will.[13]

When we act selfishly, guiding ourselves by those prudential calculations which economists describe as the motives of the market, it is not, then, some abstract self apart from the interests that engage it which we are serving, but, on the contrary, *a particular set of interests—pecuniary or other—with which the self is contingently identified.* These interests may be broad or narrow as the case may be.

The psychological egoist, if one takes James's criticism seriously, seems to be saying no more than that individuals must act in behalf of the interests they have. Since interests may be indefinitely various, ranging from those which led white youths from the North to crusade for civil rights in the deep South, to those which led some Mississippi bigots to murder several of them, the statement that all conduct is sefish reduces to the indisputable but sterile truism that all conduct is whatever it happens to be. No doubt the egoist thinks of himself as affirming more than such an empty tautology. This is because, for the most part covertly, he believes that we must act in pursuit of certain interests to the exclusion of others. These interests generally turn out in his view to be a desire for power, accumulation, glory, conspicuous display, creature comforts and so on, those interests, namely, that were in fact most visible as the "acquisitive society" came into its own in the nineteenth century. Thus construed, the statement that all men are selfish is no longer a tautology. But it happens to be false since all sorts of men—poets, scientists, philosophers or just plain vagabonds—while they may not be totally devoid of such interests, clearly value other things more.

A third kind of other-regarding conduct has a jurisprudential basis. That individuals should have regard for the needs of others and that society should make provision for the welfare of its disadvantaged members is decreed by accepted standards of morality and reflected in our rules of law. To be sure, statutory law normally confines itself to the negative requirement that we not harm our fellowmen. It does not require that, *as individuals,* we act positively in their behalf. Even when it holds parents responsible for the care of their children the care required is only minimal. On the other hand, in social legislation, so-called, we do acknowledge a collective responsibility for the care of those in need, although the acknowledgment of such legal responsibility has often been inspired by prudential considerations (for example, in Germany by Bismarck's desire to undercut socialism and to unify the Germans) and came only tardily to the United States after a long period during which the role of the state was largely restricted to the exercise of its police powers. Standards of morality advocating altruism, unsupported though they may be by the force of law, are deeply imbedded in religious traditions and command general respect although their range of application beyond the individual's kinship group varies greatly. Other-regarding conduct is, in brief, an acknowledged *duty.*

It is in terms of other-regarding conduct inspired by such a sense of duty, decreeing that we help others quite apart from whatever favorable or unfavorable inclinations we might have, that Kant would understand altruism in the distinctively moral sense:

To be beneficent when we can is a duty; and besides this, there are many minds so sympathetically constituted that, without any other motive of vanity or self-interest, they find a pleasure in spreading joy around them, and can take delight in the satisfaction of others so far as it is their own work. But I maintain that in such a case an action of this kind, however proper, however amiable it may be, has nevertheless no true moral worth, but is on a level with other inclinations, for example, the inclination to honor, which, if it is happily directed to that which is in fact of public utility and accordant with duty, and consequently honorable, deserves praise and encouragement, but not esteem. For the maxim lacks the moral import, namely, that such actions be done *from duty*, not from inclination. Put the case that the mind of that philanthropist was clouded by sorrow of his own, extinguishing all sympathy with the lot of others, and that while he still has the power to benefit others in distress, he is not touched by their trouble because he is absorbed with his own; and now suppose that he tears himself out of this dead insensibility and performs the action without any inclination to it, but simply from duty, then first has his action its genuine moral worth.[14]

It was on such a basis that Kant urged that a mother's solicitude for her child lacks moral quality unless the motive of her conduct is not her natural impulse, but her sense of duty. Unfortunately, Kant's exclusive concentration on the sense of duty, construed by him as "the necessity of acting from respect for the law,"[15] leads him to neglect the role of other standpoints than that provided by law, in particular the ethical implications of sympathy and the distinctive role *it* plays in the moral life. That role will be overlooked if, like Kant, we regard altruism as one among many instances of conduct inspired by respect for *law*.

Other-regarding conduct takes on a distinctively ethical character when by virtue of sympathetic response to an appeal from someone in distress one is required to give up, or to consider the possibility of giving up, values that he holds dear. We have, if we are normal, an aversion to the suffering of others. That has already been noted, along with some of the causal conditions which lead us to feel distressed in the presence of the suffering of others.[16] We are often able to alleviate such distress at no cost to ourselves: in such circumstances we have no conflict, are involved in no problem. The crucial problem confronts us when favorable response to an appeal for help requires us to go contrary to our established preferences, to give up something important to us whether this be the uninterrupted enjoyment of our creature comforts or loyalty to some ideal of conduct the merit of which we have always taken for granted. Sympathy for a person with a terminal illness may prompt someone heretofore always truthful to lie to him about his illness. A Southern lawyer (as in *To Kill a Mockingbird*) jeopardizes his career to come to the defense of a black man threatened by a mob. A renowned Russian cellist, Matislav Rostropovich, invites government reprisal by coming to the defense of a beleaguered friend, Nobel-prize-winning writer, Alexander Solzhenitsyn, in an open letter attacking the Russian censors and declaring that "Every man must have the right to think independently and express his opinion about what he knows . . ." If in situations like the foregoing action is not, as at the aesthetic level, impulsive; if standards or laws decreeing one course rather than another are not taken as binding; if one seriously contemplates suspension of one's preferences; if there is, in other words, a genuine tension between alternatives, we have been involved by sympathy in an ethical problem.[17]

Once again we are indebted to Dewey:

It is sympathy which carries thought out beyond the self and which extends its scope. . . . It is sympathy which saves consideration of consequences from degenerating into mere calculation, by rendering vivid the interests of others and urging us to give them the same weight as those which touch our own honor, purse, and power. *To put our-*

*selves in the place of others, to see things from the standpoint of their
purposes and values, to humble, contrariwise, our own pretensions and
claims till they reach the level they would assume in the eye of an
impartial sympathetic observer, is the surest way to obtain objectivity
of moral knowledge.* Sympathy is the animating mold of moral judgment, *not because its dictates take precedence in action over those of
other impulses (which they do not do), but because it furnishes the
most efficacious intellectual standpoint.*[18]

The foregoing is one of the few passages in the extensive
literature on benevolence which brings out its basic ethical import. Several points in this passage are noteworthy. First is the
reference to how we achieve objectivity for judgments of value.
We do so by validating our values, interests, preferences, that is
to say, by viewing them from standpoints *other* than the stand-
point they dictate. Such standpoints may be provided, we have
been urging, by the example or advice of an authority figure, by
rules of law, by standards of morality (see above, Chapter 11,
p. 178), etc. Here we are concerned with benevolence. In one
respect the procedure is not unlike that involved in validating
an existential judgment concerning, say, whether a grey blotch
on the horizon is an island or a cloud. We call in other witnesses.
Not just any witnesses, it may be noted; the witnesses must be
qualified, i.e., they must be sober, have good eyesight, etc. If we
were dealing with something like an interpretation of X ray
photographs we would have many more tests of competence.
And, of course, reliability would be enormously increased if we
could call on witnesses viewing the object from another angle.
Analogously, our values may be objects of inquiry. To see our
values from the point of view of others whose needs require us
to sacrifice, or seriously to contemplate the possibility of sacri-
ficing, them is to get a new perspective on them; to project ourselves into the position of others in need in this way and thereby
make our values objects of inquiry is part of the process of
reaching an objective judgment about them.

A second point in Dewey's comment is noteworthy. The way to obtain objectivity, he says, is to "humble" our own "pretensions." He might less tendentiously and more accurately have said to *subordinate our own needs,* but at any rate some attitude of humility with respect to our values is, as I have already urged (see above, p. 174), essential to both moral and ethical deliberation.

Finally, the view of sympathy suggested by Dewey enables us to see that the ethical relevance of benevolence does not derive simply from the circumstance that the welfare of other selves has some inexplicable priority. As he says elsewhere, self for self one is as good as another: "our own [self] is worth as much as another's."[19] Why, then, should we take the role of the other and entertain the possibility of self-sacrifice? Let us first be clear concerning what such sacrifice is.

Much confusion is caused by the erroneous assumption that the self-denial that an act of benevolence occasions invariably requires one to give up some physical comfort, some creature gratification, some sum of money or objects that money can buy. This stems from a more basic fallacy noted above of identifying selfishness with pecuniary acquisitiveness or a preoccupation with one's physical comforts and then opposing selfishness as thus understood to selflessness or altruism or benevolence. The kind of self-denial that an appeal to our benevolence may require might have nothing to do with giving up a physical comfort; indeed it could be just the opposite. An ascetic monk dedicated to prayer and meditation in a remote monastery (to take an extreme case) might be prompted to give up that kind of *austere* life in response to an appeal from oppressed countrymen, might even come to oppose the church to which he had dedicated himself if he found it, as in Spain during the Spanish Civil War of 1936, condoning if not actually allied with the oppressors of his people.[20] He would thereby have engaged in an act of self-denial, but hardly of physical enjoyments; he would be rejecting (whether provisionally or finally) the self he had been—the enjoyed self as I earlier called it. Had the monk ignored such an appeal he could as aptly be called selfish as a prosperous Madrileno opposed to any course that threatened his power and comfort. In sum, the selfish individual is one who refuses to examine the interests or standards he has, and he is that no matter what those interests or standards happen to be; the selfless individual is the contrary. It follows logically from what has been said that a concentration on the interests of others so intense as to render one insensitive to alternatives must be regarded as a form of selfishness.

"Selfishness" is used pejoratively just because it designates an individual of narrow interests and there is no contradiction in saying that such selfishness is self-defeating or self-stultifying. Consider, for example, an unregenerate misanthrope, some species of anomic man[21] ruthlessly bent upon using or exploiting everyone, even the members of his family. Such a person would not be self-serving, but self-destructive (and hence psychopathic), since, as his interests dwindled, his self would have shriveled in its isolation to virtually nothing. As G. H. Mead observed, "the matter of selfishness is the setting up a narrow self over against a larger self."[22]

The person who takes cognizance of the interests of others even when they are opposed to his own is selfless. But it is only the *enjoyed* self that is sacrificed; in an important (and decisive) sense he becomes a larger self and the outcome may be fulfillment and enhancement. He must, of course, be *aware of the possibility* of becoming such a larger or, as I have called it, *transcendent* self (see above, pp. 184–186). Such awareness is, indeed, the hallmark of the ethically conscious person. In the case of an appeal to one's sympathy, this is true even if, after a fair appraisal of such an appeal, it is rejected.

Reference to "fair appraisal" suggests that not all appeals or offers of aid are worthy. How is an appraisal to be made if in the problematic situation as defined the standards of worth on which we have heretofore relied are not available? Are we able here, as in the case of the promptings of authority, to rely on formal tests, formal in the sense that they are applicable to all appeals? "Criteria of trustworthiness"[23] are, it must be noted, available to us. Is the help rendered in such a way as to humiliate the recipient and remind him of his dependence? Will it prolong or perpetuate dependency while palliating its consequences? That, it would appear, is the result of help inspired by the sense of *noblesse oblige* or—to coin a term for its American variant—*richesse oblige*. Such help often goes by the name of charity, a once noble word which is understandably tarnished just because most charity as it has been practiced preserves invidious differences between "superiors" and "inferiors" and thereby impedes emergence of the fellow-feeling and sense of mutuality that rewards ethically authentic benevolence.

There are other tests. Is one's sympathy genuine in the sense that it is independent of conscious or unconscious calculations of self-interest as defined above)? For example, is it inspired by a need for praise? Or, by a need to dissipate guilt feelings so that one may in other areas persist in conduct that perpetuates need and dependence? It is notorious that compassion is easily counterfeited and that it is difficult to distinguish between the spurious and the genuine. Again, when we impose our idea of what people need on them instead of consulting their ideas, we promote resentment instead of reciprocal understanding and affection. We may well ask, therefore, whether the intended beneficiaries have been really consulted. It is all too easy to patronize those whom we help. No doubt other excellent tests will occur to the reader.

Benevolence is an essential ingredient of the ethical experience.[24] We are what we are by virtue of our social relationships. To the extent that it transforms these relationships it transforms us. It promises experiences of amity and brotherhood from which we would be excluded by a firm refusal to give up what we have. However, that promise cannot be fulfilled unless benevolence is genuine, unless, that is, it levels and does not preserve or raise barriers to social intercourse. Surely, we are provided here with an objective standard by reference to which, despite cultural relativists, we may measure the ethical quality of a society as well as an individual. The ethical life can hardly flourish in a society where a slave or caste or class system precludes reciprocity among its members.

It is enjoined that "Thou shall love thy neighbor as Thyself." Apart from such other problems as the injunction poses, the extension of "neighbor" is puzzling since it varies from group to group and time to time ranging from the tribalism of many groups to the Christian ideal of the universal brotherhood of man. Modern technology may well make the beggars of Calcutta and the wretched victims of the Vietnam War closer neighbors than the family down the street. Can compassion embrace the world?

We can be helped in answering this question if a difference is recognized between appeals to our feeling of sympathy and arousals of our sense of injustice. The former is personal and the *appellant* is treated as an end. Whether the closeness is physical or consanguineous, the feat of projection required of us is much easier and correspondingly more frequent. Considerations of injustice are not necessarily involved. Distress arousing our sympathy is often a result of misfortune, mishap, inadvertence. I may respond to a friend's plea for help even though his need is a consequence of his own negligence. The sense of injustice is both more general and more limited: more limited with reference to the kinds of need that evoke it, and more general in that it embraces those with whom we have no direct or personal tie. Thus we are aroused to help others by a sense of injustice when the law fails to deal with them as equals, when (relatedly) there is inequality of economic opportunity, when there is disproportion between merit and reward or punishment, when, in sum, individuals have been treated *un-fairly*, whether legally or extra-legally, by those who have the power, if they would only so exercise it, to deal fairly. Injustice betrays a flaw in our social arrangements. When on such occasions we are moved by a sense of injustice, it is to correct the conditions that make a misuse of power possible rather than directly to aid the victims of such misuse. We are involved in *social* reconstruction and to the extent that such involvement requires us to consider the abandonment of our present values we view them not from the standpoint of a specific person but rather from the point of view of what Mead called the "generalized other." We may, as he said, "take the attitude of the entire community, of all rational beings."[25]

Like law professor Edmond Cahn, who gave us a book with the title *The Sense of Injustice*, I prefer that term to "the sense of justice." His reason is that justice "has been so beclouded by natural-law writings that it almost inevitably brings to mind some ideal relation or static condition or set of perceptual standards." Cahn, on the contrary, is concerned with "what is active, vital, and experiential in the reactions of human beings."[26] Justice is the criterion by reference to which we evaluate law, if it is not, as Sidgwick reminds us, actually used interchangeably with law as when we speak of "Law Courts" and "Courts of Justice," or when, in calling for justice we demand simply that the law be enforced.[27] On the other hand, there is in the sense of injustice the seed of innovation and reconstruction; it suggests that "propulsive tendency toward the future"[28] and that constant revolt against the past with its legacy of obstacles to be surmounted which are distinctive features of the ethical life and are somehow not conveyed by the term "sense of justice."

We shall be aided in seeing the usefulness of a distinction between sympathy and the sense of injustice as incentives to other-regarding conduct by citing as illustration the storm of protest aroused some years ago by the impending execution of aryl Chessman after he had spent twelve years on San uentin's Death Row. Part of that protest was no doubt inired by simple compassion for a man whose writings during ose years made it clear that he had transformed himself om a hardened, refractory lawbreaker into an individual manistly capable of assuming a responsible role in society. He rote:

> As a young man, I was a violent, rebellious, monumental damn fool. was at odds with my society; I resisted authority. I am ashamed of at past but I cannot change it. After being brought to the death)use, the change in me and my outlook came slowly and painfully. efiantly, I stood and fought in the courts for survival, asking no iarter and expecting none. But, ironically, to have any chance for irvival, I had to turn to the law; I had to invoke the protections of ie Constitution; I had to study, often as much as 18 to 20 hours a day; had to learn to impose upon myself a harsh self-discipline; I had to iink and to be ruthlessly honest with myself; in time, I forced myself) admit, "Chessman, you have been, and to some degree still are, an rational, impossible fool. What are you going to do about it?"[29]

, greater part of the protest, which took the form of a call for xecutive clemency and literally deluged the Governor's office, 'as aroused by a sense of injustice; those who protested were utraged by a system of punishment that kept Chessman in the iadow of the gas chamber for more than a decade and romised to culminate this with the ultimate brutality of executig him—as it finally did. No doubt compassion played its part ere, too, but in this context Chessman as a person was not the)le or chief *end*—as would be the case if he were an object of enevolence; his fate was incidental to a more inclusive end, amely reconstruction of the law by which Chessman was nally destroyed and others like him would meet a similar end.)ne now takes not just the role of Chessman but of all who might find themselves in such a predicament. It is even possible for the victim of an injustice to take such a position. On the eve of the scheduled execution Governor Edmund Brown of California, at great political risk to himself, granted Chessman a reprieve "to give the people . . . an opportunity, through the Legislature, to express themselves once more on capital punishment." In one of the most remarkable letters ever sent from a prison cell Chessman wrote to Governor Brown:

> I . . . earnestly urge you to ask the Legislature to consider the question of capital punishment apart from Caryl Chessman and the Chessman case. I urge you to request that they consider framing their bill as suggested above, to exclude me. You can do this honorably by taking my life back into your hands alone. You can let me die. Indeed, as the matter now stands, you are powerless to do otherwise because of the present 4–3 vote against me in the California Supreme Court. But, at the same time, you can give your proposal to the Legislature a chance.
>
> It deserves that chance. It deserves your forceful leadership. You are right in the position you have taken. It is time to speak out, for too seldom does unenlightened humanity in this age of fear and awesome nuclear devices have a spokesman with the courage to advocate that death and hate are not and never can be an answer to the problems that beset our civilization. Mankind and future generations ever will remain in your debt and will honor your name.[30]

Caryl Chessman's sense of injustice had brought him into a relationship of identity with all the wretches who linger in death cells while a society committed to the death penalty wrestles with its conscience.

In *The God That Failed* the great Italian novelist, Ignazio Silone, asks, "From what source do some people derive their spontaneous intolerance of injustice, even though the injustice affects only others?" Silone was unable to answer. The volume, in which he and other former Communists expressed their disenchantment with communism, suggests the hazards that beset soldiers against injustice—including the hazard of alliances with those who perpetrate injustice to oppose injustice. But it also attests to the intensity of our revulsion against injustice and the way in which social protest can alter our lives, as it did the lives of Silone, Spender, Gide, Koestler, and the others who contributed to the same volume.

It is instructive, because so strikingly paralleled in the United States in recent years, to recall the "Narodniki" of the 1870's, Russian students from prosperous families who, aroused by the desperate plight of the peasants, obeyed Alexander Herzen's exhortation, "V narod!" ("To the People!"), and went to work selflessly as nurses, teachers, doctors, and even laborers in remote villages, where they sought to merge with and arouse the masses. Similarly, middle-class American students, consumed by a burning sense of injustice, journeyed from the North to the South to crusade for civil rights. The risks were not quite as great—the Narodniki were turned over to the Czarist police by suspicious peasants who persisted in regarding the Czar as their "Little Father"— but there was the same crusading zeal, the same feeling of moral outrage, the same willingness to sacrifice in behalf of an ideal of social justice.

"The sense of injustice," Professor Cahn observes, "does not provide a formula to relieve men of the duty of deliberation and decision."[31] It, too, must be tested for reliability. There are dangers. If conservatives are afflicted with reactionaries and bigots, social reformers have their fanatics. If there is too much apathy there can also be too much zeal. Over-zealousness tends to be careless of facts. It is *not* a fact, for example, that the faculties of major American universities are biased against blacks, although many blacks and many white students who are properly outraged by the indignities from which blacks have suffered say so. Over-zealousness can also be undiscriminating in its choice of means; for example, Louis Aragon, aroused once by his sense of social injustice to become a leader (and orna-

ment) of the French Communist Party, overlooked the tragedies
of Hungary and Prague, and became blind to the indignities
suffered by fellow poets wherever the Communist Party controls
their destiny.

The sense of injustice may be betrayed not only by an
excess of zeal. Reason, too, may lure it like a siren's song. Once
reason becomes sole arbiter, we impose its syllogisms on the
past only to find the past replete with inconsistencies—the contradiction, for example, of simultaneously extolling brotherly
love and the virtues of an acquisitive society, of celebrating
the Sermon on the Mount ("Ye cannot serve God and mam-
mon") and pursuing wealth. But the past, that is to say, the
established order, is not so easily discredited. Its contradictions
are not as quickly discerned by ordinary mortals as by the
French *philosophes*. Moreover, there are glues that bind the
present to the past: habits, customs, our affinity for the familiar,
the concerns involved in living from day to day—not to mention vested interests that resist change. It is proverbial that many
crimes are committed in the name of reason because these
simple truths are ignored and the hold of the past underesti-
mated. This was, of course, the burden of Burke's quarrel with
the French Revolution, as it was of the romanticist protest
against the Enlightenment, and, if Burke became querulous and
the romanticists obfuscatory, the point is nonetheless valid.

It is in part another way of saying the same thing to warn
that the sense of injustice, succumbing to impatience or a
passion for perfection, may lose itself in utopianism which flouts
the past ("He [the philosopher-king] will scrape the canvas
clean," Socrates says in the *Republic*),[32] or romanticism which
fawns upon it. Both are escapist exercises in futility. The sense
of injustice must work in the soiled and grubby and often intractable present where its victories, though not likely to be
many or large or complete, still bring their own kind of in-
vigoration and their own manner of reward. There are no slide
rules by reference to which our sense of injustice can de-

termine at what point it verges on dangerous alliances, dubious methods, carelessness with facts, excessive rationality, perfectionism, escapism, but it may be a great gain simply to be warned. Had the militants of the late 1960's heeded such warnings they might with their dedication and aptitudes have made a significant contribution to reconstructing a badly flawed society instead of wasting themselves on counter-productive adventures.

Chapter Fifteen

Individual Impulsions

A full account of promptings to action must reckon finally with those impulsions or desires which, however modified by cultural conditions and special circumstances, have their genesis in the individual's own needs. If their contribution to the ethical experience is to be properly interpreted, such impulsions must be understood not in terms of their intensity alone—although that will necessarily be an important factor in their assessment—but as providing a different standpoint from which to reexamine a way of life in which they may have been neglected or frustrated and hence as providing a basis of reevaluation and a source of possible renewal.

We reckon here, in other words, primarily with emotional or instinctual drives and the role, actual or potential, they play in character formation and the direction of conduct. One need not take sides in the many controversies that have beset instinct theory—whether instincts are preformed, inherited and unlearned, based on specific neural structures, etc.—nor need one let the term become a substitute for genuine causal explanation, to agree that instinct remains a useful label for species-characteristic behavior patterns associated with and generative of powerful drives or appetites and strong emotions initially unmediated by deliberation or reflection and therefore often appropriately described as spontaneous and nonrational.[1] At the same time it is well to heed C. H. Cooley's warning, still useful today, that,

There is . . . a wide-spread disposition among psychologists, psychoanalysts, biologists, economists, writers on education, and others who are interested in instinct but would gladly avoid history or sociology, to short-circuit their current of causation, leading it directly from instinct to social behavior, without following it into those intricate convolutions of social process through which, in the real world, it actually flows and by which it is transformed."[2]

But, whether or not behavior impelled by hunger, aggressiveness, fear, rage, sexuality, maternal love, etc. is properly called instinctive and thought of as at least in part hereditary and unlearned, it is clear that such behavior comprises a significant part of conduct and that in one or other of its manifestations it comes into conflict with habit, the dictates of law and custom and, as passion gets in the way of compassion, with the promptings of benevolence. Unfortunately, such conflict has for complex reasons been misunderstood so that all too frequently it has been viewed in terms of a Manichean opposition between good and evil, light and darkness, our spiritual as against our animal nature. And even Freud, salutary as was his teaching that drives that cannot find an outlet will be rechanneled and manifest themselves in neurotic symptoms, encouraged a misleading polarity (with confusing moral overtones) in his concept of the id as a kind of raging inferno of desire and the superego as its stern taskmaster. (See above, pp. 52–53, 60–62.)

In *Human Nature and Conduct* (1922), a minor masterpiece still untarnished by time, Dewey pointed out that in the career of any impulsive activity there are, generally speaking, three possibilities. First, the impulse may simply explosively discharge itself, blindly and unintelligently. Second, it may be suppressed. With Freud, Dewey points out that to suppress is not to eliminate. " 'Psychic' energy is no more capable of being abolished than the forms we recognize as physical. It is neither exploded nor converted, it is turned inwards, to lead a surreptitious, subterranean life." Just as a regardless indulgence in the first sense is, he says, "a sign of immaturity, crudity, savagery," a suppressed activity is the cause of all kinds of intellectual and moral pathology."[3] Third, and finally, an impulse may be sublimated. Dewey's concept of sublimation is quite different from the doctrine made famous by Freud and the difference has such important implications for moral theory that it is worth exploring.

Freud's doctrine of sublimation is distinguished in the first place by his insistence on finding a sexual basis for activities as diverse and seemingly removed from sexuality as miserliness and artistic creation. Thus miserliness is associated with an anal-erotic pleasure in holding on to the faeces, enjoyment of painting is depicted as a desexualized pleasure in playing with the faeces, surgery as a sublimation of sadistic tendencies which are erotic in nature, and so on.[4] Sublimation is for Freud a defense mechanism by which, instead of denying libidinal pleasures, they are given some other socially acceptable expression. The term "defense" is used advisedly because it suggests that, as Freud conceives of sublimation, it is often indistinguishable from actual suppression or denial ("reaction formations") of instinctual desires imposed from without by our social arrangements and institutions, with all the conflict and unhealthy neurotic symptoms attendant on such conflict. (See above, pp. 52–53, 60–62.)

Dewey specifically rejects the notion of a single psychic

force or "libido," or even of two such basic drives (e.g., a life and death instinct). Moreover, as Philip Rieff points out, "For Dewey the individual is not, as in Freud's conception, under a constant threat from the instincts lying in wait below the surface of consciousness, ready at any moment to claim their autonomy."[5] When any impulse activity, as Dewey calls it, is sublimated, it becomes, in his words, a factor coordinated intelligently with others in a continuing course of action. Thus a gust of anger may, because of its dynamic incorporation into disposition, be converted into an abiding conviction of social injustice to be remedied, and furnish the dynamic to carry the conviction into execution. Or an excitation of sexual attraction may reappear in art or in tranquil domestic attachments and services. Such an outcome represents the normal or desirable functioning of impulse; in which . . . the impulse operates as a pivot, or reorganization of habit."[6]

Clearly, for Dewey, sublimation does not mean that instinctual drives are straitjacketed and straining for release. If, for Freud, conflict, bred of just such tensions, is a tragic inevitability, casting a pall over civilization and fueling its discontent, Dewey finds it an occasion for creative reconstruction. He speaks of "utilizing released impulse" and of habit as responsive to the "transforming touch of impulse."[7] If Freud finds that morality is a yoke on the instinctual desires of the individual, Dewey finds that "Morality is an endeavor to find for the manifestation of impulse in special situations an office of refreshment and renewal."[8]

For the purpose of understanding morality (ethicality in our sense) rather than psychopathology Dewey's views are by far the more suggestive. For there is no inherent *opposition* between social regulations, on the one hand, and individual instinctual needs, on the other. So-called ego drives and communal purposes can in fact renew each other when their conflict is viewed not as a collision of opposed forces in which the greater force conquers, but as an occasion on which to view each from the point of view of the other. Ethicality (as distinguished from morality) lies, for example, neither in the old laws preserving indissoluble marriage such as those which inspired the film "Divorce, Italian Style," nor in satisfying the individual needs and feelings which such laws thwarted, but in the refusal to judge either alternative from one point of view and the *validating* of one as against the other by a kind of progressive comparison. This will not happen unless the process is viewed by the agent as one of constructing or reconstructing a self rather than serving this or that need or conforming to this or that canon or law.

Absurd as rigid anti-divorce laws are from the point of view of this writer—I deliberately take an extreme case—they command the vigorous support of a church that is the acknowledged spiritual leader of hundreds of millions (and which may yet succeed in getting these laws restored in Italy), and there could be in them residues of insight into interpersonal relations between men and women that might illuminate one's final decision at the time of choosing between alternatives. And, if the foregoing is true of canons and laws which have been found insufferable by the great majority of those who refuse to take them on blind faith, it is surely true of the feelings and emotions of incompatible partners in an indissoluble marriage. *The heart has its reasons which reason knows nothing of.* One needs not agree with the characteristic hyperbole of D. H. Lawrence that "what our blood feels is always true,"[9] nor with all the aberrational variations on this romanticist theme (e.g., Hitler's "I think with my blood"),[10] to see that our deep feelings and emotions are a conduit to reality, and may, if acknowledged and directed, give to our relations to others new vitality and new meaning. Aggression may have in it the seed of great achievement in science or civic leadership; rage may right a gross injustice; and erotic attraction, transformed as love, proverbially yields exaltation beyond our power to celebrate. Given recognition, our needs and emotions may generate deeper respect and warmer feeling for moral standards and precepts by humanizing them.

Are there tests here, too? "Reliability," "trustworthiness," are hardly right for this context. Moreover, there is danger when we subject our feelings and emotions to scrutiny of losing what is often most precious in them—their spontaneity and freshness, their *impulsiveness*, the importance of which we implicitly acknowledge in our disparagement of the inveterate calculator, the person who *always* looks before he leaps, who never fails to count the cost. We may be tempted to say with Hotspur, "I will ease my heart, / Albeit I make hazard of my head." And yet there are obvious tests, quite formal in nature, to which our emotional needs and the desire to which they give rise can be subjected. To begin with, we may ask, without passing judgment on the consequences, if the results of gratifying a desire have been taken into account. Teleological ethics contains at least that much truth. Is the desire such that its denial or pursuit, as the case may be, will disorient and disrupt us in the pursuit of all our engagements and enterprises? Is it such that it makes us dependent on precarious and exhaustible means—to recall the ancient Epicurean warning against most desire—and hence apprehensive, worried, anxiety-ridden; or may we pursue it with a zest bred of the knowledge that fulfillment can be secure and abiding? Will it end quickly in satiety and boredom or will it be self-renewing? Will the gratification of a desire generate an overwhelming need to continue indulging it so that, in effect, our action could be irreversible?

Clearly, addictive drugs, whatever their enticement as an escape from boredom or a promise of easy euphoria, would fail to pass this last test, indeed, would not deserve a hearing. The test, it may be noted again, is in an elementary sense a formal one. Competent authorities agree that the heroin addict is not aroused by the drug he takes and transformed into the "dope-fiend" and rapist–killer of popular folklore. In fact, opium is a depressant tending to dull sexual appetite and reduce violent behavior. Criminal behavior generally occurs when the addict is not under the influence of the drug but desperately needs money for a new dose. If, as has recently been proposed by a prestigious committee of the American Bar Association, heroin addicts were to be provided with the drug at little or no cost, the rampant crime committed by addicts in order to pay for their habit would disappear.[11] Moreover, contrary to popular opinion, there are no known organic diseases associated with opiate addiction, as there are with heavy smoking and drinking. The point is that, if a desire is such that its denial induces withdrawal symptoms of the kind suffered by heroin addicts, it is to be distrusted no matter what the desire is *for*.

Also, desire is obviously untrustworthy if its gratification impairs the physical capacity of the body. Such a desire is self-defeating. Again, a desire so compulsive that it monopolizes an individual's energies and attention is suspect unless it serves the bare need of survival. One thinks of a gambler's complete engrossment in games of chance, a collector's monomania for possession, a miser's passion for money, or a businessman's obsession with success in his enterprise to the neglect of all other interests and concerns. We say it best by calling such people "hooked." Genius, to be sure, calls for single-minded concentration, but it is no doubt part of the essence of genius that it works out its own salvation. Genius apart, surely one test of the kind of individual impulses under consideration is whether those who act on them suffer a loss of motivation and lapse of interest in their normal social ties and usual occupations such as is suffered, to take an extreme case, by the so-called psychedelic dropout.

There are other less easily applied and perhaps more controversial criteria. We may, if we can detach ourselves from it, wish to know of a desire, if it is genuinely what it presents itself as being. We may ask if there has been inquiry into its causes and conditions with a view to determining how deep-rooted it is. The list can be supplemented. But in each case the attitude required is the same—an attitude which ignores the intensity of the desire (save as one among many tests) or the felt quality attendant on its satisfaction, and achieves, to borrow a useful term from another area, *critical distance*. At issue is whether we possess our desires or they possess us, and, at the extreme, whether possession will give way to obsession, as with Thomas Mann's Aschenbach, who might have fled plague-ridden Venice —that "accursed morass" where he had become consumed with an undisclosed passion for a youthful stranger. Yet "he knew that he was far indeed from any serious desire to take such a step. It would restore him, would give him back himself once more; but *he who is beside himself revolts at the idea of self-possession.*" So we learn from *Death in Venice* and so it is with all the Aschenbachs, the Ahabs, the Javerts, all those who, as Scott Fitzgerald said of Gatsby, have "lived too long with a single dream"; in their different ways they are all wretched and tormented, maimed and stricken.[12] However, having put desires in their place, we must not forget that our instinctual desires are nature's voice, muted or transmuted. We do well to listen and to be wary of codes and laws that ignore them.

Chapter Sixteen

Conclusion

The position taken here is that the ethical character of an act is determined by the *way* in which an act is willed rather than by the nature of the act itself. The former has been called "agent" morality, the latter "act" morality. I follow Kant in urging that no object which "is *to be acquired*" can of itself be regarded as of moral worth[1] and agree that "an action done from duty derives its moral [ethical] worth, *not from the purpose* which is to be attained by it, but from the maxim by which it is determined, and therefore . . . [from] the *principle of volition* by which the action has taken place without regard to any object of desire."[2] We have held, in other words, that a course of conduct is not of itself *ethically* good or bad. Its ethical quality derives from an *attitude* manifesting itself on critical occasions in a distrust of one's prevailing values, and a *method* of resolving the situation of conflict with which one is thereby confronted. In such a typically ethical situation it will not be a consideration of the consequences which determines the action

234

of the will, however much they may constitute the reward or punishment of whatever action the will does undertake. The will becomes, to recur again to Kant's suggestive phrase, the "author of its own principles," which is what he meant by the freedom or autonomy of the will. The will is not determined by laws outside of it—that he called the "heteronomy of the will," which he rightly found to be the "source of all spurious principles of morality"[3]—but by its own law. This occurs, as I have argued (see above, pp. 182–188), when we *refuse* to be governed by our prevailing desires or interests or by the standards on which we have heretofore relied.

In the absence of such refusals, the laws by which we are governed are those describing the conditions (biological, psychological, social) which determine for us that we shall eat or refuse the flesh of cattle, prefer wealth to poverty, place the welfare of our country before the welfare of other countries, believe in polygamy or monogamy, defend or oppose racial and sexual equality, praise or damn socialism, and so on. There would be no place for ethics as an *autonomous science,* and ethics would properly be "reduced" to one or other of the social sciences. I hold that we may appropriately think of ethics as a science possessing its own distinctive subject matter if we differentiate, as it seems to me we must, between *experiential* and *experimental* (empirical) science. What can this distinction mean?

"Questions of intention," Durkheim has written, "are too subjective to allow of scientific treatment."[4] Recently, B. F. Skinner, well-known behaviorist, in his controversial *Beyond Freedom and Dignity,* has deplored (it would seem, querulously) the "pre-scientific" way in which "almost everyone who is concerned with human affairs—as political scientist, philosopher, man of letters, economist, psychologist, linguist, sociologist, theologian, anthropologist, educator or psychoanalyst," continues to talk about "attitudes," the "sense of responsibility," "man's inner capacities," "intentions," and the like—in sum, about a "person we can't see." The existence of such an "inner man" is a product of our ignorance and "he naturally loses status as we come to know more about behavior." As we learn more about the effects of the environment, "we have less reason to attribute any part of human behavior to an autonomous controlling agent."[5] On the other hand, some, especially phenomenologists since Husserl, have stressed the need for an experiential as distinguished from an experimental science, an Augustinian emphasis which the Bishop of Hippo would surely have applauded could experimental science have come within his ken. The distinction serves us well here. Nothing so ambitious (or obscure) as a phenomenological *metaphysics* of experience is contemplated or even suggested; I only suggest allowing for a science of experience which has as its data, at least so far as ethics is concerned, interior doubt, suspension of judgment, reevaluation, decision, the meaning to an individual of conduct determined upon in this fashion, his sense of self-direction, in sum, the very *humanity* of man as exhibited in his reflecting on himself. (Unfortunately, the term "ethology" cannot be used to designate a science of ethics, having been preempted by students of animal behavior.) Experimental (empirical) science limits itself to the direct or indirect testimony of the senses and is concerned with what is accessible to more than one observer, as when we confirm by direct observation that objects expand when heated or, indirectly, that the condensation of vapor to form visible tracks in a Wilson cloud chamber is caused by alpha particles. The science of man to the extent that it is experimental is necessarily a *behavioral* science limited to generalizations about data as observed from an "external" point of view and hence to the study of overt behavior and neurophysiological processes. The data of experiential science are neither public—at any rate in the same sense—nor observed by the individual through his senses.

The behavioralist is right to be wary of the extravagances of unchecked explorers of the *vie intérieure*. There is no intent here to question his well-founded suspicion of introspective report or his interest in imparting scientific rigor to his discipline, only his assumption that the position of the external observer is the *only* one, and his unwarranted derivation from a canon of method, highly useful in its place, of an ontological generalization, namely, that private feeling states and *meaningful* experiences are nonexistent. Whatever may be the final verdict on Max Weber's view of the subject matter of sociology (in contrast to Durkheim's) as "subjectively meaningful action," that view surely applies to the subject matter of ethics. It would be unfortunate if a narrow conception of science precluded us from a scientific approach to the self-knowledge that comes with reexamining and re-directing our lives as we do in the ethical experience.

This, I take it, is the point made by Charles Arthur Campbell in his acutely reasoned discussion of free will. It is Professor Campbell's view that "an act which is not an expression of the self's *character* may nevertheless be the *self's* act," in other words, that the self can rise above itself. Campbell contends, as we have in the foregoing pages, that this is the essence of an ethical decision and is precisely what is meant by an exercise of free will. Arguing against those who contend that this is indeterminism and that acts which do not issue from the agent's character (which is itself, of course, causally conditioned) can only be a matter of sheer chance, Campbell insists that this is *self*-determinism, and urges that, if critics are unable to find a meaning in this manner of talking, this is because "*they are looking for it in the wrong way; or better, perhaps, with the wrong orientation.*" The full passage follows:

They are looking for it from the stand-point of the *external observer;* the stand-point proper to, because alone possible for, apprehension of the physical world. Now from the external stand-point we may observe processes of change. But one thing which, by common consent, cannot be observed from without is *creative activity.* Yet—and here

lies the crux of the whole matter—it is precisely creative activity
which we are trying to understand when we are trying to understand
what is traditionally designated by "free will." For if there should be
an act which is genuinely the self's act and is nevertheless not an expression of its character, such an act, in which the act "transcends"
its character as so far formed, would seem to be essentially of the
nature of creative activity. It follows that to look for a meaning in
"free will" from the external stand-point is absurd. It is to look for it
in a way that insures that it will not be found. Granted that a creative
activity of any kind is at least *possible* (and I know of no ground for
its *a priori* rejection), there is one way, and one way only, in which
we can hope to apprehend it, and that is from the *inner* stand-point
of direct participation. . . .

Accordingly,

if the Libertarian's claim to find a meaning in a "free" will which is
genuinely the self's will, though not an expression of the self's character, is to be subjected to any test that is worth applying, that test
must be undertaken from the inner stand-point. We ought to place
ourselves imaginatively at the stand-point of the agent engaged in the
typical moral situation in which free will is claimed, and ask ourselves
whether from *this* standpoint the claim in question does or does not
have meaning for us. That the appeal must be to introspection is no
doubt unfortunate. But it would be a very doctrinaire critic of introspection who declined to make use of it when in the nature of the
case no other means of apprehension is available.[6]

All this attests to need for more than a semantic analysis of "the
language of morals," to borrow the title of R. M. Hare's suggestive book; we must press beyond language to the experience
of which our language is an expression if we are to understand
the data of ethics—a reminder that might seem to be gratuitous
were it not for the recent preoccupation of Anglo-American
philosophy with logical and linguistic analysis and hence with
what is *said* about conduct rather than conduct itself.[7]

When we look to the *way* in which an act has been willed we are in a position to appreciate the sense in which it is possible to speak meaningfully of the objectivity of moral judgments without using "objectivity" as a subterfuge for consecrating our own preferences or the values and standards prevalent in our own culture. It would be diversionary (and excessively ambitious) to probe all the complexities of this protean word.[8] Professor H. D. Aiken finds himself forced to conclude that "at least as far as ethics is concerned, traditional philosophical notions concerning the meanings of the terms 'objective' and 'subjective' must be abandoned once for all." Such notions, he observes, have been derived "from a continuous philosophical tradition for which formal logic and natural science have provided not only exemplary, but paradigm cases of objective discourse," and it is, he contends, "the uncritical application of such notions and the noetic models from which they are derived, beyond the domains of science and logic, that is ultimately responsible for the widespread moral skepticism with which at present most of us are afflicted."[9] The emotivist position (noncognitivism, and subjectivism) discussed earlier (see above, pp. 86–101) is fatally flawed in precisely this way.

It seems to me that we must grant the merit of this protest against a slavish reliance on the models of formal logic and empirical science for our understanding of all objective discourse. Still, in ethics as in the empirical sciences, if objectivity is to make sense, there must be a procedure for determining, if not the truth or falsity (since this suggests too strongly the models of which Aiken rightly complains), then the *reliability* or *unreliability* of conflicting claims that commends itself to rational men. How, to use the term proposed by Herbert Feigl and favored by Paul Taylor and others, can the judgment or choice we make be *vindicated?*[10] Two scientists may differ vigorously over whether Neptune can sustain life. But they can agree on the procedures to be employed for resolving their difference, that is to say, on what constitutes evidence that

would confirm or disconfirm the presence of life on that planet
and on how to go about getting such evidence. The case must
be similar in ethics.[11] If judgments in ethics are to have any
claim to objective status, it must be possible to justify them with
reasons—reasons, moreover, which no more here than in the
natural or behavioral sciences are a reflection of our personal
preference or bias, reasons which—it is perhaps not too paradoxical to urge—are in this sense *wertfrei* ("normatively-
neutral"). As such they can commend themselves to individuals
of differing bias and diverse preference. It must be agreed that
an adequate moral theory will enable us to understand how, in
Hare's words, "there can be useful and compelling moral argument even among people who have, before it begins, no substantive principles in common."[12] But, if this is to be accomplished, the principles employed for assessing the alternatives in
a problematic situation that is typically ethical must as H. W.
Stuart once insisted, when calling for a reversal of perspective
in ethical theory: *"First and last . . . renounce all thought or
purpose of present judgment upon the specific sorts of conduct
suggested to the individual as ways out of his perplexity."* We
must look, instead, "to the general character and status of the
authorities, the impulsions, and the appellant persons by which
the ways out are suggested."[13] I have argued that it is possible
in principle to determine the trustworthiness of such promptings
without intruding our prevailing biases or viewing them from
the standpoint of our present interests. And, if we often fall
short of complete objectivity, this is only slightly less true of the
quest for objectivity in the social sciences.

There is no difference in principle between giving up or
modifying one's present scheme of values in favor of another and
the kind of interpersonal persuasion to which Hare is referring
in the words just quoted. In both cases the dynamics are the
same: an initial suspension of judgment in a new situation that
has generated doubt of one's prevailing standards, the experimental adoption of other standpoints, their scrutiny with a view

to testing them for reliability or trustworthiness. The kind of case we make to others who do not share our values, i.e., the effort to resolve differences among those who have different value systems, will vary, of course, depending on whether the disagreement does or does not stem from different degrees of access to the relevant information. If it does, as noted earlier, persuasion will consist of citing the missing or neglected facts on the assumption that there is an underlying agreement concerning values; if it does not, persuasion will take the more difficult form involved in resolving a typically ethical problem. What we often find, of course, are situations in which we believe that differences in judgments of value can be resolved once all parties to the dispute know the facts, only to discover that the so-called facts are interpreted differently with a stubborn persistence that can only suggest a difference in basic values. At this point the dialogue need not stop. But the game will have changed and the moves will be different. Citing "facts" will be incidental. One will now speak in terms of a choice of principles to live by, of different kinds of selfhood, of alternatively possible systems of life and action; and of *viewing and criticizing each alternative from the standpoint of the other*, not, to be sure, in terms of their present appeal—terms which must necessarily favor one's prevailing preferences and arrest change —but in terms of their credentials, credentials open to critical inspection and yet honored as possibly leading to presently undiscerned and undiscernable values which the agent himself will come to prefer once he is in a position to appreciate them. This could be as true of groups with different patterns of culture as of individuals.

Professor Aiken might or might not accept the program proposed in the foregoing chapters for testing the reliability of the promptings to which we respond in a moral (in our terms, ethical) predicament, but words like the following provide welcome support for the view just expressed. After urging that we seek an understanding of moral objectivity by returning to the world of "work-a-day moral problems and judgment," he comments:

The principle of objectivity in morals is . . . essentially a principle of reconsideration. What it demands, when a question about the objectivity of a particular judgment or principle arises, is that we consider whether such a judgment or principle, as it stands, can be consistently upheld in the face of whatever other moral considerations might be thought, in conscience, to defeat it.[14]

It has been said more than once in the foregoing pages that ethicality is an achievement, not a native endowment. While here or there, even in the most hostile environment, a prophet may emerge, an Amos or Hosea, its attainment requires propitious conditions. Maturity is one of them. Freedom from the kind of grinding poverty that condemns everyone, or almost everyone, to an unremitting struggle for survival is another.[15] Ethicality can hardly emerge or survive under conditions—whose description I shall leave to social critics—that breed bigotry and fanaticism or generate total habituation to servitude and hopeless resignation to oppression. Social institutions that rest upon such a foundation subvert ethicality, as do institutions that promote or perpetuate exploitation, demand conformity, punish dissent. Totalitarian societies are no haven for that reciprocal interaction by means of which diverse views transform each other in the course of ethical deliberation.

It is at this point that one must at last come to grips with those who will cry "foul!" and charge that bias—in this case the bias of the "liberal" or "humanist" or "egalitarian"—is being palmed off as an objective ethic. After all, a society might warmly embrace Nietzsche's ideal of a world ruled by "higher" men who find their happiness in "hardness against themselves and others,"[16] spirits of "different calibre . . . rendered potent through wars and victories, to whom conquest, adventure, danger, even pain, have become a need,"[17] by the kind of "virile, noble natures" who were masters once of Rome[18] and reappeared all too briefly in the Renaissance man of *virtu*. The thought is not farfetched. Nietzsche did not have in mind the Nazi elite-guardists of the Third Reich, but they saw themselves reflected in his murky mirror and that is the kind of world the Nazis espoused before World War II. Had Germany won the war, as it nearly did, that view would have prevailed.

Two answers may be suggested. First, it is not held that the conditions referred to as indispensable to the emergence of ethical deliberation and the method of reevaluation implicit in it *ought* to prevail—only that, as a matter of fact, they must prevail *if* there are to be experiences to which the use of "ought" in an ethical sense is relevant. To say this is to make a descriptive (normatively neutral) statement; it is not to express a preference. It is not to make a value judgment of the kind expressed in the ethical predicates "good" or "right," but to indicate the conditions under which such value judgments must be made. To be sure, I may not only be citing such conditions, namely, a society in which there is freedom to dissent and in which servitude, oppression, and exploitation are minimized; *I* may find such conditions satisfying. I may find them good in any one of the four senses (aesthetic, prudential, moral, ethical) explored in the preceding chapters,[19] but that is incidental to the part *they* play in making ethical deliberation possible.

There is another answer to the charge of bias which addresses itself directly to the question of trans-cultural standards raised in our discussion of cultural relativity and its skeptical implications (Chapter one). A society in which such conditions are absent is simply not realizing its possibilities. The contention is that an authoritarian, closed society excludes its members from experiences which they would themselves prefer if only they came to know them. Contrary to Ruth Benedict, theirs is not an equally valid pattern of life (see above, p. 19), not even for them, because those who live in such a society have no way of validating it. Or, if the dialogue is interpersonal instead of trans-cultural, the contention is that the rigid, inflexible individual who refuses to reexamine his standards of value cuts himself off from experiences which he might himself find preferable if only he viewed his prevailing standards from the standpoints provided in an ethical problem. To say this is to say that before one can become a moral agent in the ethical sense he must, as Mead advised in another context, become an object to himself by taking the attitudes of others toward himself in the manifold ways that group life makes possible. Only so can he be open to all the possibilities of life.

I think it was Camus who said that, if goodness has no meaning, the world becomes absurd and men can tear each other to pieces. The world is often absurd and men do often destroy themselves as well as others because they have failed to find such meaning and are therefore spurred only by desire and bridled only by prudence. But many have found that goodness does have meaning, discovering it not in general and altogether vague principles (whether of happiness or self-realization), nor as an unanalyzable datum of immediate experience, nor in explicit moral codes or a revelation from on high. They have found it emerging as the creative outcome of a "good will" resolving in concrete situations to reckon with alternatives to one's prevailing values in the interest of a fuller life.

Notes

INTRODUCTION

Notes to pages 1–11.

1. Margaret Mead, *Coming of Age in Samoa* (New York: Penguin, 1943), pp. 143–144.
2. Charles Darwin, *The Origin of Species* (New York: Random House, Modern Library ed., 1936), p. 373.
3. Darwin, *Origin of Species*, pp. 101–102.
4. Charles Darwin, *The Descent of Man* (New York: Random House, Modern Library ed., 1936), p. 920.
5. The position described here is now known as "critical naturalism," as distinguished from the older reductionistic naturalism called "materialism." The latter would understand nature exclusively in terms of its physical manifestations; the former is pluralistic, refusing to reduce the biological, the psychological, and the social to the physical even though the physical may be temporally and causally antecedent. For a fuller account *cf.* Roy Wood Sellar's *Evolutionary Naturalism*, especially Chapter 1, or Harry Girvetz *et al., Science, Folklore, and Philosophy* (New York: Harper and Row, 1966), pp. 346–365.

6. R. N. Anshen (ed.), *Moral Principles of Action: Man's Ethical Imperative* (New York: Harper and Brothers, 1952), p. x.

CHAPTER ONE

Notes to pages 15–25.

1. See D. T. Campbell, "Distinguishing Differences of Perception from Failures of Communications in Cross-Cultural Studies," in F. S. C. Northrop and H. H. Livingston (eds.), *Cross-Cultural Understanding* (New York: Harper and Row, 1964), pp. 308–336.
2. William Graham Sumner, *Folkways* (Boston: Ginn, 1940), p. 58.
3. Melville Herskovits, *Man and His Works* (New York: Knopf, 1965), pp. 63, 76.
4. Richard Brandt, *Hopi Ethics* (Chicago: The University of Chicago Press, 1954), p. 11.
5. Ruth Benedict, *Patterns of Culture* (Boston and New York: Houghton Mifflin, 1934), p. 278.
6. Herskovits, *Man and His Works*, p. 76.
7. Benedict, *Patterns of Culture*, pp. 90–91.
8. We may also wish to question the "dignity" of practices brought to light the defense in a recent trial of six Colombian cowboys charged with the killing of sixteen nomadic Cuiba Indians whom they had asked in as guests. The Indians were slaughtered as they were eating. Two escaped to report the massacre to a priest. Five years later the cowboys were brought to trial. A news report describes one phase of the "equally valid pattern of life" of the Colombian cowboy:

   As Morin, now 33, put it: "For me, Indians are animals like deer or iguanas, except that deer don't damage our crops or kill our pigs. Since way back, Indian-hunting has been common practice in these parts." None of Morin's men suspected that they had done wrong. Marcelino Jimenez, 22, hiked for five days to a police outpost when he heard the authorities were looking for him. "If I had known that killing was a crime, I would not have wasted all that time walking just so they could lock me up," he explained during the trial. The cowboys cooperated fully with the investigating magistrate, helpfully supplying every detail of the massacre. "All I did was kill the little Indian girl and finish off two who were more dead than alive anyway," protested one of the defendants. "From childhood I have been told that everyone kills Indians. . . ."
   The defense lawyer's basic argument was that the government was unfairly trying to apply 20th century law to the *Ilaneros*, a swash-

buckling and primitive breed of cowhand, whose lives and attitudes have changed little since the days of Simon Bolivar. . . . One witness, an elderly trader, recalled that trappers used to offer him cured Indian skin along with crocodile hides and deer pelts. The Ilaneros even have a verb for Indian-hunting—*guahibiar* (which is derived from the name of another local Indian tribe, the Guahibo). (*Time*, July 10, 1972, p. 33.)

9. Clyde Kluckhohn, "Ethical Relativity: *Sic et Non*," *Journal of Philosophy*, vol. 52, p. 672, 1955.

10. Clyde Kluckhohn, "Values and Value Orientations in the Theory of Action," in *Toward a General Theory of Action*, Talcott Parsons and E. A. Shils (eds.) (Cambridge: Harvard, 1962), p. 417.

11. Ralph Linton, "Universal Ethical Principles: An Anthropological View," in R. N. Anshen, *Moral Principles of Action* (ed.) (New York and London: Harper, 1952), p. 646.

12. Herskovits, *Man and His Works*, p. 234.

13. F. J. Simoons, *Eat Not This Flesh* (Madison: The University of Wisconsin Press, 1961), p. 8.

14. S. E. Asch, "A Critique of the Psychology of Cultural Relativism," in Richard B. Brandt (ed.), *Value and Obligation* (New York: Harcourt, Brace & World, 1961), p. 483.

15. Ija Lazari-Pawlowska, "On Cultural Relativism," *Journal of Philosophy*, vol. 67, p. 580, 1970.

16. L. S. Feuer, *Psychoanalysis and Ethics* (Springfield, Ill.: Charles C Thomas, 1955), pp. 9–10.

17. Paul Taylor, "Social Science and Ethical Relativism," *Journal of Philosophy*, vol. 55, p. 33, 1958.

CHAPTER TWO

Notes to pages 26–46.

1. Friedrich Engels, *Herr Eugen Dühring's Revolution in Science* (New York: International Publishers), p. 300. (Better known as *Anti-Dühring*.)

2. Karl Marx, *A Contribution to the Critique of Political Economy* (Chicago: Charles H. Kerr), p. 11.

3. Friedrich Engels, *Anti-Dühring* in L. S. Feuer (ed.), *Marx and Engels Basic Writings* (Garden City, N.Y.: Anchor Books, 1959), p. 272. Engels's acuteness and the extent to which he adequately reflects the views of Marx is a subject of debate among

Marxian scholars. However, Engels read the full text of *Anti-Dühring* to Marx, and the latter gave it his unqualified approval.

4. R. H. Tawney, *Religion and the Rise of Capitalism* (New York: Harcourt, Brace, 1926), p. 61.

5. Plato, *Republic*, Cornford trans., VIII, 563.

6. Senator James H. Hammond, Speech in the U.S. Senate on the admission of Kansas, March 4, 1858. Reprinted in *Selections from the Letters and Speeches of the Hon. James H. Hammond* (New York: John F. Trow, 1866), pp. 318–321.

7. In this country, the most notable examples among men in high places were John Adams and John C. Calhoun.

8. Friedrich Engels, *Socialism: Utopian and Scientific* in *Marx and Engels Selected Works*, vol. II (Moscow: Foreign Languages Publishing House, 1951), p. 108.

9. Engels, *Socialism: Utopian and Scientific*, p. 110.

10. Reinhold Niebuhr, *Moral Man and Immoral Society* (New York: Scribner, 1932), p. 126.

11. John Dewey and James Tufts, *Ethics* (New York: Henry Holt and Co., 1936, rev. ed.), pp. 161–162.

12. Karl Marx, *The Eighteenth Brumaire of Louis Bonaparte* in *Marx and Engels Selected Works*, vol. I (Moscow: Foreign Languages Publishing House, 1951), pp. 249–250.

13. Karl Marx, *Capital* (Chicago: Charles H. Kerr, 1932), p. 15.

14. Friedrich Engels, Letter to Mehring, in *Marx and Engels Selected Correspondence* (New York: International Publishers, 1942), pp. 510–511.

15. Karl Marx and Friedrich Engels, *The German Ideology* (New York: International Publishers, 1960), pp. 14–15. Marx and Engels both later qualified this position in important ways. Thus Engels conceded the ideological superstructure may include a variety of ideological forms which are not equally subject to economic influence. For example, in a letter to Conrad Schmidt, he granted that law may have its own independent development: "In a modern state, law must not only correspond to the genera' economic position and be its expression, but must also be ar expression which is *consistent in itself,* and which does not, owing to inner contradictions, look glaringly inconsistent." (*Marx and Engels Selected Correspondence,* p. 481.) In a letter to M Starkenburg, he conceded that even philosophy and religion are determined by their prior manifestations and only indirectly an ultimately affected by economic factors. "It is not that the eco nomic position is the *cause and alone active,* while everythin else only has a passive effect. There is, rather, interaction on th

basis of the economic necessity, which *ultimately always asserts itself.*" (Engels to M. Starkenburg, *Selected Correspondence*, p. 517.) Even with art, Marx conceded in an unpublished introduction to the *Critique of Political Economy:* "It is well known that certain periods of highest development of art stand *in no direct connection* with the general development of society, nor with the material basis and the skeletal structure of its organization."

16. Karl Marx and Friedrich Engels, *The Manifesto of the Communist Party: Selected Works*, vol. I, pp. 41–42.

17. Engels, *Socialism: Utopian and Scientific*, p. 115.

18. V. Adoratskÿ (ed.), *Die Deutsche Ideologie, Marx-Engels Gesamtansgabe* (Moscow, 1933), Band 5, p. 227. Lenin, in an address (1920) to the Communist Youth League, declared: "We repudiate all morality taken apart from human society and classes . . . it is a fraud. Morality for us is subordinated to the interests of the class struggle of the proletariat . . ." N. Lenin, *Selected Works*, vol. II, pt. 2 (Moscow: Foreign Languages Publishing House, 1951), pp. 482–484, reprinted in S. Hook, *Marx and the Marxists* (Princeton, N.J.: Van Nostrand, 1955), pp. 195–196.

19. E. Kamenka, *Marxism and Ethics* (New York: Macmillan, 1969), pp. 11–12. Emphasis among scholars on his early works and the more "humanistic" Marx who had not yet become an avowed positivist is quite modish these days. The extent to which the views expressed in his early works continued to influence the mature Marx is a subject of debate among Marxist scholars. [*Cf.* Daniel Bell's "The 'Rediscovery' of Alienation; Some Notes along the Quest for the Historical Marx," *Journal of Philosophy*, vol. 56, pp. 933–952, 1959; E. Kamenka, *The Ethical Foundations of Marxism* (New York: Praeger, 1962).] Bell's verdict is that "it is only myth-making to read this concept [alienation] back as the central theme of Marx." (p. 935)

20. Karl Marx, *Theses on Feuerbach*, XI in L. S. Feuer, ed., *Basic Writings*, p. 245. An acute critic, Sidney Hook, has written: "Despite his refusal to appeal to ethical principles, Marx had a passionate sense of social justice which burns fiercely in everything he wrote. He would have scoffed at the idea that he was in line with the Hebrew prophets, but he sometimes spoke of the laws of history as if they were the decrees of Jehovah punishing a wicked society, and of the socialist revolution as if it were the catastrophic prelude to a new dispensation." *Marx and the Marxists* (Princeton, N.J.: Van Nostrand, 1955), p. 48.

21. Jean-Paul Sartre, "The Artist and His Conscience," reprinted in H. Girvetz and R. Ross (eds.), *Literature and the Arts: The Moral Issues* (Belmont, Cal.: Wadsworth, 1971), p. 154.

22. George Lukacs, *The Meaning of Contemporary Realism* (London: Merlin Press, 1963), p. 14.

23. Marx and Engels, *The German Ideology* (New York: International Publishers, 1960), p. 203.

24. *Cf.* Daniel Bell's "The 'Rediscovery' of Alienation: Some Notes along the Quest for the Historical Marx," *Journal of Philosophy,* vol. 56, n. 10, p. 941, 1959.

25. Karl Mannheim, *Ideology and Utopia* (New York: Harcourt, Brace, 1936), p. 49.

26. Mannheim, *Ideology and Utopia,* pp. 49–50.

27. Mannheim, *Ideology and Utopia,* p. 40.

28. Mannheim, *Ideology and Utopia,* p. 57.

29. Mannheim, *Ideology and Utopia,* pp. 82–83.

30. Mannheim, *Ideology and Utopia,* p. 40. As Mannheim uses the term, Marxists would be utopians. Marx uses the term in a completely different way to designate visionary socialists who fail to reckon with the dynamics of history.

31. Mannheim, *Ideology and Utopia,* p. 85.

32. Mannheim, *Ideology and Utopia,* p. 94.

33. Mannheim, *Ideology and Utopia,* pp. 2–3. Mannheim sometimes identifies the sociology of knowledge with the theory of ideology and sometimes differentiates them by assigning the latter the task of unmasking the "more or less *conscious* deceptions and disguises of human interest groups."

34. Mannheim, *Ideology and Utopia,* p. 4.

35. Mannheim, *Ideology and Utopia,* p. 5.

36. Mannheim, *Ideology and Utopia,* p. 31.

37. Mannheim, *Ideology and Utopia,* p. 41.

38. John C. Calhoun, *Congressional Debates,* vol. XIII, pt. I, 1836–1837, p. 566.

39. "Appeal from the New to the Old Whigs," in *The Writings and Speeches of Edmund Burke,* IV, Beaconsfield Edition (London: Bickers and Sons Ltd., 1901), pp. 174–175. Burke was referring, he says, to a natural aristocracy, including, it will be noted, the "professor of high science" and the "rich trader," but it was, using Jefferson's distinction, an artificial aristocracy that he was defending—the aristocrats composing the House of Lords and the French aristocracy, the overwhelming majority of whom were not professors of "high" or any other kind of science. Although he believed that virtue and wisdom should be recognized wherever they are found, "the road to eminence and power, from obscure condition, ought not to be made too easy, nor a thing too much

of course." (*Reflections on the Revolution in France, Writings and Speeches,* III, p. 297.)

CHAPTER THREE

Notes to pages 47–66.

1. See below, p. 70ff. Freud was untroubled by such comparisons. "It is of no concern to us . . .," he wrote, "to enquire how far, with this hypothesis of the pleasure principle, we have approached or adopted any particular, historically established, philosophical system." [*Beyond the Pleasure Principle* in J. Strachey (ed.), *Complete Psychological Works of Sigmund Freud* (London: Hogarth, 1953–1966), vol. XVIII, p. 7.]

2. Freud, *Civilization and Its Discontents,* in Strachey (ed.), *Complete Works,* vol. XXI, p. 76 (Garden City, N.Y.: Doubleday Anchor, 1958), p. 16.

3. Freud, *Introductory Lectures on Psychoanalysis,* in Strachey (ed.), *Complete Works,* vol. XVI, Lecture 22, p. 356.

4. Alasdair MacIntyre, "Sigmund Freud," *Encyclopedia of Philosophy,* vol. 3 (New York: Macmillan, 1967), p. 252a.

5. Freud, *Beyond the Pleasure Principle* (1920), in Strachey (ed.), vol. XVIII, p. 10 (New York: Bantam, 1959), p. 26.

6. Freud, *Beyond the Pleasure Principle,* p. 20.

7. Freud, *Beyond the Pleasure Principle,* p. 23.

8. Freud, *Beyond the Pleasure Principle,* p. 38.

9. Freud, *Beyond the Pleasure Principle,* p. 24.

10. Freud, *Beyond the Pleasure Principle,* p. 59.

11. Freud, *New Introductory Lectures,* in J. Strachey (ed.), *Complete Works,* vol. XXII, p. 107.

12. Ernest Jones, *The Life and Work of Sigmund Freud* (New York: Basic Books, 1961), pp. 265–280; J. C. Flugel, *Man, Morals, and Society* (New York: Viking, 1961), p. 102. *Cf.* also Clara Thompson, *Psychoanalysis: Evolution and Development* (New York: Hermitage House, 1951), Chapter 2; William McDougall, *Psychoanalysis and Social Psychology* (London: Methuen, 1936), Appendix III.

13. Dr. Heinz Hartmann, former President of the International Psychoanalytic Association, commenting on the three types of pleasure gratification associated with the id, ego, and the superego, concedes that, although these are of different kinds, "This is . . . one of the difficulties that besets every hedonistic philosophy." He

adds: "It would seem promising to attempt for this and for other reasons, a qualitative differentiation of pleasure experiences. Such an attempt Freud has not made." Dr. Hartmann believes that such a project "would not . . . be incompatible with his [Freud's] later formulations of the pleasure principle." [*Psychoanalysis and Moral Values* (New York: International Universities Press, 1960), p. 36.] But it would surely be as difficult for Freud as it was for J. S. Mill (see below, pp. 82–83) to differentiate morally among pleasures, if that is what "qualitative differentiation" implies.

14. Freud, *New Introductory Lectures*, in Strachey (ed.), *Complete Works*, vol. XXII, p. 73.

15. Freud, *Civilization and Its Discontents*, in Strachey (ed.), *Complete Works*, vol. XXI, p. 124.

16. Freud, *New Introductory Lectures*, in Strachey (ed.), *Complete Works*, vol. XXII, p. 93.

17. Karen Horney, *New Ways in Psychoanalysis* (New York: Norton, 1939), p. 187.

18. Erich Fromm, *Man for Himself* (New York: Rinehart, 1947), p. 7.

19. Freud, *Civilization and Its Discontents*, in Strachey (ed.), *Complete Works*, vol. XXI, p. 145.

20. Fromm, *Man for Himself*, p. 6.

21. Ernst L. Freud (ed.), *Letters of Sigmund Freud* (New York: Basic Books, 1969), p. 436.

22. Philip Rieff, *The Triumph of the Therapeutic* (New York: Harper & Row, 1966), p. 38.

23. The better known works in which Freud concerned himself with culture are *Totem and Taboo* (1912), *Civilization and Its Discontents* (1930), *Moses and Monotheism* (1939). For an examination of the whole issue as it pertains to Freud, see the discussions of Abram Kardiner, Ernest van den Haag, and Alex Inkeles in S. Hook (ed.), *Psychoanalysis, Scientific Method and Philosophy* (New York: New York University Press, 1959), pp. 81–128.

24. Herbert Marcuse, *Eros and Civilization* (New York: Vintage Press, 1962), p. 229.

25. Franz Alexander, Introduction to Freud's *Group Psychology and the Analysis of the Ego* (New York: Bantam, 1960), pp. xvi–xvii.

26. The criticism is directed against Professor Abram Kardiner's remark that "Freud was trapped by his earliest assumptions; and when it came to including the environmental factor in the frame of reference, he found there was just no room for it. He therefore ascribed to the [social] environmental factor a coincidental role." ("Social and Cultural Implications of Psychoanalysis," *Psychoanalysis, Scientific Method and Philosophy*, p. 89.)

27. Ernest van den Haag, "Psychoanalysis and Its Discontents," *Psychoanalysis, Scientific Method and Philosophy*, p. 106.

28. Hans Meyerhoff, "Freud and the Ambiguity of Culture," *Partisan Review*, Winter 1957, pp. 117–130. *Cf.* also Dennis H. Wrong, "The Over-Socialized Conception of Man," *American Sociological Review*, vol. 26, pp. 183–193 (April, 1961).

29. Freud, *Group Psychology and the Analysis of the Ego*, in Strachey (ed.), *Complete Works*, vol. XVIII, p. 69.

30. Freud, *Group Psychology*, p. 70.

31. Freud, *Group Psychology*, p. 124.

32. C. S. Hall and G. Lindzey, "Psychoanalytic Theory and Its Application to the Social Sciences," *Handbook of Social Psychology* (Reading, Mass.: Addison-Wesley, 1954), p. 166.

33. See Freud's *Leonardo da Vinci, A Study in Psychosexuality*, a striking example of analysis *in absentia*.

34. Hall and Lindzey, "Psychoanalytic Theory and Its Application to the Social Sciences," p. 167.

35. Freud, *Civilization and Its Discontents*, in Strachey (ed.), *Complete Works*, vol. XXI, pp. 113–114. (My emphasis.)

36. Freud, *The Complete Introductory Lectures on Psychoanalysis*, J. Strachey (trans.) (New York: Norton, 1966), Lecture 33, p. 598.

37. See Freud's *Totemism and Taboo* (1912–1913), in Strachey (ed.), *Complete Works*, vol. XIII. He recurs to this theme in *Group Psychology and the Analysis of the Ego*, Chapter X (1921), in *Complete Works*, vol. XVIII.

38. "The Influence of Sigmund Freud Upon Sociology in the United States," *American Journal of Sociology*, XLV, no. 3, pp. 356–374, November, 1939.

39. Philip Rieff, *Freud: The Mind of the Moralist* (Garden City, N.Y.: Doubleday, 1961), p. 275.

40. Meyerhoff, "Freud and the Ambiguity of Culture," p. 117.

41. See Chapters 1 and 7 of my *Evolution of Liberalism*. As I point out there Bentham was so dominated by such an orientation "that he could offer his services as a lawmaker, after scant concessions to the 'influence of time and place,' to such disparate peoples as the English, the Russians, and the Latin Americans. Underneath the differences wrought by ancient custom and rooted habit there apparently resides a natural man whose fundamental sameness renders him equally amenable to the legislative wisdom of a Benthamite whether he resides in Cambridge or the Cameroons." (New York: Collier, 1950), p. 44.

42. Freud, *Civilization and Its Discontents,* in Strachey (ed.), *Complete Works,* vol. XXI, p. 144.

43. The anti-psychologism of Emile Durkheim, whose classical study, *Suicide,* is generally regarded as having initiated the modern science of sociology, is expressed in injunctions such as the following: *"The determining cause of a social fact should be sought among the social facts preceding it and not among the states of the individual consciousness."* [*The Rules of Sociological Method* (New York: Free Press, 1964), p. 110.]

    Alfred L. Kroeber, in an influential article, "The Superorganic," while unfortunately hypostatizing the social by calling it a "substance," thought of social evolution as "A new factor . . . which was to work out its own independent consequences" and urged that "Civilization as such begins only where the individual ends; and whoever does not in some measure perceive this fact . . . can find no meaning in civilization, and history for him must be only a weary jumble or an opportunity for the exercise of art." (*American Anthropologist,* XIX [1917], pp. 193, 208–209.

44. See Freud, *Group Psychology and the Analysis of the Ego,* in Strachey (ed.), *Complete Works,* vol. XVIII, pp. 93ff.,

45. Freud, *The Ego and the Id,* in Strachey (ed.), *Complete Works,* vol. XIX, p. 54.

46. Shakespeare recurs to this theme in *Lear:*

> Thou rascally beadle, hold thy bloody hand!
> Why dost thou lash that whore? Strip thine own back;
> Thou hotly lust'st to use her in that kind
> For which thou whipp'st her . . .

47. Freud, *The Ego and the Id,* p. 54. (My emphasis.)

48. Ernest Jones, "The Genesis of the Superego," in Clara Thompson *et al.* (ed.), *An Outline of Psychoanalysis* (New York: Random House, Modern Library ed., 1955), p. 39.

49. Jones, "The Genesis of the Superego," p. 42.

50. George H. Mead, *Mind, Self, and Society* (Chicago: The University of Chicago Press, 1934), p. 255. (My emphasis.)

51. Herbert Fingarette, *The Self in Transformation* (New York: Basic Books, 1963), pp. 146–147.

52. Fingarette, *The Self in Transformation,* p. 154.

53. Freud, *The Future of an Illusion,* in Strachey (ed.), *Complete Works,* vol. XXI, p. 53.

54. Freud, *The Complete Introductory Lectures,* Lecture 9, pp. 146–147.

55. Morris Ginsberg, *On the Diversity of Morals* (London: William Heinemann, 1956), p. 68.

56. Merton Gill, "The Present State of Psychoanalytic Theory," *Journal of Abnormal and Social Psychology,* vol. 58, pp. 1–2.

57. Alfred L. Kroeber, "Totem and Taboo in Retrospect," *The American Journal of Sociology,* vol. XLV, p. 446, 1939–1940.

58. Gill, "The Present State of Psychoanalytic Theory," p. 7.

59. See, for example, his distinction in *Man For Himself* between an "authoritarian" conscience and the "humanistic" conscience, the latter characterized not as the superego of Freudian theory, but as an "expression of our true selves," as "our own voice . . . independent of external rewards and sanctions," as "the reaction of our total personality to its proper functioning or dysfunctioning," (p. 158).

CHAPTER FOUR

Notes to pages 67–85.

1. W. J. Oates (ed.), *The Stoic and Epicurean Philosophers* (New York: Random House, 1940), p. 35.

2. Jeremy Bentham, *Introduction to the Principles of Morals and Legislation,* in J. Bowring (ed.), *The Works of Jeremy Bentham,* I (Edinburgh: W. Tait, 1838–1843), 1ff.

3. The full passage runs as follows:

   The only proof capable of being given that an object is visible, is that people actually see it. The only proof that a sound is audible, is that people hear it. . . . In a like manner, I apprehend the sole evidence it is possible to produce that anything is desirable is that people do actually desire it. J. S. Mill, *Utilitarianism* in Samuel Gorovitz (ed.), *Critical Essays* (New York: Bobbs-Merrill, 1971), Ch. IV.

   It has often been pointed out that Mill achieved plausibility for his statement because of its ambiguity. "Visible" means capable of being seen; "desirable" could mean capable of being desired but is almost always used to mean ought to be desired, so that there is no real analogy between the two terms as Mill supposed. Great minds sometimes fall into simple errors.

4. B. F. Skinner, *Beyond Freedom and Dignity* (New York: Knopf, 1971), p. 107.

5. As Dewey noted,

The self, like its vital basis the organism, is always active; . . . it acts by its very constitution, and hence needs no external promise of reward or threat of evil to induce it to act. . . . Observation of a child, even a young baby, will convince the observer that a normal human being when awake is engaged in activity; he is a reservoir of energy that is continually overflowing. The organism moves, reaches, handles, pulls, pounds, tears, molds, crumples, looks, listens, etc. . . . nothing is more intolerable to a healthy human being than enforced passivity over a long period. It is not action that needs to be accounted for, but rather the cessation of activity. Dewey and Tufts, *Ethics* (New York: Henry Holt, rev. ed., 1932), p. 320.

6. *Principles of Morals and Legislation,* Ch. IV, iv.

7. S. C. Pepper, "The Equivocation of Value," *University of California Publications in Philosophy,* vol. 4, p. 110, 1923. For a discussion of the difference between the older hedonism and contemporary theories of value, see R. B. Perry, *General Theory of Value* (Cambridge, Mass.: Harvard University Press, 1926, 1950), pp. 606–609; and George Santayana, *Life of Reason,* I (New York: Scribner's, 1932), pp. 237–238.

8. R. B. Perry, *General Theory of Value* (New York: Longmans, 1926), pp. 115–116.

9. Perry, *General Theory of Value,* p. 307. Cf. Perry, "The Independent Variability of Purpose and Belief," *Journal of Philosophy,* vol. 18, pp. 169–180, 1921.

10. David Prall, "A Study in Theory of Value," *University of California Publications in Philosophy,* vol. 3:2, p. 216, 1921.

11. Perry, *General Theory of Value,* p. 128.

12. For a more detailed discussion of differing views concerning "valuing" and "evaluating," including those held by C. I. Lewis, John Dewey *et al.,* see Paul Taylor's *Normative Ethics* (Englewood Cliffs, N.J.: Prentice-Hall, 1961), especially Part I.

13. Perry, *General Theory of Value,* p. 179. (His emphasis.)

14. Perry, *General Theory of Value,* pp. 357–358.

15. Perry, *General Theory of Value,* p. 308. The statement raises the issue as to whether judgments are part of the structure of interests or a causal antecedent. The equivocation is unfortunate, inasmuch as a decision on this issue would necessarily have wide implications.

16. Perry, *General Theory of Value,* p. 318.

17. David Prall, "The Present Status of Theory of Value," *University of California Publications in Philosophy,* vol. 4, p. 84, 1923.

18. Thomas Hobbes, *The Leviathan,* Part I, Ch. VI.

19. Spinoza, *Ethics,* Pt. III, Prop. IX, Note.

20. Prall, "Present Status of Theory of Value," p. 94.
21. Prall, "A Study in the Theory of Value," *University of California Publications in Philosophy,* vol. 3:2, pp. 199–200, 1921.
22. Prall, "A Study in the Theory of Value," p. 201.
23. Prall, "Present Status of Theory of Value," p. 95.
24. Perry, *General Theory of Value,* p. 629. "Observe," noted Dewey, "that the . . . theory of Robinson, Perry and Prall implies a denial of the genuine reality of doubt, uncertainty. It holds that it is a mere seeming, due to a personal failure to reduce the present case to the proper combination of old ones." ("Valuation and Experimental Knowledge," *Philosophical Review,* vol. 31, p. 335, 1922.)
25. Max Otto, "Morality as Coercion and Persuasion," *International Journal of Ethics,* vol. 31, p. 11, 1920–1921.
26. Prall, "A Study in the Theory of Value," p. 263. Prall refers here to the "culture" or technical training of the well-schooled and consequently sensitive artist. *Cf.* his *Aesthetic Judgment* (New York: Crowell, 1929), e.g., p. 327, and "The Esthetic Heresy," *Journal of Philosophy,* vol. 18, pp. 516–526, 1921.
27. Prall, "A Study in the Theory of Value," p. 257.
28. Prall, "A Study in the Theory of Value," p. 257. Professor Perry's statement is somewhat clearer. Even though mistaken interests are *"none the less* valuable" and objects of correct interests are not as such better than objects of incorrect interests, Perry employs the "principle of correctness" as a basis according to which values may be graded for the reason that "a mistaken interest is relatively unstable because of the likelihood that the subject will sooner or later be convinced of his error." (*General Theory of Value,* p. 614; see also the preceding and following pages, 611–615.) Perry employs the principle in rather a different context than that here engaging the attention of Prall. Prall is attempting —and quite properly, if inconsistently—to distinguish between the value judgments of the expert and of the neophyte. In doing so, he employs a qualifying term (higher), of which we can only surmise that Prall avails himself because of the connotation which the term carries over from a philosophy of value which he explicitly rejects. Presumably the judgment of a novice is bad, i.e., wrong, as he will come to see when he acquires experience. Perry employs the principle of correctness to grade interests on the basis of the truth or falsity of the mediating judgment. To mistakenly suppose that this painting is a Titian appears to be rather different than to mistakenly like the work of a bad, not really competent or good painter. But just as the latter in the use of these epithets begs the question in presupposing a way of determining the valuableness of objects (which is what grading of value amounts to)

in which more than *merely* liking is involved, so does the former. Even though I may have falsely judged this painting to be a Titian, I value it. Why should that value be at the mercy of the possibility of my discovering that some obscure Venetian painted it instead (provided, of course, it is not its monetary value I prize rather than the painting), unless the determination of such possibilities is more intrinsic to valuableness than spokesmen of the interest theory can in all strictness admit. Factual compulsion does lead them to such admissions. There *is* the instability which Perry notes. But it needs to be explained as well as noted and such explanations will require a revised conception of the nature of value.

29. Prall, "A Study in the Theory of Value," p. 258.

30. Mill, *Utilitarianism*, Ch. II.

31. Mill, *Utilitarianism*, Ch. II.

32. This failure is even more obvious in the writings of other sponsors of this theory of value. Professor DeWitt Parker writes, ". . . while desires are never generically evil, they are sometimes morally evil. They are morally evil when they frustrate desires on a higher [*sic*] level than themselves, desires such as love and ambition. As opposed to love, for example, cruelty is evil; as opposed to ambition, sloth is evil. But apart from relation to such interests of higher order, it is meaningless to speak of immoral desires." ("Value as Any Object of Any Interest," *International Journal of Ethics*, vol. 40, p. 470, 1930. My emphasis.) It would seem that Mill's classical blunder has been corrected in vain.

33. Perry, *General Theory of Value*, pp. 134–135.

34. Perry, *Realms of Value* (Cambridge, Mass.: Harvard University Press, 1954), p. 92.

35. John Dewey, *Quest for Certainty* (New York: Minton, Balch, 1929), p. 258.

CHAPTER FIVE

Notes to pages 86–101.

1. Wittgenstein, *Tractatus Logico-philosophicus* (London: Rutledge and Kegan Paul, 1961), 4, 112.

2. Wittgenstein, *Philosophical Investigations* (New York: Macmillan, 1958), 38.

3. Wittgenstein, *Investigations*, 109.

4. Rudolf Carnap, "The Elimination of Metaphysics Through Logical Analysis of Language," in A. J. Ayer (ed.), *Logical Positivism* (New York: Free Press, 1959), p. 61.

5. Carnap, "The Elimination of Metaphysics," p. 69.

6. Cited by Carnap, "The Elimination of Metaphysics," p. 73.

7. Carnap, "The Elimination of Metaphysics," p. 76.

8. In the early formulations of the verifiability principle by logical positivists, this meant, in F. Waismann's view, that unless a statement can be verified conclusively it is devoid of meaning; or, modified significantly, as by C. G. Hempel, that a sentence has cognitive meaning only if it is translatable into empiricist language, i.e., a language the terms of which designate properties that are in principle observable. (See "The Verifiability Principle," *Encyclopedia of Philosophy*, vol. 8, pp. 240–246.)

9. That is, "What we mean when we invoke the predicate concept (in an analytic judgment) is already included in what we mean by the subject concept." (D. W. Hamlyn, "Analytic and Synthetic Statements," *Encyclopedia of Philosophy*, vol. I, p. 106a.)

10. H. Reichenbach, *Elements of Symbolic Logic* (New York: Macmillan, 1947), p. 17.

11. Reichenbach, *Elements of Symbolic Logic*, p. 17. Words may be considered in their (a) *semantic*, (b) *syntactic*, or (c) *pragmatic* aspect. The first concerns what the word stands for, the second its relation to other words, the third the purpose of its user.

12. A. J. Ayer, *Language, Truth and Logic* (New York: Dover, 1952), p. 107.

13. Ayer, *Language, Truth and Logic*, p. 109.

14. A. J. Ayer, "On the Analysis of Moral Judgments," *Philosophical Essays* (New York: Macmillan, 1954), p. 237.

15. A. P. Brogan, "A Criticism of Mr. A. J. Ayer's Revised Account of Moral Judgments," *Journal of Philosophy*, vol. 56, p. 272, 1959.

16. C. L. Stevenson, "The Emotive Meaning of Ethical Terms," in A. J. Ayer (ed.), *Logical Positivism*, p. 269.

17. Stevenson, "The Emotive Meaning of Ethical Terms," p. 269. (His emphasis.)

18. Stevenson, "The Emotive Meaning of Ethical Terms," p. 273.

19. C. L. Stevenson, *Facts and Values* (New Haven: Yale, 1963), pp. 1–2.

20. Plato, *Republic*, Cornford trans., VI, 492.

21. Joseph Margolis, "On the Ethical Defense of Violence and Destruction," in V. Held *et all.* (ed.), *Philosophy and Political Action* (New York: Oxford, 1972), pp. 70–71.

CHAPTER SIX

Notes to pages 105–116.

1. H. A. Prichard, "Does Moral Philosophy Rest on a Mistake?," *Mind,* vol. 21, pp. 27–28, 1912. Reprinted in *Readings in Ethical Theory,* W. Sellars and J. Hospers, eds. (New York: Appleton-Century-Crofts, 1970), 2nd ed., pp. 86–96; *Ethical Theories,* A. I. Melden, ed. (Englewood Cliffs, N.J., Prentice-Hall, 1967), pp. 526–538.

2. Prichard, "Does Moral Philosophy Rest on a Mistake?," p. 37.

3. Later to become Sir David Ross, the distinguished editor of the Oxford edition of the works of Aristotle.

4. Sir David Ross, *The Right and the Good* (Oxford: The Clarendon Press, 1930), p. 17.

5. Ross, *The Right and the Good,* p. 39.

6. Ross, *The Right and the Good,* p. 19.

7. Ross, *The Right and the Good,* p. 19.

8. Ross, *The Right and the Good,* p. 19.

9. Dewey, *Ethics,* p. 304.

10. G. E. Moore, *Principia Ethica* (Cambridge: Cambridge University Press, 1903), p. 6.

11. Moore, *Principia Ethica,* p. 7.

12. Moore, *Principia Ethica,* p. viii.

13. G. E. Moore, *Ethics* (New York: Oxford, 1965), p. 83.

14. Moore's utilitarianism is sometimes called "ideal utilitarianism" to distinguish it from the hedonistic utilitarianism of Bentham and Mill.

15. See Moore, *Principia,* pp. 40–41.

16. For an extensive discussion of Moore's ethical views, including his defense of them from criticisms such as those cited above, see P. A. Schilpp (ed.), *The Philosophy of G. E. Moore* (Evanston: Northwestern University Press, 1942).

17. R. M. Hare, *The Language of Morals* (New York: Oxford 1964), p. 72.

18. G. Warnock, *Contemporary Moral Philosophy* (London: Macmillan, 1967), p. 7.

CHAPTER SEVEN

Notes to pages 117–126.

1. R. M. Hare, *Freedom and Reason* (London: Oxford, 1963), p. 2. See also *Language of Morals* (New York: Oxford, 1952), p. 31.
2. Hare, *Language of Morals,* p. 13.
3. Hare, *Language of Morals,* p. 25.
4. Hare, *Language of Morals,* p. 40.
5. In a famous paragraph of *A Treatise on Human Nature* (1739) Hume remarks on authors who make observations concerning human affairs, "When of a sudden I am surpriz'd to find, that instead of the usual copulations of propositions, *is,* and *is not,* I meet with no proposition that is not connected with an *ought,* or an *ought not . . .* as this *ought,* or *ought not,* express some new relation or affirmation, 'tis necessary that it shou'd be observ'd and explain'd; and at the same time that a reason should be given, for what seems altogether inconceivable, how this new relation can be a deduction from others, which are entirely different from it." To take this precaution, Hume adds "would subvert all the vulgar systems of morality." T. H. Green and T. H. Grose (eds.), *Philosophical Works* vol. 2 (Scientia Verlag Aalen, 1964) Book III, Pt. I, Sec. I, pp. 245–246.
6. Hare, *Freedom and Reason,* p. 2.
7. Hare, *Language of Morals,* p. 28.
8. Hegel, *Philosophy of Law,* cited by Karl Popper in *The Open Society and Its Enemies* (Princeton, N.J.: Princeton, 1950), p. 263.
9. Kant, *Perpetual Peace* (New York: Columbia, 1939), p. 51.
10. "The truth in naturalism is that moral terms do indeed have descriptive meaning. It is not the only element in their meaning, and it is therefore misleading to refer to it, as do the naturalists, as *the* meaning of a moral term; but in view of possessing this descriptive meaning moral judgments are universalizable, and naturalism has the merit of implying this." Hare, *Freedom and Reason,* p. 21.
11. Hare, *Freedom and Reason,* p. 12.
12. Hare, *Language of Morals,* p. 177.
13. Hare, *Freedom and Reason,* p. 30.
14. Hare, *Freedom and Reason,* pp. 89–90.
15. Hare, *Freedom and Reason,* p. 18.

16. Hare, *Freedom and Reason*, p. 5.
17. G. Warnock, *Contemporary Moral Philosophy* (London: Macmillan, 1967), pp. 43–44.

CHAPTER EIGHT

Notes to pages 127–139.

1. John Dewey, "The Need for a Recovery in Philosophy," in *Creative Intelligence* (New York: Holt, 1917), pp. 7–8.
2. Dewey, *Reconstruction in Philosophy* (New York: Henry Holt and Co., 1920), p. 87.
3. Dewey, *The Quest for Certainty* (New York: Minton, 1929), pp. 166–167.
4. Dewey, *Reconstruction in Philosophy*, p. 156.
5. Dewey, "In Reply to Some Criticisms," *Journal of Philosophy*, vol. 27, p. 273, 1930.
6. Dewey, *Quest for Certainty*, p. 274.
7. Dewey, *Experience and Nature* (New York: Norton, 1925), p. 130.
8. Dewey, *Experience and Nature*, p. 154.
9. Dewey, *Experience and Nature*, p. 157.

That a perception is cognitive means, accordingly, that it is used; it is treated as a sign of conditions that implicate other as yet unperceived consequences in addition to the perception itself. That a perception is *truly* cognitive means that its active use or treatment is followed by consequences which fit it appropriately into the other consequences which follow independently of its being perceived. (*Quest for Certainty*, p. 323.)

10. Dewey, "Valuation and Experimental Knowledge," *Philosophical Review*, vol. 31, p. 329, 1922.
11. Dewey, *Experience and Nature*, p. 398.
12. Dewey, "Valuation and Experimental Knowledge," p. 329.
13. Dewey, "Valuation and Experimental Knowledge," p. 332.
14. Dewey and Tufts, *Ethics* (New York: Henry Holt and Company, rev. ed., 1932), p. 291.
15. Dewey, "The Logic of Judgments of Practice," *Journal of Philosophy*, vol. 12, p. 516, 1915.
16. Dewey, "The Objects of Valuation," *Journal of Philosophy*, vol. 15, p. 254, 1918.

17. Dewey, *Quest for Certainty*, p. 261.
18. Dewey, *Quest for Certainty*, p. 263.
19. Dewey, *Ethics* (New York: Henry Holt, 1st ed., 1908), pp. 206–207. (All other references are to the revised editions) I prefer this formulation to the version in the revised *Ethics* (pp. 173–175).
20. Dewey, *Reconstruction in Philosophy*, p. 165.
21. Dewey, *Reconstruction in Philosophy*, p. 174.
22. H. Hartmann, *Psychoanalysis and Moral Values* (New York: International Universities Press, Inc., 1960), pp. 39–40.
23. This is the essence of the acute criticism of Dewey's ethical theory written for the Dewey volume of the Library of Living Philosophers (Evanston and Chicago: Northwestern University Press, 1939), pp. 293–333, by H. W. Stuart.
24. Dewey, *Ethics*, rev. ed., p. 422.
25. Dewey, *Quest for Certainty*, p. 259.
26. Dewey, *Quest for Certainty*, p. 273.
27. Dewey, *Quest for Certainty*, p. 274.
28. Dewey, *Ethics*, p. 302.
29. George Geiger, *John Dewey in Perspective* (New York: McGraw-Hill, 1958), p. 102.
30. Dewey, *Quest for Certainty*, p. 273.
31. "On this level" is an interesting qualification suggesting a belief that there are levels at which we ought not to feel compelled "to follow the law as it is on our books."

CHAPTER NINE

Notes to pages 143–152.

1. A number of distinguished social scientists, e.g., Weber and Cooley, would say that, quite apart from ethics and its subject matter, this must be true of all the social sciences. In a widely quoted passage R. M. MacIver writes that those who defend the behaviorist or "objective" position in social science:

fail to perceive the essential difference from the standpoint of causation, between a flying paper before the wind and a man flying before a pursuing crowd. The paper knows no fear and the wind no hate, but without fear and hate the man would not fly nor the crowd pursue. If we try to reduce it to its bodily concomitants we merely substitute the concomitants for the reality expressed as fear. We denude the world of meaning for the sake of a theory . . . [*Society: An Introductory Analysis,* new edition with C. H. Page (New York: Rinehart, 1949), p. 628.]

2. "Evil" seems to have dropped out of favor among ethicists as a synonym for "bad," probably because of its dogmatic overtones, a fate which has also befallen "virtue."

3. I share Mr. Hare's view that "A judgment is not moral if it does not provide . . . a *reason* for *doing* something." (*The Language of Morals,* p. 31. My emphasis.) This view is defended in differing ways by such writers as Kurt Baier (*The Moral Point of View; A Rational Basis for Ethics,* Ithaca, N.Y.: Cornell University Press, and Stephen Toulmin (*The Place of Reason in Ethics,* Cambridge, Mass.: The University Press, 1950).

4. See Professor Paul W. Taylor's discussion of the difference in his *Normative Discourse* (Englewood Cliffs, N.J., Prentice-Hall, 1961), pp. 72–76.

5. G. J. Warnock, *Contemporary Moral Philosophy* (London: Macmillan, 1967) p. 76.

6. His play, *The Crucible,* was obviously inspired by this experience.

7. C. A. Baylis, "Grading, Values, and Choice," *Mind,* vol. 67, p. 487, 1958. It is not necessary for my purpose to linger here for a discussion of the already thoroughly explored distinction between "comparisons" and "ranking" (Baier, *The Moral Point of View,* pp. 11ff.) or, to use Paul Taylor's nomenclature, "grading" and "ranking" (*Normative Discourse,* pp. 5–9.)

8. Alexander Sesonske, *Value and Obligation* (New York: Oxford, 1964), p. 12. On the other hand, a work such as Paul W. Taylor's *Normative Discourse* with its wealth of subtle distinctions is an important contribution to value theory that fills in the gaps left by those of us who work with a broader brush.

CHAPTER TEN

Notes to pages 153–160.

1. Dewey, *Ethics,* rev. ed., p. 316.

2. The conjunctives suggest that ambiguities lurk here. Does value attach to the water that quenches my thirst, i.e., to the *object of* interest; to the satisfaction of the interest or the feeling I have

when I quench my thirst, which some would call the objective of interest distinguished from the object; or, to the interest itself, that is, the anticipation of fulfillment, whether designated in motor (behavioral) or motor-affective terms? *Cf.* De Witt Parker, "Value as Any Object of Any Interest," *International Journal of Ethics,* vol. XL, pp. 465–473, July, 1930. For R. B. Perry, for example, value is constituted by the interest itself, not its satisfaction. Homer Dubs reminds us that in an earlier book (*The Moral Economy*) Perry identified value with the actual state of fulfillment or satisfaction of a particular interest. However, I am not interested here in resolving these ambiguities.

3. Dewey, *Ethics,* p. 212.

4. David Prall, "A Study in Theory of Value," *University of California Publications in Philosophy,* vol. 3, p. 201, 1921. Santayana has remarked that our aesthetic judgment "is necessarily intrinsic and based on the character of immediate experience, and never consciously on the idea of an eventual utility in the object." [*The Sense of Beauty* (New York: Scribner, 1936), p. 20.]

5. David Prall, "Value and Thought Process," *Journal of Philosophy,* vol. 21, p. 122, 1924.

6. Involved here, of course, is an issue of central importance—the relation of art and morals. For a systematic exploration of this issue, see Harry Girvetz and Ralph Ross (eds.), *Literature and the Arts: The Moral Issues* (Belmont, Cal.: Wadsworth, 1971).

7. Dewey, *Ethics,* p. 211.

8. See my *Evolution of Liberalism,* Chapters 1, 7.

9. Sidney Zink, "The Moral Effect of Art," *Ethics,* vol. LX, pp. 261–274, 1950, reprinted in E. Vivas and M. Krieger (eds.), *The Problems of Aesthetics* (New York: Rinehart, 1953), pp. 545–561.

10. Immanuel Kant, *Fundamental Principles of the Metaphysic of Morals,* T. K. Abbott (trans.), Library of Liberal Arts ed. (New York: Bobbs-Merrill, 1949), p. 59.

CHAPTER ELEVEN

Notes to pages 161–175.

1. See Hugo Bedau's useful discussion of this distinction as it pertains to military service in his "Military Service and Moral Obligation," in V. Held *et al.* (eds.), *Philosophy and Political Action* (New York: Oxford, 1972), p. 135.

2. Immanuel Kant, "So act as to treat humanity, whether in thine own person or in that of any other, in every case as an end withal, never as a means only." (*Fundamental Principles of the Metaphysic of Morals*, p. 46.) (See notes for Chapter 10.)

3. It is difficult not to agree with H. L. A. Hart who finds it "absurd to speak of having a moral duty not to kill another human being or an obligation not to torture a child." ("Legal and Moral Obligation," reprinted in A. I. Melden's *Essays in Moral Philosophy* [Seattle: University of Washington Press, 1958], p. 82.) One wonders why Professor Hart limited himself to the torture of *children!* In any case (and he seems inadvertently in his limitation to suggest this), the reason for the absurdity to which Hart refers may be that by virtue of social conditioning our aversions are in such instances so strong and irresistible that the sense of obligation need not be enlisted.

4. "Person" is used in the Kantian sense, as when he says that "rational beings are called persons because their very nature points them out as ends in themselves, that is, as something which must not be used merely as means . . ." (*Fundamental Principles of the Metaphysic of Morals*, p. 45).

5. It is not useful to linger here for distinctions between act-utilitarianism and rule-utilitarianism or to explore the difference between utilitarianism in its strictly hedonistic version and such other teleological doctrines as *eudamonism* (happiness as the goal) and perfectionism (the realization of human excellence as the goal). The reader may wish to consult such excellent texts as Richard Brandt's *Ethical Theory* (Englewood Cliffs, N.J.: Prentice-Hall, 1959) or William Frankena's *Ethics* (Englewood Cliffs, N.J.: Prentice-Hall, 1963).

6. John Rawls, *The Theory of Justice* (Cambridge, Mass.: Harvard, 1971), p. 26.

7. The words of Albert Camus, written in 1958 during the most tragic days of the French-Algerian crisis, are worth recalling:

Reprisals against civilian populations and the use of torture are crimes in which we are all involved. The fact that such things could take place among us is a humiliation we must henceforth face. Meanwhile, we must at least refuse to justify such methods, even on the score of efficacy. The moment they are justified, even indirectly, there are no more rules or values; all causes are equally good, and war without aims or laws sanctions the triumph of nihilism. Willy-nilly, we go back in that case to the jungle where the sole principle is violence. Even those who are fed up with morality ought to realize that it is better to suffer certain injustices than to commit them even to win wars, . . . [*Resistance, Rebellion and Death* (New York: Knopf, 1969), p. 114.]

Similarly, Jean-Paul Sartre wrote grimly:

> In 1943, in the Rue Lauriston [Paris Gestapo Headquarters], French-men were screaming in agony and pain. . . . In those days the outcome of the war was uncertain and the future unthinkable, but one thing seemed impossible in any circumstances: that one day men should be made to scream by those acting in our name.
> There is no such word as impossible: in 1958, in Algiers, people are tortured regularly and systematically. Everyone . . . knows this is so, but almost no one talks of it. . . . France is almost as mute as during the Occupation, but then she had the excuse of being gagged.

He goes on:

> Appalled, the French are discovering this terrible truth: that if nothing can protect a nation against itself, neither its traditions nor its loyalties nor its laws, and if fifteen years are enough to transform victims into executioners, then its behavior is not more than a matter of opportunity and occasion. Anybody, at any time, may equally find himself victim or executioner.

He concludes:

> Happy are those who died without ever having had to ask themselves: "If they tear out my fingernails, will I talk?" But even happier are others, barely out of their childhood, who have not had to ask them-selves that *other* question: "If my friends, fellow soldiers, and leaders tear out an enemy's fingernails in my presence, what will I do?" [Sar-tre's Preface to Henri Alleg's *The Question* (London: John Calder, 1958), pp. 11–12.]

8. Or we might defend the action of Federal Health officers who for thirty years allowed 400 indigent black men known to have syphilis to go untreated despite the discovery that penicillin could cure their disease. The officials had excellent "utilitarian" reasons. The blacks were subjects of a study started in Tuskegee, Alabama in 1932 (ten years before penicillin) to learn the course of un-treated syphilis. The study, writes Jane E. Brody, a correspondent of the *New York Times:*

> has raised once again a major dilemma for medical research that con-cerns the ancient issue of means and ends: Assuming that some ex-perimentation on human beings is necessary to medical progress, how can these studies be performed in a way that does not violate the basic rights of man? . . .

None of the men in the study were ever treated for their disease, and at least seven eventually died of the late effects of syphilis. . . . The study's subjects may never have been told in terms they understood what was wrong with them.
One of the study's 74 survivors, Charles Pollard, an intelligent although uneducated farmer in Tuskegee, told a reporter, "they never mention syphilis to me—not even once."

The *Times* correspondent continues:

The ethics of the study would have been questioned regardless of who the subjects were, but the fact that Federal doctors had selected poor, uneducated men—and not one of them a white man—further inflamed the issue. As one white Southerner remarked, "The worst segregationist in Alabama would never have done this."
Even with a score of proclamations, codes, declarations, statements and guidelines formulated since the Nurenburg code that are now supposed to be applied to all human experimentation, many questionable studies have been done in recent years and, to loud cries of "human guinea pigs," several have become embroiled in public controversy. Almost without exception, they involve members of minority or disadvantaged groups. (*New York Times,* July 30, 1972. © 1972 by The New York Times Company. Reprinted by permission.)

Suppose, however, the human subjects had been chosen by lot. He would be a stubborn utilitarian who would insist that in the interest of curing illness the experiment could now go forward.

9. What Susan Anthony's counterparts in today's liberation movement would say of Aquinas's interpretation of natural law as it pertains to woman might be unprintable. He found her "defective and accidental . . . a male gone awry," adding that she is probably "the result of some weakness in the [father's] generative power . . ."

10. "Jural" and "moral" would do just as well.

11. Austin and Bentham both insisted that the moral desirability of a rule does not establish it as a rule of law any more than the inconsistency of a law with rules of morality renders it less a law. The view was affirmed by Oliver Wendell Holmes, Jr. in his influential essay "The Path of Law" (10 *Harvard Law Review,* 457, 1897), and J. C. Gray wrote in his *The Nature and Sources of the Law* (1909) of the "great gain in its fundamental conceptions which Jurisprudence made during the last century [with] . . . the recognition of the truth that the Law of a State . . . is not an ideal, but something which actually exists." He noted that it "is

not that which ought to be, but that which is. To fix this definitely in the Jurisprudence of the Common Law, is the feat that Austin accomplished." Sec. (213). Cited by H. L. A. Hart, "Positivism and the Separation of Law and Morals," reprinted in F. A. Olafson (ed.), *Society, Law and Morality* (Englewood Cliffs, N.J.: Prentice-Hall, 1961), p. 445.

12. Plato, *Republic*, II, 359–360.

13. Philip Selznick, *International Encyclopedia of the Social Sciences*, vol. 9, p. 51b.

14. H. L. A. Hart, *The Concept of Law* (Oxford: Clarendon Press, 1961), pp. 55–56.

15. *Cf.*, for example, Thelma Z. Lavine's "Note to Naturalists on the Human Spirit" (*Journal of Philosophy*, vol. 50, pp. 145–154, 1953) and Ernest Nagel's "On the Method of *Verstehen* as the Sole Method of Philosophy" (*Journal of Philosophy*, vol. 50, pp. 154–157, February 26, 1953).

16. Hart, *The Concept of Law*, p. 12.

17. "Conduct" is preferred to "behavior" because it includes motives and attitudes, i.e., the "internal" as well as what we do.

18. It is on such "acceptance" as a kind of not-further-analyzable datum that Hart relies, thereby justifying Kurt Baier's charge that his account of obligation is a "sophisticated attitudinal (emotive) theory." ("Moral Obligation," *American Philosophical Quarterly*, vol. 3, no. 3, p. 217, July, 1966.)

19. H. W. Stuart, "A Reversal of Perspective in Ethical Theory," *The Philosophical Review*, vol. 29, p. 343, 1920.

20. Kant, *Fundamental Principles of the Metaphysic of Morals*, p. 19n.

21. Hart, *The Concept of Law*, p. 85.

22. Recognition of the point would make it easy to see that problems of the kind raised by deontologists like Sir David Ross (see above pp. 108–110) are quite artificial. He writes in a criticism of utilitarianism:

> Suppose . . . that the fulfillment of a promise to A would produce 1000 units of good for him, but by doing some other act I could produce 1,001 units of good for B, to whom I have made no promise; the other consequences of the two acts being of equal value; should we really think it . . . our duty to do the second act and not the first? I think not. We should, I fancy, hold that only a much greater disparity of value between the total consequences would justify us in failing to discharge our *prima facie* duty to A. After all, a promise is a promise, and is not to be treated so lightly as the theory we are examining [utilitarianism] would imply. (*The Right and the Good*, pp. 34–35.)

One need only ask how great a disparity to see that deontologists as well as teleologists involve moral theory in absurd calculations of consequences which never in fact occur.

23. G. E. Moore, *Principia Ethica,* p. 147.
24. David Hume, *On the Passions,* Sec. II, para. 1.
25. Frederich Nietzsche, *The Antichrist,* in Oscar Levy (ed.), *Complete Works,* H. Zimmerman (trans.) (New York: Russell and Russell, 1964), vol. 16, pt. 43, p. 187.

CHAPTER TWELVE

Notes to pages 176–189.

1. This still implies, let it be clear, a refusal to judge a course of conduct where judgment implies evaluation from the viewpoint of one's own interests.
2. This is not to deny that such a sense of self-integrity can degenerate into so squeamish a concern for one's virtue as to verge on moral hypochondria.
3. H. W. Stuart, whose account this partly parallels, suggests three main heads: "the authorities, institutional and otherwise, which the individual acknowledges; his own private impulses and desires; and the appeals, whether actually spoken or imputed to others by himself, which other living beings make to [the individual]." "Reversal of Perspective in Ethical Theory," *Philosophical Review,* vol. 29, p. 350, 1920.
4. Paul W. Taylor, *Normative Discourse* (Englewood Cliffs, N.J.: Prentice-Hall, 1961), p. 131.
5. Aristotle, *Nichomachean Ethics,* Book 1.7.
6. Nicholas Halasz, *Captain Dreyfus* (New York: Simon and Schuster, 1955), p. 68. This is an excellent and highly readable account of the Dreyfus case.
7. Incidentally, this story has a happy ending. After Dreyfus was exonerated, Col. Picquart was installed by a contrite France as Minister of War! And, fittingly, Zola's remains now rest in the Pantheon.
8. Nowell-Smith, *Ethics* (London: Penguin, 1954), p. 190.
9. *The Complete Introductory Lectures on Psychoanalysis,* J. Strache (trans.), Lecture 21, p. 522.
10. Plato, *Apology,* XXVIII, 38.

11. One can ignore T. H. Green's metaphysics and still feel the weight of his observation that man:

> In a certain sense, makes [experience] instead of merely waiting to be made by it. He is capable of being moved by an idea of himself, as becoming that which he has it in him to be—an idea which does not represent previous experience, but gradually brings an experience into being, gradually creates a filling for itself, in the shape of arts, laws, institutions, and habits of living, which, as far as they go, exhibit the capabilities of man, define the idea of his end, afford a positive answer to the otherwise unanswerable question, what in particular it is that man has it in him to become. [*Prolegomena to Ethics* (Oxford: Clarendon Press, 1899), p. 443, # 352.]

12. George Mead, *Philosophy of the Present* (Chicago: Open Court Publishing Co., 1932), p. 84.

13. Dewey, *Ethics*, pp. 250–251. (See notes for Chapter 8.)

14. Taylor, *Normative Discourse*, pp. 5ff. Professor A. P. Brogan in an article entitled, "The Fundamental Value Universal" (*Journal of Philosophy*, vol. 16, pp. 96ff., 1919) undertakes to prove "that the relation 'better' is a sufficient fundamental universal for the theory of value and that it is the only value universal which can be taken as fundamental." Dewey places himself in explicit accord with this observation. ("Valuation and Experimental Knowledge," *Philosophical Review*, vol. 31, p. 334, note 2, 1922.)

15. Immanuel Kant, *Fundamental Principles of the Metaphysic of Morals*, p. 65.

16. Dewey constantly stressed the creative role of choice. In the *Ethics*, for example, he observes that when we have to make up our minds concerning what we *"really"* want, "every such choice sustains a double relation to the self. It reveals the existing self and it forms the future self." In the choice resulting from moral deliberation a person "shapes the self, making it, in some degree, a new self . . . [and] gives a lasting set to his own being" (p. 317). For an excellent account of Existentialist ethics *cf.* Mary Warnock, *Existentialism* (London, New York: Oxford, 1970).

CHAPTER THIRTEEN

Notes to pages 190–204.

1. Kenneth Keniston, *The Uncommitted* (New York: Harcourt, Brace & World, 1960), p. 228.

2. Keniston, *The Uncommitted,* pp. 230–231.

3. Keniston, *The Uncommitted,* pp. 231–233.

4. The phenomenon is manifest, among other places, in the colleges and universities in the form of a growing hostility to required courses and a demand for "student power," i.e., greater student participation in determining the content of the curriculum and the selection and promotion (or demotion) of the faculty.

5. Even so perceptive a thinker as Hannah Arendt overlooks this distinction. Although asserting that authority does not rely on coercion—"where force is used, authority has failed"—she adds:

> Authority, on the other hand, is incompatible with persuasion, which presupposes equality and works through a process of argumentation. . . . Against the egalitarian order of persuasion stands the authoritarian order, which is always hierarchical. If authority is to be defined at all, then, it must be in contradistinction to both coercion by force and persuasion through arguments. ["What is Authority?" in *Between Past and Future* (New York: Viking, 1961), p. 93.]

Clearly, what is needed is a recognition of the difference between authoritarianism and reliance on or recourse to authority.

A poet has been more perceptive than Dr. Arendt. W. H. Auden in *Secondary Worlds* observes:

> I can either obey or disobey the order. I may obey it for one of two reasons:
>
> 1. Out of an irresistible passion of fear at the consequences of disobedience. In that case, I am forced to obey, and the act is not mine.
>
> 2. Because I accept the authority of him who gives the command, I believe that he is wiser than I, and that he wishes me well. In this case, my lying down is *my* act (p. 134).

6. Philip Selznick, *International Encyclopedia of the Social Sciences,* vol. 9, p. 54a.

7. H. L. A. Hart, *The Concept of Law,* p. 7. (See notes for Chapter 11.)

8. "Law, considered merely as order, contains . . . its own implicit morality. This morality of order must be respected if we are to create anything that can be called law, even bad law." ("Positivism and Fidelity to Law," *Harvard Law Review,* 1958, reprinted in F. A. Olafson (ed.), *Society, Law, and Morality* (Englewood Cliffs, N.J.: Prentice-Hall, 1961), p. 481.

9. A bill, outlawed by the U.S. Constitution, for attaining, i.e., punishing for treason or felony, without a judicial trial.

10. The English Reform Act of 1832, which enfranchised the middle class, did not abolish property qualifications for voting, nor were they completely abolished in the Reform Act of 1867. For a long time the states in this country limited voting to male property owners almost exclusively, and it was not until 1860 that most states provided for universal white male suffrage. In France the ideal of universal manhood suffrage proclaimed by the Revolution of 1789 was not effectively realized until 1875. The reign of Louis Philippe, Orleanist "Citizen King," was marked by the ascendancy of the bourgeoisie, but only 200,000 could vote in a population of about 30 million.

11. Anti-draft riots in New York destroyed $1,500,000 of property and resulted in the killing or wounding of one thousand persons.

12. Plato, *Republic*, Cornford trans., I, 338.

13. Marx differed from the Sophists like Thrasymachus and from the so-called Neo-Machiavellians by limiting the generalization to societies in which there is private ownership of the means of production.

14. To be sure, much important legislation gives one segment of the population benefits that are provided by another, whether this be aid to the aged, public education, or compulsory military service. But such legislation is consensual, is thought to serve the common good and is presumably an outcome of open consideration of competing claims.

15. Professor John Rawls cites two principles associated with the conception of justice as fairness, principles by which "free and rational persons concerned to further their own interests" would initially govern the assignment of basic rights and duties and the division of social benefits if, by hypothesis, "no one [knew] his place in society, his class position or social status, . . . his fortune in the distribution of natural assets and abilities, his intelligence, strength, and the like." These would be as follows: "First: each person is to have an equal right to the most extensive basic liberty compatible with a similar liberty for others. Second: social and economic inequalities are to be arranged so that they are both (a) reasonably expected to be to everyone's advantage, and (b) attached to positions and offices open to all." [*The Theory of Justice* (Cambridge, Mass.: Harvard, 1971), pp. 11–12, 60.]

16. "Suppose the laws and the commonwealth were to come and appear to me as I was preparing to run away . . . and were to ask . . ."

17. Rawls, *The Theory of Justice*, p. 62.

CHAPTER FOURTEEN

Notes to pages 205–225.

1. C. H. Cooley, *Human Nature and the Social Order* (New York: Schocken Books, 1964), p. 136.

2. L. G. Wispè, "Sympathy and Empathy," *International Encyclopedia of the Social Sciences*, vol. 15, p. 441.

3. For an acute study of empathy, especially as it bears on the role of the psychotherapist, *cf.* H. Fingarette's *The Self in Transformation*, Chapter 6. For a discussion of the role of empathy in the aesthetic experience and an emphasis on the extent to which motor sets are involved, *cf.* H. S. Langfeld, *The Aesthetic Attitude* (New York: Harcourt, Brace, 1920), pp. 109–127, 136–138) reprinted in E. Vivas and M. Krieger (eds.), *The Problems of Aesthetics* (New York: Rinehart, 1952), pp. 315–325.

4. Peter Kropotkin, *Mutual Aid: A Factor of Evolution* (London: Heinemann, 1902). For an interesting account of Social Darwinism see Richard Hofstadter's *Social Darwinism in America* (Philadelphia: University of Pennsylvania Press, 1945).

5. For an excellent account, from the point of view of an outstanding geneticist, of the erroneous ethical implications derived from the Darwinian doctrine of natural selection, see George Gaylord Simpson's *The Meaning of Evolution* (New Haven: Yale, 1949), especially Chapter XVIII. He observes that "it was neither established that the tooth-and-claw ethic is inherent in evolution as a whole nor that what is inherent in evolution as a whole constitutes a fit guide for human life." He adds, "Literal struggle is *not* the essence of natural selection" (p. 299), noting that "selection in favor of harmonious or co-operative group association is certainly common" (p. 223).

6. Whatever the verdict concerning his animalizing humans, Darwin surely tended to humanize animals. The pathetic fallacy consists of imputing human traits to nonhuman, even physical, objects. In *The Descent of Man* (New York: Modern Library ed., Chapter IV, p. 476), Darwin wrote: "It must be called sympathy that leads a courageous dog to fly at anyone who strikes his master." He added: "Besides love and sympathy, animals exhibit other qualities connected with the social instincts, which in us would be called moral; and I agree with Agassiz that dogs possess something very like a conscience."

7. Abraham Tucker, *The Light of Nature Pursued* (London: R. Faulder & T. Payne, 1805), vol. VII, p. 164.

8. Cited by Walton H. Hamilton, "Acquisition," *Encyclopedia of the Social Sciences,* 1st ed., vol. I, p. 421b.

9. Adam Smith, *The Wealth of Nations* (New York: Random House, 1937), Book IV, Chapter ii.

10. Smith, *The Wealth of Nations,* Book I, Chapter ii.

11. Bernard de Mandeville, *Fable of the Bees* (London: Oxford, 1924), Part I.

12. Joseph Butler, *Five Sermons* (New York: Library of Liberal Arts ed., 1950), p. 14.

13. William James, *Principles of Psychology* (New York: Henry Holt and Company, 1890), vol. I, pp. 318–320, 323. (James's emphasis.)

14. Immanuel Kant, *Fundamental Principles of the Metaphysic of Morals,* pp. 15–16. (See notes for Chapter 10.)

15. Kant, *Metaphysic of Morals,* p. 18.

16. Much remains to be done in studying sensitiveness to the distress of others as related to maturation in the individual (see L. Murphy, *Social Behavior and Child Personality* (New York: Columbia, 1937).

17. In a perceptive book Professor Richard Taylor, after noting that "compassion is the moral incentive *par excellence,*" adds that it is "the very irrationality of compassion, the residual capacity to respond with tenderness and love *when all one's reason counsels otherwise,* that confers upon a compassionate act its sweetness, beauty and nobility." [*Good and Evil* (New York: Macmillan, 1970), pp. 206, 217. My emphasis.] Although usage encourages the reference to "irrationality," it would be better to speak of the "nonrationality" of compassion (reserving "irrationality" for self-destructive behavior), understanding that the transcending of reason, as Taylor puts it, is simply the refusal to be governed by a calculation of consequences the outcome of which would be determined by one's prevailing values. It is to reject prudential and jurisprudential considerations for another way of guiding one's conduct. As Taylor says, "Service to the common good inevitably requires one to subordinate his interests, at times, to the interests of others, and *not* with any expectation or hope that this will even in the long run promote his own good" (p. 220).

I am indebted to Professor Taylor for reminding me of Schopenhauer's stress on the same point. Disinterested acts of justice and disinterested loving-kindness are, Schopenhauer notes, the only kinds of action to which we attribute moral worth. Such "absence of all egoistic motivation is . . . *the criterion of an action* of moral worth." We are moved to action of this kind by virtue of

the phenomenon of compassion, that is, "the immediate participation . . . primarily in the suffering of another." How this comes
about is the "great mystery of ethics." Unfortunately, Schopenhauer throws no light on its solution by affirming it to be a subject of "metaphysical speculation" and referring it to his metaphysics. [*On the Basis of Morality* (New York: Bobbs-Merrill,
Library of Liberal Arts ed., 1965), pp. 143–146. His emphasis.]
Schopenhauer postulates three fundamental incentives embracing
all possible motives: egoism (desire for one's own weal), compassion (desire for another's weal) and malice (desire for another's woe). The latter two, although opposites, are alike in being devoid of self-interest.

18. Dewey, *Ethics*, pp. 297–298.

19. John Dewey, *Human Nature and Conduct* (New York: Modern
Library ed., 1930), p. 269.

20. There is no intent here to re-fight a tragic civil war which even
the Spanish would like to forget. In fairness it should be added
that the Spanish Catholic hierarchy has been changing.

21. Social scientists have taken over Durkheim's term "anomic" or
"anomy" to designate what might be called a state of normless-
ness. According to R. M. MacIver, "Anomy signifies the state of
mind of one who has been pulled up by his moral roots, who has
no longer any standards but only disconnected urges, who has no
longer any sense of continuity, of folk, of obligation." *The Ram-
parts We Guard* (New York: Macmillan, 1950), p. 84. *Cf.* also
David Riesman's *The Lonely Crowd* (New Haven: Yale, 1950),
pp. 278ff., and Robert K. Merton's *Social Theory and Social
Structure* (New York: Free Press, 1957), pp. 161–170.

22. G. H. Mead, *Mind, Self and Society* (Chicago: The University of
Chicago Press, 1934), p. 388.

23. I have borrowed this term from H. W. Stuart.

24. For a discussion of current views which deny that any social content or concern is intrinsic to morality, see W. K. Frankena, "Recent Conceptions of Morality," in H. Castañeda and G. Nakhni-
kian (eds.), *Morality and the Language of Conduct* (Detroit:
Wayne State University Press, 1965).

25. Mead, *Mind, Self and Society*, pp. 155–156, 379.

26. Edmond Cahn, *The Sense of Injustice* (New York: New York
University Press, 1949), p. 13. Although I do not agree with Professor Cahn's Hobbesian interpretation that "The sense of injustice is the equipment by which a human being discerns assault,
recognizes oppression of another as a species of attack upon himself, and prepares defense," I find his statement that the ethica

function of justice "become(s) evident in the *sense of injustice*" highly suggestive. ("Justice," *International Encyclopedia of the Social Sciences*, vol. 8, pp. 346–347; his emphasis.)

27. Henry Sidgwick, *The Methods of Ethics*, 7th ed. (London: Macmillan, 1907, 1922), p. 265.

28. Georges Gurvitch, " 'Moral Man' and 'Immoral Society'," *Philosophical Review*, vol. 52, p. 543, 1943.

29. Reprinted in H. K. Girvetz (ed.), *Contemporary Moral Issues*, 2nd ed. (Belmont, Cal.: Wadsworth, 1968), p. 145.

30. Girvetz (ed.), *Contemporary Moral Issues*, p. 148. So far as I know, the only published text of this letter appears in my anthology, *Contemporary Moral Issues*. Some might question the letter's sincerity. This writer was then on leave, serving on Governor Brown's personal staff and in an unusual position to observe. I am completely convinced of Chessman's sincerity. Chessman was convicted of assault and kidnapping. Assault alone is not a capital crime in California. The kidnapping charge was a strictly technical one. Governor Brown, who was opposed to capital punishment, could not under California law commute the sentence of Chessman, a twice-convicted felon, without a recommendation—which was refused—from the State Supreme Court. The legislature, called into special session by the Governor, voted against repeal of capital punishment.

31. Cahn, *The Sense of Injustice*, p. 13.

32. Plato, *Republic*, Cornford trans., VI, 500.

CHAPTER FIFTEEN

Notes to pages 227–233.

1. Even one so hostile to the concept of instinct as the experimental psychologist, F. A. Beach, concedes:

   Although there are militant opponents of the instinct doctrine among present day psychologists, it is undoubtedly correct to say that the concept of instincts as complex, unlearned patterns of behavior is generally accepted in clinical, social, and experimental psychology. ("The Descent of Instinct," *The Psychological Review*, vol. 62, pp. 401–409, November 1955.)

2. C. H. Cooley, *Human Nature and the Social Order*, p. 29. Cooley was among the first to warn in his great classic against tendencies to explain war as due to an "instinct of pugnacity," or sociability

in one or other of its forms as the outcome of a "gregarious instinct" or "instinct of the herd." "War," he wrote,

is rooted in many instinctive tendencies, all of which have been transformed by education, tradition, and organization, so that to study its
sources is to study the whole process of society. . . . Indeed, I am not
aware that there is any . . . evidence of the existence of a gregarious
instinct as there is of an instinct of fear or anger . . . (p. 28).

3. John Dewey, *Human Nature and Conduct*, pp. 146–148. (See
notes for Chapter 14.) *Cf.* also *Ethics*, pp. 202–203. (See notes
for Chapter 8.)

4. *Cf.* Karen Horney, *New Ways of Psychoanalysis* (New York:
Norton, 1939), p. 54. Dr. Clara Jones writes of Freud:

The solution of sublimation is seen best exemplified in the attitude
towards money. Pleasure in the feces becomes sublimated in pleasure
in money. The child's feeling of power in controlling feces becomes
the feeling of power in the manipulation of money. The extreme character development here would be the miser.

Parsimonious and stingy people also have anal characters, and even
the sharp businessman has "anal" traits.

Another type of sublimation of anal libido has to do with pleasure in
handling feces. This, according to Freud, accounts for the sculptor and
painter, who manipulate objects and materials.

Psychoanalysis: Evolution and Development (New York: Hermitage
House, 1951), p. 66.

5. Philip Rieff, *Freud: The Mind of the Moralist*, p. 33. (See notes
for Chapter 3.) *Cf.* also Konrad Lorenz's widely read work *On
Aggression* (German ed., 1963, English trans. 1966), in which
the noted ethologist treats aggression on a "hydraulic" model as
an instinctual drive which accumulates more and more pressure
until finally released, even—when the pressure has built up
enough—without a stimulus.

6. Dewey, *Human Nature and Conduct*, p. 146.

7. Dewey, *Human Nature and Conduct*, p. 97.

8. Dewey, *Human Nature and Conduct*, p. 157.

9. Letter to Ernest Collings, January 17, 1913.

10. Someone has called this the power of positive non-thinking.

11. Heroin addicts are said to spend about $70 per day on the
habit. In most cases they must steal to support it.

12. How the "footnotes" on Plato abound! Recall that "master pa
sion" which, first championing the "mob of idle appetites," at la

as leader of the soul, "takes madness for the captain of its guard and breaks out in frenzy;" and "if it can lay hold upon any thoughts or desires that are of good report and still capable of shame, it kills them or drives them forth, until it has purged the soul of all sobriety and called in the partisans of madness to fill the vacant place." (*Republic*, Cornford trans., IX, 572.)

CHAPTER SIXTEEN

Notes to pages 234–244.

1. Kant, *Fundamental Principles of the Metaphysic of Morals*, p. 45. (Kant's emphasis.)

2. Kant, *Fundamental Principles of the Metaphysic of Morals*, p. 17. (Kant's emphasis.)

3. Kant, *Fundamental Principles of the Metaphysic of Morals*, p. 57.

4. Emile Durkheim, *The Rules of Sociological Method* (New York: Free Press, 1964), p. 95. Elsewhere in the same work Durkheim urged that the data of the sociologist, what is given to him as the point of departure of his science, "is not the idea that men form of value, for that is inaccessible, but only the values established in the course of economic relations; not conceptions of the moral ideal, but the totality of rules which actually determine conduct . . ." (p. 27). On the other hand, he conceded that "a deliberate intention is itself something objectively real" (p. 92) and agreed that "we are not incapable of self-control; we can restrain our impulses, habits, and even instincts, and we can arrest their development by an act of inhibition" (p. 101).

5. B. F. Skinner, *Beyond Freedom and Dignity* (New York: Knopf, 1971), pp. 9, 14, 101.

6. C. A. Campbell, "Is Free Will a Pseudo-Problem?" *Mind*, vol. 60, pp. 462–463, 1951. Reprinted by permission of the author and the editor of *Mind*. Also reprinted in Richard B. Brandt, ed., *Value and Obligation* (New York: Harcourt, Brace & World, 1961), pp. 685–706; Paul Edwards and Arthur Pap, eds., *A Modern Introduction to Philosophy*, 3rd ed. (New York: Free Press, 1973), pp. 67–82. *Cf.* also H. W. Stuart, "Dewey's Ethical Theory," in P. A. Schilpp (ed.), *The Philosophy of John Dewey* (Evanston: Northwestern University, 1939), and the reference to H. L. A. Hart above, pp. 247–249. I am concerned here not with the free will versus determinism issue as such—which has been sufficiently discussed elsewhere [*Cf.* Brand Blanshard, "The Case for Determinism" and Paul Edwards, "Hard and Soft Determin-

ism" in *Determinism and Freedom,* S. Hook, ed. (New York: Collier, 1961), pp. 19-30, 117-125]—but with the methodological issue raised by Campbell which has been central to the present approach.

For a brief but excellent discussion of this issue in the context of a critique of behaviorism with special emphasis on the psychology of B. F. Skinner, see Ralph Ross, *Obligation, A Social Theory* (Ann Arbor: University of Michigan Press, 1970), Chapters 1, 2.

7. As George Geiger points out in his useful study of Dewey, to get at the meaning of value we must seek more than verbal clarity or logical consistency; we must look to "the process of human decision, of decision emerging from a problematic situation." [*John Dewey in Perspective* (New York: McGraw-Hill, 1964), p. 115.]

8. In common usage objectivity is opposed to (a) subjectivity, (b) relativity and (c) bias in making judgments, seeking evidence, reaching conclusions. Each of these polarities is beset by ambiguity and confusion. In the case of (a) objectivity is an existential predicate designating (i) what is real as distinguished from what is subjective or unreal (e.g., the actual killing of one's father as distinguished from a dream or fantasy that one has killed one's father); or (ii) a *kind* of reality or kind of data amenable, as in the natural sciences, to observation by more than one person, in contrast to private feeling states, motives, intentions, attitudes, dispositions, etc. In the case of (b) relativity is often used to designate the relationship of every object of knowledge to what Lovejoy calls a "percipient event," thereby making it nonsense to speak of objective knowledge as opposed to relative knowledge. In the case of (c) objectivity is a methodological predicate referring to the degree in which the quest for evidence is unaffected by our desires and values and is often said, as by Marx and Mannheim, to be *unattainable* in the social sciences, not to mention ethics.

9. H. D. Aiken, "The Concept of Moral Objectivity," *Reason and Conduct* (New York: Knopf, 1962), pp. 134, 138. The same point is made by Professor Paul Taylor:

Their (the radical skeptics') basic error is to misconstrue the nature of our reasoning about value judgments. . . . They consider verification and validation purely in terms of reasoning in the empirical science and in mathematics, respectively. . . . Both the argument for and th (intuitionist) argument against radical skepticism rest on the false a sumption that there are only two ways of reasoning about anything . the way we reason in mathematics and the way we reason in the er pirical sciences. . . . We are overlooking what *is distinctive* about eval ative reasoning. We are trying to fit it into some preconceived logical pattern . . . (*Normative Discourse*, pp. 105–106.)

10. See Feigl's "Validation and Vindication: An Analysis of the Nature and the Limits of Ethical Arguments" in Wilfred Sellars and John Hospers (eds.), *Readings in Ethical Theory*, 1st ed. (New York: Appleton-Century-Crofts, Inc., 1952), pp. 667–680; and Paul W. Taylor, *Normative Discourse*, pp. 125–150.

11. Carl Wellman finds that

> There are at least twelve features of the language of ethics [suggesting] that it is an objective form of discourse—ethical utterances can be incompatible with one another, we dispute about ethical issues, ethical sentences are formulated in the declarative mood, we speak of them as true or false, we ask ethical questions, the individual may wonder if his ethical conviction is mistaken, some ethical arguments are formally valid, ethical reasoning is always possible, and it is usually necessary we distinguish between relevant and irrelevant considerations, rational methods of persuasion are to be preferred to sheer propaganda, and we apply the terms 'valid' and 'invalid' to ethical arguments." ("Emotivism and Ethical Objectivity," *American Philosophical Quarterly*, vol. 5, p. 92, 1968.)

12. R. M. Hare, *Freedom and Reason*, p. 187. An acute analysis of "grading"—a term preferred by some to evaluating—lapses into disappointing vagueness when its author, Oxford philosopher J. O. Urmson, in his concluding comments, addresses himself to the problem of how to reconcile differences of opinion about what grading criteria (i.e., standards of *evaluation*) to adopt in a given situation. "Is there not," he asks, "a right and wrong about it; . . . are we to say that the distinction . . . between higher and lower, enlightened and unenlightened, moral codes is chimerical"? Professor Urmson believes that appeal can be made to "criteria" of enlightenment, but he neglects to spell them out.

> We cannot hope now to give a complete and clear list of these criteria; no doubt they are vague; and it is easier to employ criteria than to recognize them. . . . Surely one criterion would be that the reasons for adopting the criteria are not superstitious or magical; that some reasons can be given would seem to be another. Again, the contrast between the health, wealth, and happiness of people living under different moral codes cannot prove the superiority of one code over another, but it does seem to be a criterion of enlightenment. ["On Grading," in Anthony Flew (ed.), *Logic and Language* (Garden City, N.Y.: Anchor Books, 1965), pp. 408–409.]

I am not aware that Professor Urmson has elaborated elsewhere on these suggestions. The passage cited is, I believe, typical of the vagueness that beclouds this critical issue. Be that as it may, the kind of reversal of perspective proposed here and the formal criteria of trustworthiness that have been outlined may at least suggest the program of which he is in need.

13. H. W. Stuart, "A Reversal of Perspective in Ethical Theory," *Philosophical Review*, vol. 29, p. 351, 1920. (My emphasis.) In more recent literature Richard Brandt's "Qualified Attitude Method," if I understand it correctly, more closely approximates the position I am defending than anything I have read. See his *Ethical Theory* (New York: Prentice-Hall, 1959), Chapter 10.

14. Aiken, "The Concept of Moral Objectivity," *Reason and Conduct*, p. 163.

15. *The Mountain People* (New York: Simon and Schuster, 1972), Colin M. Turnbill's recent study of the African Iks, provides an interesting description of the shocking callousness with which even children are treated in a group suffering constantly from hunger.

16. Friedrich Wilhelm Nietzsche, *The Antichrist in Complete Works*, Part 57, p. 218. (See notes for Chapter 11.)

17. Nietzsche, *The Genealogy of Morals* (New York: The Modern Library, 1927), p. 715, second essay, #24).

18. Nietzsche, *The Antichrist*, Part 58, p. 222.

19. In the fourth or ethical sense only, of course, if I partake of a culture in which such conditions prevail.

Selected Readings

CHAPTER ONE

Asch, S. E., "A Critique of the Psychology of Cultural Relativism," in Richard Brandt (ed.), *Value and Obligation* (New York: Harcourt, Brace & World, 1961), pp. 473–485.

Bidney, David, "The Concept of Value in Modern Anthropology," in A. L. Kroeber (ed.), *Anthropology Today: An Encyclopedic Inventory* (Chicago: University of Chicago Press, 1953).

Brandt, Richard, *Hopi Ethics* (Chicago: University of Chicago Press, 1954).

Dewey, John, "Anthropology and Ethics," in W. F. Ogburn and A. Goldenweiser (eds.), *The Social Sciences and Their Interrelations* (Boston: Houghton, Mifflin, 1927), pp. 24–36.

Edel, May and Abraham, *Anthropology and Ethics* (Springfield, Ill.: Charles C Thomas, 1959).

Hartung, F. E., "Cultural Relativity and Moral Judgments," *Philosophy of Science,* vol. 21, no. 2, pp. 118–126, 1954.

Herskovits, Melville, *Man and His Works* (New York: Knopf, 1965), Chapter 5.

Kluckhohn, Clyde, "Values and Value Orientations in the Theory of Action," in T. Parsons and E. A. Shils (eds.), *Toward a General Theory of Action* (Cambridge: Harvard, 1962).

———, "Ethical Relativity: *Sic et Non,*" *Journal of Philosophy,* vol. 52, pp. 663–677, 1955.

Lakin, R. D., "Morality in Anthropological Perspective," *Antioch Review*, vol. 21, no. 4, pp. 422–440, 1961.

Lazari-Pawlowska, Ija, "On Cultural Relativism," *Journal of Philosophy*, vol. 67, pp. 577–584, 1970.

Linton, Ralph, "Universal Ethical Principles: An Anthropological View," in R. Anshen (ed.), *Moral Principles of Action: Man's Ethical Imperative* (New York and London: Harper, 1952), pp. 645–660.

————, "The Problem of Universal Values," in R. F. Spencer (ed.), *Method and Perspective in Anthropology: Papers in Honor of Wilson D. Wallis* (Minneapolis: University of Minnesota Press, 1954), pp. 145–168; reprinted in R. Brandt (ed.), *Value and Obligation* (New York: Harcourt, Brace & World, 1961), pp. 460–472.

Nielsen, Kai, "Anthropology and Ethics," *The Journal of Value Inquiry*, vol. 5, pp. 253–266, 1971.

Taylor, Paul W. "Social Science and Ethical Relativism," *Journal of Philosophy*, vol. 55, pp. 32–44, 1958.

Wellman, Carl, "The Ethical Implications of Cultural Relativity," *Journal of Philosophy*, vol. 60, pp. 169–184, 1963.

CHAPTER TWO

Marx and Engels were not moral philosophers and did not write systematically about the problems of ethics. Those observations that bear directly on moral theory are scattered throughout the Marx-Engels corpus. Marxist epigones of recent years have concentrated on his early, humanistically oriented work, but Marx himself repudiated the *Economic-Philosophic Manuscripts of 1844*, and their relevance for an understanding of the basic tenets of Marxism is debatable, whatever their intrinsic merit as a suggestive discussion of alienation and "reification." The most useful anthology for readers interested in Marx's politics and philosophy is:

Karl Marx and Friedrich Engels. *Basic Writings on Politics and Philosophy*, Lewis S. Feuer (ed.) (Garden City, New York: Doubleday, 1959).

Source readings of particular relevance to the present topic are:

Karl Marx and Friedrich Engels, *The German Ideology* (New York: International Publishers, 1960).

————, *The Manifesto of the Communist Party* in *Marx and Engels Selected Works*, I (Moscow: Foreign Languages Publishing House, 1951).

Engels, *Herr Eugen Dühring's Revolution in Science (Anti-Dühring)*, as excerpted in Lewis S. Feuer (ed.), *Marx and Engels. Basic Writings on Politics and Philosophy*, pp. 270–280.

❉   ❉   ❉   ❉   ❉

Bell, Daniel, "The 'Rediscovery' of Alienation: Some Notes Along the Quest for the Historical Marx," *Journal of Philosophy*, vol. 56, pp. 933–952, 1959).

Cox, R. H. (ed.), *Ideology, Politics, and Political Theory* (Belmont, Cal.: Wadsworth, 1969).

Fromm, Erich, *Marx's Concept of Man* (New York: Ungar, 1961).

Hook, Sidney, *Marx and the Marxists* (Princeton, N.J.: Van Nostrand, 1955), especially pp. 45–47, 88–89, and excerpts on Communist morality from Lenin's *Selected Works*, pp. 195–196.

———, "The Enlightenment and Marxism," *Journal of the History of Ideas*, vol. 29, no. 1, pp. 93–108, 1968.

Kamenka, E., *Marxism and Ethics* (New York: Macmillan, 1969).

———, *The Ethical Foundations of Marxism* (New York: Praeger, 1962).

Lichtheim, George, "The Concept of Ideology," *History and Theory*, vol. IV, no. 2, pp. 164–195, 1965.

Mannheim, Karl, *Ideology and Utopia* (New York: Harcourt, Brace, 1936).

Merton, Robert K., *Social Theory and Social Structure*, rev. ed. (New York: Free Press, 1957), Chapters 12, 13.

Mullins, W. A., "On the Concept of Ideology in Political Science," *The American Political Science Review*, vol. 66, pp. 498–510, 1972.

Nagel, Ernest, *The Structure of Science* (New York: Harcourt, Brace & World, 1961), pp. 498–502.

Plamenatz, John, *Ideology* (New York: Praeger, 1970), pp. 32–45.

Popper, Karl, *The Open Society and Its Enemies* (London: Routledge, 1945), Chapters 22, 23.

Wolff, Kurt H., "Sociology of Knowledge and Sociological Theory," in Llewellyn Gross (ed.), *Symposium on Sociological Theory* (Evanston, Ill.: Row, Peterson, 1959), pp. 567–602.

CHAPTER THREE

Feuer, L. S., *Psychoanalysis and Ethics* (Springfield, Ill.: Charles C Thomas, 1955).

Fingarette, Herbert, *The Self in Transformation* (New York: Basic Books, 1963), Chapters 3, 4.

Flugel, J. C., *Man, Morals, and Society* (New York: Viking, 1961).

Freud, Sigmund, *The Standard Edition of the Complete Psychological Works of Sigmund Freud,* James Strachey (ed.), (London: Hogarth Press, 1953–1966):
Beyond the Pleasure Principle (1920, vol. 18)
Civilization and Its Discontents (1930, vol. 21)
The Ego and the Id (1923, vol. 19)
Group Psychology and the Analysis of the Ego (1921, vol. 18)
Introductory Lectures on Psychoanalysis (1915–1917, vols. 15–16)
New Introductory Lectures on Psychoanalysis (1933, vol. 22)
Totem and Taboo (1912–13, vol. 13)

Fromm, Erich, *Man for Himself* (New York: Rinehart, 1947).

Gill, Merton, "The Present State of Psychoanalytic Theory," *Journal of Abnormal and Social Psychology,* vol. 58, pp. 1–8, 1959.

Ginsberg, Morris, "Psycho-Analysis and Ethics" in *On the Diversity of Morals* (New York: Macmillan, 1952), pp. 54–78.

Hall, C. S., and Gardner Lindzey, "Psychoanalytic Theory and Its Applications in the Social Sciences," *Handbook of Social Psychology,* I (Reading, Mass.: Addison-Wesley, 1954), pp. 143–175.

Hartmann, Heinz, *Psychoanalysis and Moral Values* (New York: International Universities Press, Inc., 1960).

Holt, R. R., "Freud" in *International Encyclopedia of the Social Sciences,* vol. 6, pp. 1–10.

Horney, Karen, *New Ways in Psychoanalysis* (New York: Norton, 1939), Chapters 2, 11, and 13.

Inkeles, Alex, "Psychoanalysis and Sociology" in Sidney Hook (ed.), *Psychoanalysis, Scientific Method and Philosophy* (New York: Grove Press, 1959), pp. 117–129.

Kardiner, Abram, "Social and Cultural Implications of Psychoanalysis," in Sidney Hook (ed.), *Psychoanalysis, Scientific Method and Philosophy* (New York: Grove Press, 1959), pp. 81–103.

Marcuse, H., *Eros and Civilization* (New York: Vintage Press, 1962)

McDougall, William, *Psycho-Analysis and Social Psychology* (London: Methuen, 1936).

Meyerhoff, Hans, "Freud and the Ambiguity of Culture," *Partisan Review,* vol. 24, pp. 117–130, 1957.

Rieff, Philip, *Freud: The Mind of the Moralist* (New York: Doubleday, 1961).

———, *The Triumph of the Therapeutic; Uses of Faith After Freud* (New York: Harper and Row, 1966), Chapters 1–4.

Thompson, Clara, *Psychoanalysis: Evolution and Development* (New York: Hermitage House, 1951).

van den Haag, Ernest, "Psychoanalysis and Its Discontents," in Sidney Hook (ed.), *Psychoanalysis, Scientific Method and Philosophy* (New York: Grove Press, 1959), pp. 104–116.

CHAPTER FOUR*

Lewis, C. I., *An Analysis of Knowledge and Valuation* (LaSalle, Ill.: Open Court, 1946), Chapters 12, 13, 14.

Nowell-Smith, P. H., *Ethics* (London: Pelican Books, 1954), Chapter 10.

Parker, DeWitt, "Value as Any Object of Any Interest," *International Journal Of Ethics*, vol. 40, pp. 465–495, 1930.

Parker, DeWitt, Homer H. Dubs, and Charner M. Perry, "Symposium on R. B. Perry's *General Theory of Value,*" *International Journal of Ethics*, vol. 40, pp. 465–495, 1929–1930.

Pepper, S. C., *The Sources of Value* (Berkeley: University of California Press, 1958).

Perry, R. B., *General Theory of Value; Its Meaning and Basic Principles Construed in Terms of Interest* (New York: Longman's, Green, 1926), reissued in 1950.

———, *Realms of Value* (Cambridge, Mass.: Harvard University Press, 1954).

Prall, David, *Aesthetic Judgment* (New York: Thomas Y. Crowell, 1967).

Taylor, Paul W., *Normative Discourse* (Englewood Cliffs, N.J.: Prentice-Hall, 1961), Chapters 1, 2, 3.

Toulmin, S. E., *The Place of Reason in Ethics* (Cambridge: Cambridge University Press, 1950), Chapter 3.

CHAPTER FIVE

Ayer, A. J., *Language, Truth and Logic* (New York: Dover, 1952), Chapter VI.

———, "On the Analysis of Moral Judgments," *Philosophical Essays* (London: Macmillan, 1954), pp. 231–249.

Blanshard, Brand, "The New Subjectivism in Ethics," *Journal of Philosophy and Phenomenological Research*, vol. 9, pp. 504–511, 1949, reprinted in Paul Edwards and Arthur Pap (eds.), *A Modern Introduction to Philosophy*, 3rd ed. (New York: Free Press, 1973), pp. 338–345.

See Selected Readings, Chapter Eight, note.

Brandt, Richard B., *Ethical Theory* (Englewood Cliffs, N.J.: Prentice-Hall, 1959), Chapter 9.

Carnap, Rudolph, "The Elimination of Metaphysics Through Logical Analysis of Language," A. J. Ayer (ed.), *Logical Positivism* (New York: Free Press, 1959).

Hudson, W. D., *Modern Moral Philosophy* (Garden City, N.J.: Doubleday, 1970), Chapter 4.

Margolis, Joseph, *Values and Conduct* (Oxford: Clarendon Press, 1971).

Moore, Asher, "Emotivism: Theory and Practice," *Journal of Philosophy*, vol. 55, pp. 375–382, 1958.

Ross, Ralph, *Obligation, A Social Theory* (Ann Arbor: University of Michigan Press, 1970), Chapter 3.

Schuster, Cynthia A., "C. I. Lewis and Emotive Theories of Value, or, Should Empirical Ethics Declare Bankruptcy?" *Journal of Philosophy*, vol. 54, pp. 169–181, 1957.

Stevenson, C. L., *Ethics and Language* (New Haven: Yale, 1944).

———, *Facts and Values* (New Haven: Yale, 1963).

———, "Ethical Fallibility," in Richard De George (ed.), *Ethics and Society* (Garden City: Anchor Books, 1966), pp. 197–217.

———, "The Emotive Conception of Ethics and Its Cognitive Implications," *Philosophical Review*, vol. 59, pp. 291–304, 1950.

———, "Brandt's Questions about Emotive Ethics," *Philosophical Review*, vol. 59, pp. 528–534, 1950.

Toulmin, S. E., *The Place of Reason in Ethics* (Cambridge: Cambridge University Press, 1956), Chapter 4.

Urmson, J. O., *The Emotive Theory of Ethics* (New York: Oxford, 1968).

Warnock, G., *Contemporary Moral Philosophy* (London: Macmillan, 1967), Chapter 3.

Warnock, M., *Ethics Since 1900* (Oxford: Oxford University Press, 1960), Chapter 4.

Wellman, Carl, "Emotivism and Ethical Objectivity," *American Philosophical Quarterly*, vol. 5, pp. 90–100, 1968.

CHAPTER SIX

Edwards, Paul, *The Logic of Moral Discourse* (New York: Free Press, 1955), Chapter 4.

Gass, William H., "The Case of the Obliging Stranger," *Philosophical Review*, vol. 66, pp. 193–204, 1957.

Frankena, W. K., "The Naturalistic Fallacy," *Mind*, vol. 48, pp. 464–477, 1939; reprinted in W. Sellars and J. Hospers (eds.), *Readings in Ethical Theory* (New York: Appleton-Century-Crofts, 1970), pp. 54–62.

Hudson, W. D., *Modern Moral Philosophy* (Garden City, N.J.: Doubleday, 1970), Chapter 3.

Lucas, J. R., "Ethical Intuitionism II," *Philosophy*, vol. 46, pp. 1–11, 1971.

Moore, G. E., *Principia Ethica* (Cambridge: Cambridge University Press, 1903).

Nowell-Smith, P. H., *Ethics* (London: Penguin Books, 1954), Chapters 2, 3, 4.

Prichard, H. A., "Moral Obligation," reprinted in *Moral Obligation* (London: Oxford, 1968), pp. 87–163.

———, "Does Moral Philosophy Rest on a Mistake?" *Mind*, vol. 21, pp. 21–37, 1912; reprinted in *Moral Obligation* (London: Oxford, 1968), pp. 1–17.

Ross, W. D., *The Right and the Good* (Oxford: Clarendon Press, 1930).

———, *Foundations of Ethics* (Oxford: Clarendon Press, 1939).

Schilpp, P. A. (ed.), *The Philosophy of G. E. Moore* (Evanston: Northwestern University Press, 1942), pp. 43–176, 535–623.

Strawson, Peter F., "Ethical Intuitionism," *Philosophy*, vol. 24, pp. 23–33, 1949; reprinted in R. Brandt (ed.), *Value and Obligation* (New York: Harcourt, Brace & World, 1961), pp. 347–357.

Toulmin, S. E., *The Place of Reason in Ethics* (Cambridge: Cambridge University Press, 1950), Chapter 2.

Warnock, G. J., *Contemporary Moral Philosophy* (London: Macmillan, 1967), Chapters II, VI.

CHAPTER SEVEN

Braithwaite, R. B., "R. M. Hare, *The Language of Morals*," *Mind*, vol. 63, pp. 249–262, 1954.

Foot, Philippa, "Moral Arguments," *Mind*, vol. 67, pp. 502–513, 1958.

Geach, Peter, "Good and Evil," *Analysis*, vol. 17, pp. 33–42, 1956.

Hare, R. M., *Language of Morals* (New York: Oxford, 1964).

———, *Freedom and Reason* (New York: Oxford, 1965).

Hudson, W. D., *Modern Moral Philosophy* (Garden City, N.J.: Doubleday, 1970), Chapter 5.

MacIntyre, Alasdair, "Imperatives, Reasons for Action, and Morals," *Journal of Philosophy*, vol. 62, pp. 513–524, 1965.

———, *A Short History of Ethics* (New York: Macmillan, 1966), pp. 260–264.

Madell, Geoffrey, "Hare's Prescriptivism," *Analysis*, vol. 26, pp. 37–41, 1965.

McCloskey, H. J., "Hare's Ethical Subjectivism," *Australasian Journal of Philosophy*, vol. 37, pp. 187–200, 1959.

Toulmin, S. E., *The Place of Reason in Ethics* (Cambridge: The University Press, 1950), Chapter 2.

Warnock, G., *Contemporary Moral Philosophy* (London: Macmillan, 1967), Chapter IV.

Warnock, Mary, *Ethics Since 1900* (London: Oxford, 1960), Chapters 2, 3.

Zink, Sidney, "Objectivism and Mr. Hare's *Language of Morals*," *Mind*, vol. 66, pp. 79–87, 1957.

CHAPTER EIGHT

Dewey, John, *Ethics*, in collaboration with J. H. Tufts (New York: Henry Holt and Company, rev. ed., 1932). Part II, "Theory of the Moral Life" is by Dewey and is reprinted separately with that title (New York: Holt, Rinehart and Winston, 1960.)

———, *Reconstruction in Philosophy* (New York: Henry Holt and Company, 1920); New ed. (Boston: Beacon Press, 1949), Chapter VII.

———, *Human Nature and Conduct* (New York: Henry Holt and Company, 1922).

———, *Experience and Nature* (Chicago: Open Court, 1925), Chapter X.

———, *The Quest for Certainty* (New York: Minton, Balch & Co., 1929), Chapter X.

———, *Logic, the Theory of Inquiry* (New York: Henry Holt and Company, 1938), Chapter IX.

———, "Theory of Valuation," in *International Encyclopedia of Unified Science* (Chicago: University of Chicago Press, 1939).

Geiger, George, *Philosophy and the Social Order* (New York: Houghton, Mifflin, 1947).

———, *John Dewey in Perspective* (New York: Oxford, 1958).

Hook, Sidney, "The Desirable and Emotive in Dewey's Ethics" in S. Hook (ed.), *John Dewey: Philosopher of Science and Freedom* (New York: The Dial Press, 1950), pp. 194–216.

————, "The Ethical Theory of John Dewey" in *The Quest for Being* (New York: Dell, 1963), pp. 49–70.

Kennedy, Gail, "Science and the Transformation of Common Sense: The Basic Problem of Dewey's Philosophy," *Journal of Philosophy,* vol. 51, pp. 313–325, 1954.

Lewis, C. I., *An Analysis of Knowledge and Valuation* (La Salle, Ill.: Open Court, 1946), Book III.

Stuart, H. W., "Dewey's Ethical Theory" in *The Philosophy of John Dewey,* Library of Living Philosophers, I (Evanston and Chicago: Northwestern University Press, 1939), pp. 291–335.

Taylor, Paul W., *Normative Discourse* (Englewood Cliffs, N.J.: Prentice-Hall, 1961), Chapters 1, 2, 3.

White, Morton, "Value and Obligation in Dewey and Lewis," *Philosophical Review,* vol. 58, no. 4, pp. 321–329, 1949.

＊　＊　＊　＊　＊

The inclusion in their chronological order of the series of articles in which Professor Dewey and Professor David Prall brought their well-known differences to the attention of philosophers may afford some convenience to students of value theory. Even though much has been said in these articles which might have been left unsaid, their direct reference to each other renders them sufficiently useful for us to forgive the repetitiousness entailed by their separate printing. Others entered this specific controversy (Perry, Picard, Brogan, Costello, Robinson, etc.), but reference to them is purposely omitted. Plato endeared the dialogue to students because in it we have an opportunity to pursue the dialectical development of two (or more) opposed sets of ideas working themselves out, not in separation from each other, but through the impact of the opposition generated in each stage of their development. Unfortunately the single authorship of a dialogue imparts a partiality to it which prevents it from fully realizing this expositional ideal. Only Plato could write the *Theaetetus.* In a sense the series of articles to which we refer possesses many of the advantages of the dialogue without this fatal flaw. The discussion, incidentally, extended over a period of eight years. This was indeed a periodical controversy! The essays are as follows:

Dewey, "The Logic of Judgments of Practice," *Journal of Philosophy,* vol. 12, no. 19, pp. 505–523, 1915. (Reprinted with variations and some expansion in *Essays in Experimental Logic,* University of Chicago Press, 1916, pp. 349–389).

Prall, "A Study in Theory of Value," *University of California Publications in Philosophy,* vol. III, no. 2, pp. 179–290, 1918–1921, especially Chapter 4, "Dewey's Pragmatic Theory of Valuation."

Dewey, "Valuation and Experimental Knowledge," *Philosophical Review,* vol. 31, pp. 325–351, 1922.

Prall, "The Present Status of Theory of Value," *University of California Publications in Philosophy,* vol. IV, no. 2. pp. 77–103, 1923.

Prall, "In Defense of a 'Worthless' Theory of Value," *Journal of Philosophy*, vol. 20, pp. 128–137, 1923.

Dewey, "Value, Liking, and Thought," *Journal of Philosophy*, vol. 20, pp. 617–622, 1923.

Dewey, "The Meaning of Value," *Journal of Philosophy*, vol. 22, pp. 126–133, 1925.

Dewey, "Value, Objective Reference, and Criticism," *Philosophical Review*, vol. 34, pp. 313–332, 1925.

Prall, "Value and Thought Process," *Journal of Philosophy*, vol. 31, pp. 117–125, 1924.

CHAPTER NINE

Baier, Kurt, *The Moral Point of View* (Ithaca, N.Y.: Cornell, 1958), Chapter 1.

Brandt, Richard, *Ethical Theory* (Englewood Cliffs, N.J.: Prentice-Hall, 1959), Chapter 1.

Dewey, John (with James Tufts), *Ethics,* rev. ed. (New York: Henry Holt & Company, 1936), Chapters 1, 10.

Frankena, William K., *Ethics* (Englewood Cliffs, N.J.: Prentice-Hall, 1963), Chapter 1.

Hill, Thomas E., *Ethics in Theory and Practice* (New York: Thomas Crowell, 1956), pp. 1–19.

Moore, G. E., *Principia Ethica* (Cambridge: The University Press, 1929), Chapter 1.

Nowell-Smith, P. H., *Ethics* (London: Penguin Books, 1954), Chapters 1, 2.

Toulmin, Stephen, *The Place of Reason in Ethics* (Cambridge: The University Press, 1950), Chapters 9, 10.

Warnock, G. J., *Contemporary Moral Philosophy* (London: Macmillan, 1967), Chapter 5.

CHAPTER TEN

Campbell, C. A., "Moral and Non-Moral Values: A Study in the First Principles of Axiology," *Mind*, vol. 44, pp. 273–299, 1935; reprinted in W. Sellars and J. Hospers (eds.), *Readings in Ethical Theory* (New York: Appleton-Century-Crofts, 1970), pp. 169–187.

Dewey, John, "Value, Liking and Thought," *Journal of Philosophy*, vol. 20, pp. 617–622, 1923.

————, *The Quest for Certainty* (New York: Minton, Balch & Co., 1929), Chapter X.

————, *Experience and Nature* (New York: Norton, 1925), Chapter X.

———— (with James Tufts), *Ethics*, rev. ed. (New York: Henry Holt and Company, 1932), Chapter XI.

Lewis, C. I., *An Analysis of Knowledge and Valuation* (La Salle, Ill.: Open Court, 1946), Chapters 12, 13, 14.

Melden, A. I., "Two Comments on Utilitarianism," *Philosophical Review*, vol. 60, pp. 508–524, 1951; reprinted in Samuel Gorovitz (ed.), *Utilitarianism* (New York: Bobbs-Merrill, 1971), pp. 117–128.

Pepper, Stephen, *The Sources of Value* (Berkeley: University of California Press, 1958).

Perry, R. B., *The General Theory of Value* (New York: Longman's, Green, 1926).

————, *Realms of Value* (Cambridge, Mass.: Harvard University Press, 1954).

Prall, David, *Aesthetic Judgment* (New York: Thomas Y. Crowell, 1967).

Santayana, George, *The Sense of Beauty* (New York: Charles Scribner, 1896), Part 1.

CHAPTER ELEVEN

Baier, Kurt, "Moral Obligation," *American Philosophical Quarterly*, vol. 3, pp. 210–226, 1966.

Brandt, Richard, *Ethical Theory* (Englewood Cliffs, N.J.: Prentice-Hall, 1959), Chapters 15–16.

————, "The Concepts of Obligation and Duty," *Mind*, vol. 73, pp. 374–393, 1964.

Dewey, John (with James Tufts), *Ethics* (New York: Henry Holt and Company, 1932), Chapter XII.

Frankena, W. K., *Ethics* (Englewood Cliffs, N.J.: Prentice-Hall, 1963), Chapter 3.

Hart, H. L. A., "Legal and Moral Obligation," in A. I. Melden (ed.), *Essays in Moral Philosophy* (Seattle: University of Washington Press, 1958), pp. 82–108.

————, "Positivism and the Separation of Law and Morals," *Harvard Law Review*, vol. 71, pp. 593–629, reprinted in F. A. Olafson (ed.), *Society, Law, and Morality* (Englewood Cliffs, N.J.: Prentice-Hall, 1961).

————, *The Concept of Law* (Oxford: The Clarendon Press, 1961).

Nowell-Smith, P. H., *Ethics* (London: Pelican Books, 1954), Chapter 14.

Rawls, John, *The Theory of Justice* (Cambridge: Harvard University Press, 1971).

Ross, Ralph, *Obligation, A Social Theory* (Ann Arbor, Mich.: The University of Michigan Press, 1970).

Sartorius, Rolf, "Utilitarianism and Obligation," *Journal of Philosophy,* vol. 66, pp. 67–81, 1969.

Sesonske, Alexander, "Rightness, Moral Obligation, and Goodness," *Journal of Philosophy,* vol. 50, pp. 608–616, 1953.

————, *Value and Obligation* (New York: Oxford, 1964).

CHAPTER TWELVE

Baier, Kurt, *The Moral Point of View,* abridged ed. (New York: Random House, 1965), Chapter 5.

Brandt, Richard B., *Ethical Theory* (Englewood Cliffs, N.J.: Prentice-Hall, 1959), Chapter 10.

Dewey, John (with James Tufts), *Ethics* (New York: Henry Holt and Company, 1932), Chapters 14, 15.

Sharp, F. C., *Ethics* (New York: Appleton-Century-Crofts, 1928), Chapters 22, 23.

Stuart, H. W., "A Reversal of Perspective in Ethical Theory," *Philosophical Review,* vol. 29, pp. 340–354, 1920.

Taylor, Paul W., *Normative Discourse* (Englewood Cliffs, N.J.: Prentice-Hall, 1961), pp. 41–47, 125–150.

CHAPTER THIRTEEN

Brandt, Richard B., *Ethical Theory* (Englewood Cliffs, N.J.: Prentice-Hall, 1959).

Fuller, Lon L., "Positivism and Fidelity to Law," *Harvard Law Review,* vol. 71, pp. 630–672, 1958; reprinted in F. A. Olafson (ed.), *Society, Law, and Morality* (Englewood Cliffs, N.J.: Prentice-Hall, 1961), pp. 471–505.

————, *The Morality of Law* (New Haven: Yale, 1964).

Hart, H. L. A., *The Concept of Law* (Oxford: The Clarendon Press, 1961), Chapter VIII.

Kantorowicz, Hermann, *The Definition of Law* (Cambridge: Cambridge University Press, 1958), pp. 41–51.

Nowell-Smith, P. H., *Ethics* (London: Penguin Books, 1954), Chapter 11.

Rawls, John, *The Theory of Justice* (Cambridge: Harvard, 1971).

Stuart, H. W., "A Reversal of Perspective in Ethical Theory," *Philosophical Review*, vol. 29, pp. 340–354, 1920.

Wasserstrom, Richard A., "The Obligation to Obey the Laws," *UCLA Law Review*, vol. 10, pp. 780–807, 1963; reprinted in Samuel Gorovitz (ed.), *Utilitarianism* (New York: Bobbs-Merrill, 1971), pp. 285–305.

CHAPTER FOURTEEN

Brandt, Richard, *Ethical Theory* (Englewood Cliffs, N.J.: Prentice-Hall, 1959), Chapter 14.

Brunton, J. A., "Egoism and Morality," *Philosophical Quarterly*, vol. 6, pp. 289–303, 1956.

Butler, Joseph, *Five Sermons* (New York: Library of Liberal Arts ed., 1950), especially *Preface* and Sermons II, V.

Cahn, E. N., *The Sense of Injustice* (New York: New York University Press, 1949).

Dewey, John (with James Tufts), *Ethics* (New York: Henry Holt and Company, 1932), pp. 324–336.

Feinberg, Joel, "Psychological Egoism," in J. Feinberg (ed.), *Reason and Responsibility* (Encino, Cal.: Dickenson, 1971), pp. 489–500.

Fromm, Erich, *Man for Himself* (New York: Rinehart, 1947), Chapter IV, 1.

Hospers, John, "Baier and Medlin on Ethical Egoism," *Philosophical Studies*, vol. 12, pp. 10–16, 1961.

Katz, Joseph, "On the Nature of Selfishness," *Journal of Philosophy*, vol. 45, pp. 96–103, 1948.

Lawrence, Nathaniel, "Benevolence and Self-Interest," *Journal of Philosophy*, vol. 45, pp. 457–463, 1948.

Mead, G. H., *Mind, Self and Society* (Chicago: University of Chicago Press, 1934), pp. 298–303.

Medlin, Brian, "Ultimate Principles and Ethical Egoism," *The Australasian Journal of Philosophy*, vol. 35, pp. 111–118, 1957. Reprinted in *Reason and Responsibility* (see under Feinberg, Joel), pp. 523–527.

Nagel, Thomas, *The Possibility of Altruism* (New York: Oxford, 1970).

Nielsen, Kai, "Egoism in Ethics," *Philosophy and Phenomenological Research*, vol. 19, pp. 502–510, 1959.

Nowell-Smith, P. H., *Ethics* (London: Penguin Books, 1954), Chapter 10.

Sidgwick, Henry, *Methods of Ethics*, 7th ed. (London: Macmillan, 1907, 1922), Chapter IV.

Stace, W. T., *The Concept of Morals* (New York: Macmillan, 1962), Chapter 7.

Stuart, H. W., "Altruism and Egoism," *Encyclopedia of the Social Sciences*, 1st ed., vol. II, pp. 14–16.

Taylor, Richard, *Good and Evil* (New York: Macmillan, 1970), Chapter 15.

CHAPTER FIFTEEN

Beach, F. A., "The Descent of Instinct," *The Psychological Review*, vol. 62, no. 6, pp. 401–409, 1955.

Cooley, Charles H., *Human Nature and the Social Order* (New York: Charles Scribner, 1902), especially the Introduction.

Dewey, John, *Human Nature and Conduct* (New York: Henry Holt and Company, 1922, reprinted in Modern Library ed., Random House), see especially Sections VI, VII.

Freud, S., "Dissection of the Personality," in Strachey (ed.), *The Complete Introductory Lectures on Psychoanalysis* (New York: Norton, 1966), pp. 521–544.

Horney, Karen, *New Ways of Psychoanalysis* (New York: Norton, 1939), especially Chapter III.

Rieff, Philip, *Freud: The Mind of the Moralist* (New York: Doubleday, 1959) (paperback), especially Chapter 2.

CHAPTER SIXTEEN

Aiken, Henry David, "The Concept of Moral Objectivity," *Reason and Conduct* (New York: Knopf, 1962), pp. 134–170.

Bambrough, Renford, "A Proof of the Objectivity of Morals," *American Journal of Jurisprudence*, vol. 14 (1969), pp. 37–53.

Blanshard, Brand, "The Case for Determinism," in S. Hook (ed.), *Determinism and Freedom* (New York: Collier, 1961) pp. 19–30.

Brandt, Richard B., *Ethical Theory* (New York: Prentice-Hall, 1959), Chapter 10.

Campbell, C. A., "Is Free Will a Pseudo-Problem?" *Mind*, vol. 60, pp. 441–465, 1951; reprinted in *In Defense of Free Will* (London: George Allen & Unwin, 1967), Chapter I.

Dewey, John, *The Quest for Certainty* (New York: Minton, Balch & Company, 1929), Chapter X.

Edwards, Paul, "Hard and Soft Determinism," in S. Hook (ed.), *Determinism and Freedom* (New York: Collier, 1961), pp. 117–125.

Nielsen, Kai, "Why Should I Be Moral?" *Methods*, vol. 15, pp. 275–306, 1963; reprinted in W. Sellars and J. Hospers (eds.), *Readings in Ethical Theory* (New York: Appleton-Century-Crofts, 1970), pp. 747–768.

Stuart, H. W., "The Logic of Self-Realization," *University of California Publications in Philosophy*, vol. I, pp. 175–205, 1904.

Taylor, Paul, *Normative Discourse* (Englewood Cliffs, N.J.: Prentice-Hall, 1961), pp. 151–188.

Toulmin, S. E., *Place of Reason in Ethics* (Cambridge: The University Press, 1950).

Index

Index

Absolutism, 2, 18, 24, 125, 136, 137
Aiken H. D. 239, 241–42, 280–81n.
Alexander, F., 55, 252n.
Altrusim, 213; see also Benevolence, Sympathy
Anshen, R. N., quoted 9, 246n.
Aquinas, St. Thomas, 268n.
Arendt, H., 272n.
Aristotle, 31, 112, 179, 270n.
Asch, S. E., 23, 247n., 283
Auden, W. H., 1, 272n.
Austin, J., 169, 196, 268n.
Authority, moral role of, 183, 190–204
    and authoritarianism, 194–95, 272n.
    and law, 170, 196
    tests of, 195–96, 196–204
Ayer, A. J., 96–97, 117, 118, 259n., 287

Baier, K., 264n., 269n., 292, 294
Bambrough, R., 296
Baylis, C. A., 151, 264n.
Beach, F. A., 277n., 296
Bedau, H., 265n.
Behavioralism, 147, 236–37; see also Skinner, B.F.
Bell, D., 250n., 285
Benedict, R., 15, 18–19, 20, 24, 243, 246n.
Benevolence, 205–219; see also Sympathy

Bentham, J., 33, 48, 52, 70, 73–74, 107, 133, 154, 169, 253n., 255n., 268n.; see also Hedonism, Utilitarianism
Bidney, D., 283
Blackstone, 208–209
Blanshard, B., 279n., 287, 296
Braithwaite, R. B., 289
Brandt, R., 17, 21, 246n., 283, 288, 292, 293, 294, 295, 296
Brogan, A. P., 97, 259n., 271n.
Brunton, J. A., 295
Burgess, E. W., 59
Burke, E., 45–46, 198, 224, 250–51n.
Butler, Bishop J., 107, 210, 275n., 295

Cahn, E., 220, 223, 276n., 277n., 295
Calhoun, J., 17–18, 45, 250n.
Calvinism, 30–31
Campbell, C. A., 237–38, 279n., 292, 297
Camus, A., 244, 266n.
Capital punishment, 167; see also Chessman case
Carnap, R., 88, 89, 118, 258n., 258n., 259n., 288
Cartesians, see Descartes
Chessman case, 220–222
Conscience, 63, 100, 148, 170, 177, 187, 191
    and Freud, 52–53, 55, 64, 187

301